Beezy Marsh is an award-winning journalist who spent more than twenty years making the headlines in newspapers including the *Daily Mail* and the *Sunday Times*. Today she writes fiction, as well as memoir and biography, and somehow finds time for a blog about her life as an imperfect mother to two young boys, in between tackling a never-ending pile of laundry and doing the school run. Family and relationships are at the heart of her writing and she is a firm believer that sisters, mothers and wives are the glue which binds everything together.

Also by Beezy Marsh

Keeping My Sisters' Secrets
Mad Frank and Sons
Mr Make Believe

All My Mother's Secrets

BEEZY MARSH

PAN BOOKS

First published 2018 by Pan Books
an imprint of Pan Macmillan
20 New Wharf Road, London N1 9RR
Associated companies throughout the world
www.panmacmillan.com

ISBN 978-1-5098-9270-9 (UK)
ISBN 978-1-5290-0278-2 (Canadian edition)

3 5 7 9 8 6 4 2

A CIP catalogue record for this book is available from the British Library.

Typeset by Palimpsest Book Production Ltd, Falkirk, Stirlingshire
Printed and bound by CPI Group (UK) Ltd, Croydon, CR0 4YY

*For the women who worked
tirelessly to keep their families together
through two world wars.*

We are the laundry girls,
The laundry girls are we.
Washing powder on our faces,
That's how it should be.
Some say we're common,
Common we may be,
If it wasn't for us laundry girls
Where would the rich men be?

Song, Anon., early twentieth century

Prologue

Acton, May 1934

Her tears had dried, but Annie's throat was still hoarse from crying as the tram clattered down the High Street, taking her away from her family and the run-down streets she called home.

They'd never had much, struggling to get by, just like everyone else round their way, but they'd stuck together through everything life could throw at them. That had always been enough, until now.

Annie clasped the worn leather handles of her carpet bag. Everything she owned had been hurriedly stuffed in there and she'd gone without even writing a note. Even after the countless quarrels that families have, she could never have imagined she'd leave home like this, lifting the latch and sneaking away up the front path. But that was before her whole world had turned upside down.

Secrets, half-truths – her head was spinning just trying to make sense of it all. Only one thing was certain: finding out had changed everything.

As the tram arrived at the bustling terminus in Shepherd's Bush, she wiped her eyes and stood up, smoothing the creases from her skirt and straightening her green felt cloche hat.

Annie stepped down, joining the crowd of people who had places to go, catching a bus up to the West End of London.

Her heart was pounding but she lifted her chin and forced a smile as the bus conductor took her penny fare.

Whatever the future held, there was no going back.

1

Soapsud Island,
November 1918

Monday was washday.

Annie watched the women struggling up Acton Lane, towards the communal laundry at the baths, with bundles of clothing tied up in sheets and slung over their shoulders.

For sixpence you could get a nice hot bath, if you could afford it, but the women's task was to get their clothes clean, bashing their laundry against the washboards at the sinks. Some were bow-legged under the weight of the week's dirty washing, which would be boiled, scrubbed, washed, rinsed, put through the wringer, starched and pegged out to dry before the day was done; not just hung up any old how on the washing line, either. There was an order to things; it had to be neatly done, on lines in the back yard, or the neighbours would talk.

A lucky few housewives had a handcart to wheel the laundry up the narrow winding lane, bordered on either side by rows of glum, sooty little terraced houses. The less fortunate bore their burden, followed by a gaggle of runny-nosed children who should really have been in school, shouldn't they?

Outside the grocer's shop up on the High Street, a couple of women tutted as they raised their handbags at the passing spectacle, as if to shield themselves from the disorder of the lower classes. They'd come from the big houses, over the other side of the town, in West Acton, but the war meant people weren't so choosy about where they were seen these days. Word got around about any shop that did a half-decent loaf and didn't try to short-change you or give you a little under what you'd paid for.

The smell of freshly baked bread wafted out of the bakery down the road, making Annie's stomach rumble; she hadn't had time to have anything more than a quick cuppa for breakfast once she'd filled the copper in the scullery – that had taken six buckets of water. Then she'd put the whites in to soak while she popped up the road to the shop.

She caught sight of the ladies' gloved hands and felt her rough, cracked knuckles. It made her want to cry, having her hands in such a terrible state, but her mother had told her time and time again there was no shame in bearing the marks of a hard day's work. It was just that she dreaded the arrival of winter when the keens would crack and bleed and she'd spend every night with her swollen fingers coated in lanolin to try to soothe them, or dunking them in warm, salty water to stop them getting infected.

The two ladies stopped twittering away to each other like a pair of linnets and looked her up and down. The toes of their polished boots were just peeking out of their long skirts and the pure white lace collars of their blouses sat perfectly against their slender throats. One had a watch on a long gold chain around her neck and the other had a beautiful amethyst brooch pinned to the lapel of her fur-tipped coat. Annie met their gaze, just as her mother had taught her.

She fumbled to do up the buttons on her cardigan, to make herself look as smart as she could. Her long chestnut hair hung in loose bunches secured by ribbons and her blunt fringe was the work of her mum's scissors. They'd probably notice that her black woollen pinafore had seen better days and the collar of her blouse was fraying, but at least it was bleached and starched nicely. She had come here to do some shopping, just like them, and her money was as good as anybody else's.

Annie made a great show of undoing the clasp on her purse; there was no handbag, she couldn't afford one of those. But she had worked hard for her purse, which was getting a little worn now.

The women watched her intently as she chose two apples, and the greengrocer slipped them into a little brown paper bag for her: 'Nice morning, Annie. But you're running a bit late today, aren't you?'

She shuffled her feet a bit, trying to hide her impatience as he weighed out a small brown loaf and popped a couple of tiny little rolls on the scales too. The make-weights were the best bit, because she liked to munch on one of those on the way back home, even though they were half stale, like the bread; that was how the shops had to sell it, with the war on. It was supposed to stop people eating too much. Her stepdad, Bill, hated the bread these days anyway, because it was made of brown flour, which played havoc with his insides. That meant there was more left for everyone else, which was a blessing.

She needed to get up to the butcher's to get some liver for his tea or she'd never hear the end of it, but it was already gone eight o'clock. She'd try to nip back up the road in her lunch break and pray to God that Bill didn't give her a thick ear for good measure. There was just so much more to do these days, with Mum expecting again.

It made Annie's stomach lurch to see Mum heaving that great bump around in front of her as she made her way down the steep staircase to head out to work. There was no banister for her to cling on to: the bedroom doors on either side opened straight on to the stairs, which led down to a thin, dark passageway into the scullery. This baby was going to be bigger than the last one, you mark my words, that's what Nanny Chick said. There would be six of them in the house once the baby came. At least they didn't have to share with another family, like so many of her friends did, because that only led to fights over who was going to use the copper on washdays and who was spending too long in the lavvy in the yard.

Clutching her shopping tightly in its brown paper bag, Annie ran, as fast as she could, back down Acton Lane, under the railway arch and down her street, Fletcher Road, to deliver the shopping back home to Nanny Chick. Then she was off again, scampering along Beaumont Road, past the carts which were already delivering their loads from the big houses up in Holland Park, with laundry hands heaving wicker hampers off the back, while the blinkered horses stood idle. There were shouts of 'Morning!' as she darted past, while a couple of housewives stood on their steps, arms folded, watching her. It would give them something to gossip about later.

It seemed the whole terrace had been enveloped in some strange fog which had seeped through the letterboxes and steamed up the windows. Annie knew the temperature inside those houses would be rising, forcing sweat from the brows of the washerwomen, but the rule was to keep the windows tightly closed to make drying easier, especially in the colder weather. The laundries all had such wonderful names gaily painted on the arched wooden gates to their yards: Sweet Lavender, Honeysuckle Villa, the Cambrian Hand Laundry and even the Blanchisserie Royale (which no one could even pronounce without getting their knickers in a twist, so they just called it 'Blanche's'); they all sounded so charming that the posh folk probably thought their drawers were being dunked in a babbling brook and dried in a field full of wild flowers. That thought always made Annie hoot with laughter.

The old washerwomen still nattered about the days when it was Acton-in-the-Fields, not so long ago, but that was a world away from what Annie and the other laundry-maids knew. This was London's Washtub, where row upon row of sooty terraces were stuffed to the gunnels with women and girls scrubbing with all their might to lift the dirt from the collars and cuffs of the well-to-do for shillings; where grimy back yards were criss-crossed with washing lines and the Laundry Missus prayed nightly that no stray smuts would land on the clean sheets before they were pressed and packed.

This grubby little network of streets, where every family worked alongside each other from dawn to dusk in the searing heat and the damp of the hand laundry, was Annie's world.

She turned into Antrobus Road. The green wooden gates of the Hope Cottage Laundry were flung open, and the yard was already a hive of activity, with hampers being carted into the sorting room at the back.

Every day was washday for Annie in Soapsud Island.

'You're late!'

Mrs Blythe, the Laundry Missus, was an absolute harridan, especially with the younger laundrymaids.

Annie had barely set foot over the threshold of the little terraced house before the old dragon was peering at her through her thick glasses, tapping her wristwatch and scolding her poor time-keeping. She knew that Annie had extra chores, what with her mother being in the family way again, but she wasn't prepared to make any allowances.

No. Mrs Blythe felt it was her duty, plain and simple, to boss the likes of Annie about from morning till night, and she'd probably dock her a few pennies' pay at the end of the week too. Some of the girls from the laundry around the corner in Fairlawn Road said *their* Missus wasn't always a proper cow, so it didn't have to be that way. Annie had said as much at tea break once and Bill had raised his hand to her for that, so she kept those thoughts to herself these days.

The Missus thought Bill walked on water, which was a true miracle, given that he spent most of his days sneaking a tot from the laundrymen's beer from the barrel under the stairs, when he should have been lugging laundry hampers around the place or heaving the wet sheets out of the washtubs with the other laundry hands. Before the war, she'd employed four fellas to help with the heavy lifting and would bark orders at them all day but now she'd only got Bill – who'd got signed out of the Army with lumbago – and Chas, who was too old to fire a gun, the recruiting office had said so when he volunteered.

The Missus knew decent men were hard to come by, so she was prepared to turn a blind eye to Bill's malingering. And Bill knew how to butter her up, bringing her a nice pig's trotter from the butcher's now and again. 'Ooh, William, you are so kind to an old widder like me, you spoil me!' she'd cry and clap her hands together, tucking the brown paper parcel under her rocking chair, next to her tea caddy. Then she'd turn to the youngest laundrymaids, who were supposed to be busy learning how to mark the customers' clothes with tiny, perfect letters and numbers in red cotton on a white hankie. 'What are you gawping at? Get on with it!' she'd yell, and half a dozen heads would stop peering around the door from the packing room and go back to their work until the Missus was satisfied they'd done it neatly enough, otherwise they'd have to unpick every letter and number and do it all over again. Annie remembered those days and how she'd seemed to be endlessly pricking her thumb with the needle. Some of the girls were only just turning twelve and should really have been at school but their dads were away fighting and so Mrs Blythe said they could come along to the laundry with their mums to earn a few shillings extra. It had been the same for her, when her family needed her to start earning, so Annie had to admit, begrudgingly, perhaps Mrs Blythe wasn't all bad.

No one was sure exactly how long the Missus had been in the laundry business, but she'd come out of Notting Hill with her husband and their four daughters when there were still cows and lambs at the end of the road rather than rows of grimy houses and a pub. Her grey hair reminded Annie of a wire-wool pot-scrubber. All her children were grown up and married now and had moved out to run their own laundries in Kensal Town. Mr Blythe had upped and died before the war and left her to it in Acton, but apart from taking the morning off to bury him, she still ran that laundry like clockwork. Every minute her girls worked was noted down in a ledger on her knee and every piece they ironed was checked by her beady eyes and sent back if it didn't come up to scratch. Some of the washerwomen swore she had another set of eyes in the back of her head because not so much as a handkerchief left Hope Cottage in the wrong hamper.

Only Annie's gran, her mum's mum, Nanny Chick, called her by her first name, Eliza, because she had worked in Notting Hill too, back in the nineties, but you could see by the way Mrs Blythe's lantern jaw set tight that she didn't like that one bit, especially in front of the younger girls.

'The others are already hard at it. You'd best go and join 'em,' she barked at Annie's back, as she made her way down the dank corridor with its peeling flowered wallpaper and into the dingy wash house, which had a solitary window overlooking the yard.

The wash house was once just a scullery, but it had been extended so that it now took up most of the patch of earth out at the back which the laundry rather proudly claimed as its 'drying grounds'. On warm days, Bill sometimes clambered up the ladder to put a clothes horse on the flat roof because the tiny yard was filled with sheets flapping about like a ship in full sail. Annie had prayed, on more than one occasion, that he might miss his footing on the way back down that rickety old ladder, but to no avail.

Three sinks with cold taps ran the length of the wall under the window, and on tables next to them half a dozen women were busy with scrubbing boards set across zinc baths. On the other side of the room were two huge galvanized iron pans with little stoves under them. These were the 'coppers' that were used to heat the water for the washing. The steam was rising steadily, meaning the coals were well alight. The coppers were four times as big as the one Annie had at home and took the laundrymen a good ten minutes to fill to the brim, making them hawk up spit from the effort of lugging the buckets. Next to the coppers were wooden tubs which came almost up to Annie's waist, for soaking the colours in.

The tiled floor was already awash with water – it slopped out of buckets and sploshed over the sides of sinks. Cold, wet feet were probably one of the worst bits of the job, especially in the winter. By the end of the day,

Annie's feet would be wet through again and she'd have to stuff newspaper down the toes of her boots and sit them by the fire to try to dry, which made the leather all hard and crusty when she put them back on in the morning. And while the laundresses' feet were freezing, their faces would be sweating from the rising steam which hit the cold whitewashed walls, ran down in rivulets and formed puddles everywhere. It couldn't have been much worse to be aboard a ship in the middle of a stormy sea, with waves crashing up the sides of the boat and water sluicing about all over the deck.

The laundrymen were supposed to mop it up, but it was like fighting a losing battle, Bill said, and so he usually gave up before he'd even started and the water lapped over the top of Annie's toecaps by lunchtime and they all had to be careful not to slip.

'Well, look what the cat's dragged in. Nice of you to turn up,' said Bill, sticking his head around the door of the sorting room, where Annie's friend Vera and a new girl were busy yanking dirty linen from the hampers: whites for boiling in the copper and colours for soaking in the wooden tubs. Bill wasn't a tall bloke but he was stocky, with huge muscles on his forearms from all the heavy lifting. His pudgy face reminded Annie of dough and there was more than a bit of a paunch over the top of his trousers because Bill liked his food, as she knew only too well. His hair was cut short, right up over his ears, just as it had been when he was a reservist in the Army, but the top bit was longer, greasy and black with flecks of grey around the ears, and he was forever brushing it out of his face.

Annie had never asked how old he was – she wouldn't have dared – but she'd guess he was a bit older than her mum, so he must be the wrong side of forty. He gave a gap-toothed grin as he spoke, as if he was just ribbing her, but his eyes weren't smiling.

'Oh, leave off, Bill,' said Bessie, giving Annie a little hug. She was one of the bob-a-day washerwomen who wouldn't take any nonsense from the likes of Bill or any of the laundrymen. She was as broad around the beam as some of the carthorses and her threat of 'I'll squash you like ants' wasn't taken lightly. Bessie was like a mother hen to the laundrymaids. She'd lost her only son somewhere called the Western Front in the war; when he died she'd put on black and only ever wore that colour now. His name was mentioned in whispers around the laundry once when she didn't show up for work and Mum went around to her house to check on her. After that, Bessie never missed a day, but Annie saw there were tears in her eyes sometimes, when she'd sing to herself while she was scrubbing.

'She was just helping her mum as usual, weren't you, chicken?' said Bessie. 'Now, come on, there's work to be done.' She gave Annie's pale cheeks a little pinch. 'You need some meat on you, girl! Been going without again to feed up that brother of yours, ain't you?'

Annie shook her head, but they both knew she was lying. Meat was rationed and Annie felt her little brother George, who was coming up to four, needed it more than she did. Mum wouldn't have her going without, so Annie had got really good at slipping food into the pocket of her cardigan when no one was looking. Annie picked up a pristine white apron from the basket in the corner and put it on over her clothes. She could wrap her apron strings around her and tie them in a bow at the front these days because her waist was so tiny.

The new girl in the sorting room smiled at her. She had raven hair pulled into two neat plaits, much neater than Annie's hair, which she had barely had time to tie a ribbon in this morning.

'I'm Esther,' she said, smiling to reveal a gap in between her front teeth, which Nanny Chick always said meant that a person was going to travel.

Vera seemed to be in a bit of a mood this morning, scowling to herself as she marched about, stiff as a board, her dirty blonde ponytail swishing about. Her pinafore was almost bursting at the seams because it was too small and her mum couldn't afford a new one. With her long legs encased in black woollen stockings and her thin arms jutting out in front of her, she reminded Annie of a wooden doll. She thrust a box of soapflakes into Annie's hands and then turned to the newcomer, wrinkling her little button nose: 'We ain't got time for idling, Esther, so you'd better go and get the soda.'

The water in Acton was supposed to be the softest in London, but that was just a silly story peddled by the laundry owners because the scum still formed in the water, as sure as night followed day, so handfuls of soda were needed in each copper to get things clean.

While Esther was busy getting the box of soda down from the shelf in the sorting room and Annie was sprinkling soapflakes into the boiling water, Vera hissed at Annie: 'She's a bleedin' Kraut!'

'Don't be daft!' said Annie, spinning round. 'She didn't sound German to me.'

'But her grandad is, which makes her a half Kraut or a quarter or something,' said Vera, conspiratorially, her eyes narrowing to slits. 'Girls up at the Cambrian told me. She could be a spy!'

Esther came back with the soda and a wicker basket full of whites.

'Did you check 'em for stains?' said Vera abruptly, ''Cos the Missus'll do her nut if you start boiling things with stains on. We've got to treat them first, see?'

'I know, that's what they taught me down at the other laundry,' said Esther, rather hurt. 'I've made a pile of things over there to spot-treat with borax.'

Vera looked a bit deflated but she wouldn't let it lie: 'Well, I think you'll find we do things a bit differently round here at Hope Cottage, don't we, Annie? It's a better class of laundry than the Cambrian. Only the best work here!'

Annie gave Esther an apologetic little shrug.

'Come on, girls!' boomed Bessie from the sink. 'There's three washboards here standing idle.'

Bill was bailing hot water out of one of the coppers and into wooden tubs to soak the dirtiest colours. The smell of those filthy clothes mingling with the steam almost made Annie retch. She darted over to the wash house door to take a breath of fresh air before rolling her sleeves up. Then she grabbed a bar of Sunlight and her scrubbing board and plunged her hands into the hot water, wincing as the soap found its way into her cracked skin. 'One, two, three, sweet Jesus, four . . .' she counted under her breath, willing the smarting to stop. By the time she reached ten, it was usually better. She grabbed a dirty plaid cotton dress from the basket at her feet and started to rub it hard against the washboard, forcing the dirt out. Her arms were strong from all the scrubbing but not as big as the likes of Bessie, who had forearms like giant hams from years of elbow grease at the sinks.

'Put yer backs into it!' said Bessie. 'And, Annie, not too much soap per piece, remember? There's a war on.'

The suds started to work into a lather and Annie found herself wandering into a daydream about the life of the girl who wore the dress, up at one of the big houses in Holland Park, to take her mind off the ache in her neck and shoulders. She turned the dress inside out and started to scrub again, with renewed vigour, noting the name stitched in neat red cotton in the collar: 'Verity Felstone'. What was Verity doing now? Annie held up the garment. Verity Felstone was probably about the same size as she was.

Perhaps she was nearly fourteen too.

2

November 1918

Ten shillings a week: that was all Annie and the other laundrymaids earned for working from eight till eight and a half-day Saturdays. Even the poorest blokes prided themselves on bringing home about a pound a week, and they didn't work much harder than the girls in Soapsud Island.

Mondays and Fridays were Annie's favourite days, though, because she got to see the horses. Annie felt the apple in the pocket of her cardigan. She was waiting for the right moment to sneak out into the yard.

Through the window she spied Ed, the carman, leaning on the gates having a smoke, in his shirtsleeves and waistcoat. He was only a couple of years older than Annie, but with so many blokes away fighting, he had shouldered the responsibility of a grown man's job. He stood around, his hands jammed in his trouser pockets, like the other carmen in the street, and he had that habit of talking out of the side of his mouth while he dangled a ciggie between his lips. But he hadn't the lines and creases of the old-timers and his skin was still smooth, apart from a few downy wisps on his upper lip. Annie couldn't help noticing that, or the way his grey eyes lit up when she came out for a chat.

Bill was nowhere to be seen, which meant he was either having a sly drink in the cupboard under the stairs or lurking in his other favourite hiding place, the lavvy in the yard. The National Loaf, on rations, was just another excuse for a longer sit down, as far as he was concerned. With Bessie off making a mid-morning cuppa for everyone on the stove in the packing room at the front of the house – and the Missus making sure she didn't use too much tea – Annie seized her moment to sneak out. She stepped outside into the yard and felt the cold air hit her lungs.

Ed knew her routine. It was their little secret, the mid-morning snack for Moses, the horse. He pursed his lips for a moment as he inhaled one last time from his roll-up before chucking it to one side. 'C'mon then, Annie,' he said in a mock whisper, pulling his cap down over his head, so that he looked quite silly. 'The coast's clear.'

'I got him a good one today,' said Annie, crossing the yard quickly before she was spotted.

Out in the street, Moses was waiting patiently. Ed never bothered to tie him up, he was such a good horse; he probably knew the route better than his driver and was content to stand still until it was time for him to leave. The cartwheels stood almost as high as the horse's back and the covered carriage bore the name 'Hope Cottage' on both sides. Underneath was painted: 'A country laundry – all items finished by hand', which was supposed to lure more customers, as the cart made its way around London. Annie thought this was a bit ridiculous because you only had to set foot in Soapsud Island, with its laundries jammed cheek by jowl with back-to-backs, to know that it wasn't the countryside.

Moses had a coat which was glossy black, like the lettering on the cart, and Annie held the apple out to him, just as Ed had shown her. Moses took a bite and chewed it and as he did so, Annie felt the softness of his muzzle. She spoke to him, quietly: 'There you go, boy,' and patted his strong neck. She was sure he liked that.

The other girls wouldn't go near the horses for love nor money, Vera least of all because she had got run over by one of the carts when she was little and had a scar which ran from her knee right up the outside of her leg. She showed it to Annie sometimes, to warn her from going too near Moses. The scar was still raised and red, even though it had happened years ago. But there was something calm about the horses, which Annie liked. What was more, you could whisper your secret thoughts in their ears and they would never tell anyone.

Bessie appeared at the sorting room door with a steaming tin mug of tea and motioned for Annie to get back into the yard. She knew full well what Annie got up to feeding those horses when no one was watching, and there was no harm in it, but she wouldn't have her idling too long.

Vera and Esther sat on the back step and drank theirs, gratefully sipping the scalding liquid.

'So, is your dad away fighting, then?' said Vera, watching Esther closely.

'No, he died when I was little, so it's just me and Mum now,' said Esther quietly, 'and Grandad.'

'My dad's away at the Front,' said Vera, before Annie could say sorry to Esther, or tell her that she knew how it felt to have lost her father. 'My dad says the only good German is a dead German.' And she spat on the ground, right in front of Esther's feet, a glob of spittle, glistening on the cobbles.

The colour rose in Esther's cheeks and she looked away.

Vera got up. 'I've gone off me tea,' she said. 'Smells bad out here. Smells rotten, in fact, like a stinking Hun.'

Annie could see the tears welling in Esther's eyes. She reached out and touched her arm.

'It's all right,' said Esther, moving her arm away from Annie's touch. 'You don't have to be friends with me. It was the same at the Cambrian. They made me leave in the end. Everyone knows about my family. Everyone hates me.'

'I don't hate you,' said Annie. 'I don't even know you, Esther, but you seem like a nice sort.'

'My grandfather is from a place called Belarus, near Russia, but he's naturalized British,' Esther said, gazing into the distance. 'Not that it makes any difference round here. He's had so many bricks through the window of his cobbler's shop up in Churchfield Road, he's had to close it.' She blinked, looked away and then wiped her tears with the corner of her apron.

Annie pulled her to her feet. Esther was just a girl, like her, who needed to work to earn money to help the family. If she was seen crying on her first day at the laundry, it could well be her last. The Missus didn't like a fuss.

'Come on, we'd better get back to it,' said Annie. 'Just ignore Vera, she'll come round, you'll see.'

Bill was poking and prodding at the next lot of sheets in the copper in the wash house while Vera started rinsing the coloured cottons, pointedly ignoring both Annie and Esther.

Annie got the muslin bag of Dolly Blue to put in the final rinse of the sheets, to bring them up nice and white. There was something pleasing about seeing how white the linen turned once it had gone through the bluing rinse. That little blue bag was like magic if you ever got stung by a wasp. It took the pain right away, Bessie had showed her that. She was just dunking the Dolly Blue in one of the tubs when there was the most almighty commotion at the front of the house. She could hear the Missus shouting, 'No, you can't come in!' and Bill moved faster than she'd ever seen him shift in her life.

Annie and Esther followed, with Bessie in hot pursuit – she was never one to miss the chance to pick up good gossip.

Annie's mother, Emma, was making her way down the stairs from the ironing room. She was the top ironer in the whole laundry, which made Annie proud, a silk-presser and baby-pleater, who did all the fancy work on the finest of the clothes. More than that, she was the unofficial deputy for the Missus, the go-between for the rough washerwomen, who would listen to reason when it came from her lips.

She moved slowly but determinedly, her starched apron swishing on top of her full skirt and her blouse still done all the way up to the neck, despite the heat and the huge bump she was carrying.

'I know you're in there, girls!' came a voice through the letterbox. 'You should be in school! Come out now and you won't get into trouble.'

'There's no kids in here, love,' said the Missus, leaning against the door. 'This is a respectable laundry business!'

Six little bodies cowered under the table in the packing room. Bill went in and grabbed a sheet, throwing it over the table, so they were obscured.

'Open the door if you've nothing to hide!'

Emma stepped forwards and opened the latch.

'Whatever is the matter?' she said, calmly. 'Can't you see we are working?'

A tall woman, as slim as an ironing board, stood glowering at her. 'I'm Miss Frobel, the headteacher of Rothschild Road School,' she said. 'And I believe some of my pupils are moonlighting here instead of attending lessons. It simply will not do.'

'Well, I'd invite you in, Miss Frobel, but a laundry is a dangerous place with lots of hot irons – you might get your fingers burned – so of course there are no children here,' said Emma. She was smiling but the note of determination in her voice was unmistakable.

The teacher craned her neck to get a view down the hallway.

'It is a private business,' said Emma, firmly. 'So, if you don't mind, you should be on your way before someone calls the police, because you are causing quite a disturbance, if you don't mind my saying so. People will think we're being robbed!' Heads were poking out of doors and windows the length of Antrobus Road to see what the fuss was all about.

Miss Frobel stiffened and clasped the top her little walking cane, which was shaped like a bird: 'You haven't heard the last of this!' And she stormed off down the front path.

Mrs Blythe collapsed in her rocking chair and started fanning herself: 'Oh, that's all we need! Thank goodness you saw her off, Em.'

'You might need to tell the girls to go to school for the next few days at least,' said Emma. 'Just in case she comes back.'

'But I need them here!' cried Mrs Blythe. 'It's bad enough losing half my best pressers to the munitions factory – and they needn't think they're coming back here with their yeller fingers touching all my white linens after the way they left me in the lurch!' Yellow hands were the telltale signs of the munitions factory girls, whose fingers were stained from the explosive powder they packed into the shells.

'And Mavis even left to drive a blooming tram up in Ealing. I've never heard anything like it in all my life!' Mrs Blythe was never going to let that one drop, either, even though Mavis, one of her rough ironers, had been gone a full six months. Annie had stepped in to cover some ironing duties and was already on collars and cuffs, not that Mrs Blythe seemed to have noticed.

'Whatever will I do when you are off having the baby?' said Mrs Blythe, wringing her hands, warming to her theme. 'Oh, I shan't cope, I shan't!' Her jowls jiggled as she shook her head.

Bill got a glass out from the cupboard under the stairs and opened the tap of the beer barrel and poured her a drink to shut her up. That usually worked.

'There, there,' said Emma, patting Mrs Blythe on the shoulder, as if she were soothing a child. 'I won't be gone long, you'll see. I was barely off two weeks with George, was I now?'

Annie felt that funny, queasy feeling in her stomach again, watching her mother's belly and thinking about how little rest her mum must have had the last time the baby came. Nanny said she was still as white as a sheet and wincing when she fastened her back into her corsets so she could come back to work at the laundry.

Bill puffed his chest out and adjusted his neckerchief as he gave Emma a little peck on the cheek: 'She's a diamond, my Emma is, Mrs Blythe, a proper diamond.'

My mum is a diamond, thought Annie, because she is worth so much more than you.

Annie turned to go back to work in the wash house but she couldn't help murmuring under her breath, 'She wasn't always yours.'

3

November 1918

Annie lay awake that night, trying to remember her father's face.

Her little brother, George, nestled like a sparrow next to her, his legs all tiny and spindly sticking out of his nightshirt and his chest puffed out. She did her best to keep him warm because she didn't want him crying for their mother. That would only make Bill angry and he would come lumbering in and yell, 'Be quiet, for God's sake stop whining or I'll give you something to whine about!' That would upset Mum too and she would stand there saying, 'No, Bill – don't, please, he'll be quiet now, won't you, George?' with such a pleading look in her eyes.

Annie would shush him as best as she could, but poor George's bones ached and there were dark circles under his eyes. It wasn't anyone's fault. It was just the way things were, but Annie couldn't help noticing he was a lot smaller than the other kids in the street who were the same age as him.

She listened to the windows rattle as another train passed by and George's wheezing started up again. As she closed her eyes tightly, she tried to imagine her father's face once more, but there was nothing – only the dim glow of the gas lamp from the hallway throwing shadows up the wall.

In the crook of her arm, she held a little china doll dressed in a faded gingham pinafore. Raggedy Annie was her most precious thing in the world, apart from her brother, of course. She was her constant companion and took pride of place on her pillowslip because *he* had given it to her when she was first born. That's what Nanny Chick had told her.

She didn't remember that, of course, or the long journey on the train, to go and stay with Nanny's sister, Annie's Great-Aunt May, in Suffolk when she was still a baby. She tried and tried to remember Mum bringing her to the farm and waving goodbye, so that she could go to work every day in the laundries back in London. She tried even harder to remember Dad holding her close and kissing her goodbye at the station; he must have done that as he pressed Raggedy Annie into her arms. Her doll's pinafore would have been brand new then. And with her black hair tumbling down her back, and her little painted shoes on her feet, Raggedy Annie must have been the smartest doll in the whole of London town.

Instead, Annie's earliest memories were of gathering firewood with her cousins in the winter and of long summers when she ran through the wheat fields and helped with the harvest; of being carried on the farm boys' shoulders as they made their way back to the big house in the fading light, her skin tingling from the heat of a full day in the Suffolk sunshine.

Twice a year, her mother and Nanny Chick would come to visit her, telling her she was lucky to be in the fresh air of 'Silly Suffolk' with Great-Aunt May, and away from the heat and damp of the laundry. 'Oh, you don't want to be back in the pea-soupers, my girl,' Nanny Chick would say, bouncing her on her knee. 'Great-Aunt May needs you to help her run the house here and keep your little cousins in check, doesn't she?'

Great-Aunt May would nod in agreement and say Annie was the best helper, as children ran pell-mell around the farmhouse kitchen. She was a widow, with three strapping grown-up sons who worked on the farm and were so kind and gentle with Annie, treating her like one of their own, swinging her high in the air to make her laugh and never scolding her when she was caught sticking her fingers in the cream or scrumping apples with her cousins.

But she was still just a little girl then. Raggedy Annie was with her as she clung to her mother's skirts when it was time for Mum to leave to go back to London, even though Great-Aunt May spoiled her rotten and gave her a kitten to play with.

When Annie started at the village school, some of the other girls teased her because her mother and father didn't live with her. Raggedy Annie sat beside her in the rocking chair by the grate in the kitchen as Great-Aunt May explained she was more loved than most children because her mother worked very hard and her father was working hard too, just so she could have some fresh air. Then, out of the blue, in the summer of 1915, her mum sent word that she needed Annie's help back at home. Annie was ten and old enough to come back to London on the train on her own.

Raggedy Annie was packed up in a little suitcase with Annie's clothes: her pinafores, her flannelette nightie, her itchy woollen stockings and her comb. Nanny Chick met her at Liverpool Street Station, with a special slice of a meat pie wrapped in brown paper, and they took the tram all the way to Acton, munching as they went. Annie marvelled at the big houses and the fancy carriages and even motor cars; there were shops with meat hanging up outside and glass jars in the windows of the pharmacies and children playing in the dusty streets. There were ladies dressed so smartly with flowers on their hats and gentlemen walking along beside them, smoking or carrying walking canes. The best bit was as they passed Hyde Park: a parade of soldiers, marching along in green uniforms, with their guns slung over their shoulders and a tall fella with an enormous moustache shouting orders to them as they stepped in time.

When they got off at Acton High Street, which was bustling with people, Annie couldn't help noticing they were dressed differently to those up in town. Their clothes were clumsier-looking, older, dirtier and, rather than fashionable dresses, the women wore plain coats, buttoned and belted, and dark felt hats, without the flowers on the top which Annie had found so pretty to look at on the journey. The coalman's lorry was wending its way down the road and the motor-buses had to chug past the milkman's dray as he sold milk by the pint from churns on the back. A totter had parked up to call out for rag and bone, and he had a tarpaulin over the top of his cart. The sharp, sickly-sweet smell of that caught Annie in the nostrils and made her cough.

'That's for the tallow factory down Packington Road,' said Nanny Chick, hurrying past. 'Hold your breath.'

They walked down the lane and under a grimy railway arch and then it was a sharp right turn into Fletcher Road, where Mum was waiting for her on the doorstep. It was just as Nanny had described it, with a big bay window at the front and a little window above it and a short front path that took no more than two steps to skip up. 'This is home,' said Nanny Chick, giving her hand a little squeeze.

Mum had a big surprise to show her in the scullery at the back of the house, the best thing ever, better than a kitten – her own little brother George. She fell in love with him then, his long fingers curling around the shawl Mum had knitted for him and his eyes tightly shut. She knew then she'd protect him forever, because she was his big sister.

Annie asked when Daddy would be coming home. Her mother turned away and poked at the fire. Nanny Chick told her softly: 'He has gone away to war and is fighting at the Front with all the other brave men. We don't talk about him no more. It makes your mother sad, see?'

Annie ran upstairs and flung herself on the bed and sobbed, clutching Raggedy Annie, whose painted face just stared back at her, her pouty red lips frozen in a smile. She hated everything then, even her doll, so she threw her on the floorboards and the china on her nose got chipped, which made Annie cry even more.

She felt her mother's hand on her shoulder and turned

and buried her face in her lap. 'I'm so sorry, Annie,' Mum said. 'But we will be all right: you, me and George and Nanny Chick. I promise you.'

'I hate you!' shouted Annie, and she saw the pain of her words register in her mother's eyes. 'Why didn't you tell me he had gone to the war?'

Mum sighed and looked away. 'Annie, I didn't want to burden you with it, not while you were away from home,' she said.

'But I wanted to meet him. I wanted to see him and now I can't!' She pummelled the bedspread with her fists as huge sobs racked her little shoulders.

Mum's skirts rustled as she stood up for a moment and went over to a little wooden box on top of the chest of drawers in the corner. She lifted the lid and took something out and brought it over to Annie.

'I have some things that he wanted to give you right here, but you have got to stop crying, Annie, because you are a big girl now and you're going to wake the baby if you carry on like this.'

'I don't want things from him, I have Raggedy Annie. I just want Daddy back and you made me stay on the farm until he'd gone away!' she wailed.

The bedroom door creaked open. It was Nanny Chick.

'What a lot of fuss and nonsense. You are a very lucky girl to have been out in all that fresh air, and it was the best place for you. It was where your father wanted you to be,' she said. 'So, you stop crying now like your mother says. I need you to think about baby George and so does your mum.' Nanny sat down on the bed, beside Mum, and stroked Annie's hair, her tone softening. 'Crying won't change anything, chicken. See what your mum has for you and then I will put the kettle on and make us all a nice cup of tea.'

Annie sat up and wiped her eyes. It was useless to protest because Nanny was always right, she knew that, and a cup of tea was the answer to all life's problems as far as she was concerned.

Mum opened her hand to reveal a small silver ring and a little brass horse on a gilt chain. 'See, Annie,' she said, offering them. 'These are for you, from Daddy. I didn't bring them to Silly Suffolk in case they got lost and I knew Raggedy Annie would be taking care of you, right enough, but now you are a grown-up girl and helping me out in London, you can have them in your own little box, like treasure.'

Annie slipped the ring onto her finger and picked up the little horse charm and put the chain over her head. She tried to smile a bit, just for her mum's sake, because this was a special gift from her father.

'He would be so proud of you,' said Mum, giving her a hug. She made a little choking sound, as if she was stifling a sob.

'Well, that's better,' said Nanny Chick, putting her hand on Mum's arm, as if to say, That's enough, now. She turned to Annie: 'You look like a proper lady, with your jewellery on. No more tears. Do you promise?'

'No more tears,' said Annie, not knowing what she was going to do with the empty, sick feeling inside her.

*

Annie kept her promise to Nanny Chick for a very long time, but there were more tears not long after the New Year, in January 1917. She remembered the month because of the bitter cold, which seemed almost to prod at her every time she scurried up the stairs at bedtime.

One evening, after a long day at work, Mum and Nanny called her away from the fireside and sat her down at the table and told her they had very sad news.

'Your daddy isn't coming home,' Nanny explained gently, as Mum sat there in silence, her fingers pressing themselves together, almost as if she were about to pray.

Annie ran to her mother, blinded by tears, and hugged her tightly, wishing it was all a dream. In her mind she was staring down into the well at the farm; it was so pitch black down there, it used to scare Annie silly. Now she was tumbling head over heels into that well and falling, into the darkness. She was hot and cold at the same time and the blackness was right in the pit of her stomach.

'Every day he is up in heaven, looking down on you, feeling proud of everything you do,' said Mum, stroking Annie's hair.

Over the weeks that followed, she used to hear Mum crying to herself softly at night, when she thought Annie was sleeping, and that would make her sob too, until her pillowcase was cold and damp. And sometimes Mum would be counting the pennies on the kitchen table and Nanny would have to put the kettle on because Mum was crying again, especially when the rent man came knocking and Annie's boots didn't fit any more.

Then, one day in the summer, Nanny Chick said Mum

should let her hair down a bit and go with the other laundry workers to Southend for the day. Annie skipped all the way down to Bollo Lane with Mum that morning to see the big charabanc and shout, 'Throw yer mouldies out!' in the hope of catching the pennies that the laundresses would chuck out to the kids. There was something about the way that Bill, one of the laundry hands, helped Mum get on that charabanc that Annie didn't care for. And he ruffled George's hair too, which Annie didn't like either. His mouth was curling at the corners as he gave Annie a little wave goodbye, but his eyes weren't smiling.

Bill was a regular visitor to the house after that, and he started calling Annie 'doll' and 'duck', which she hated. She spat in his tea once when he wasn't looking, and when she went to the church, All Saints, with Nanny Chick on Sundays she prayed to God to make Bill go away but that didn't work, so she whispered all her fears to Raggedy Annie before she went to sleep at night instead. In her dreams, her father came home from the war and he marched into Hope Cottage. He towered over the Missus and Bill and he was six feet tall and so handsome, all the laundresses gasped. He swept Mum up in his arms and then turned to Annie, saying: 'We can be a proper family again.'

But there was no homecoming when she woke up the next day, nor the day after that. There was just Bill, turning up at their house with a bunch of flowers and wearing a collar and a tie, not just his usual shirt and waistcoat. And he told Nanny Chick he wanted to 'make an honest woman of Emma'. Mum was the most honest person

Annie knew in the whole world in any case, so she couldn't see the point of it, but they got married just before Christmas and then Mum's stomach started to get big. Annie had her hands full then, helping Nanny Chick around the house and with George, as well as in the laundry. Most girls started there at twelve but she'd gone a bit earlier than most, to help out her family.

The main thing was that Bill took her favourite spot on a wooden stool by the fire every night in the scullery and she had to sit on the rag rug in the evenings if she wanted to warm her toes. He wasn't funny and kind like Great-Aunt May's sons had been at the farm. In fact, he almost relished telling her off or finding fault.

'Ain't you getting a bit old for that dolly, Annie?' he asked her one night, as he toasted some bread and dripping, taking all the best bits for himself. His greying hair flopped forwards over his face as he threw another lump of coal on the fire, making the flames flicker, and he coughed and spat into the grate. There was a glint in his inky blue eyes as he spoke, and Annie knew better than to answer him. She just smiled and shrugged her shoulders. 'What's the matter, girl? Cat got your tongue?'

Annie didn't take Raggedy Annie downstairs any more after that, in case Bill took her away. Her doll stayed on her bed, out of his grasp, her face still frozen in a little smile.

It was the same every night once November had Soapsud Island in its icy grip, and 1918 was no different. George kept Annie awake half the night, lying next to her in the bed, wheezing and spluttering.

When she did eventually fall asleep, she was woken by the windows rattling every time a train went past because the railway line was just over the back yard. When it wasn't the trains it was the noise from the pigs kept in the backs the other side of the tracks. There were patches of land down the side of the houses that were still fields, but some people even kept the animals in their back yards, not just to have something to fatten up for themselves to eat, but to sell on. Nanny Chick said they'd been driven out of Notting Hill because of the fear of disease and had come further west, out to Acton-in-the-Fields, and then Soapsud Island had grown up around them. They were far enough away not to smell – well, unless it was high summer – but the oinking and squealing when they had their babies running about was enough to wake the dead. George liked to look at them playing in the dirt because it made him laugh, but she couldn't help dreaming of bacon frying on the range in the scullery, without Bill helping himself first.

Nanny Chick said the change in the season had brought George's chest on again and she was threatening to mix him up one of her tonics. She had a great big red book, called *Consult Me for All You Want to Know*, which sat on a shelf over the range and had all sorts of recipes in it, everything from a cough medicine to corned beef hash. That and the Bible were the only two books in the house, and it was fair to say that Nanny's red book was probably more important to her. Nanny's cooking was a worry but her medicines – Gawd, just the thought of how vile they tasted was enough to make you get better, sharpish.

Annie was just checking that George was tucked up in a shawl in the scullery when Nanny Chick pulled a cork from the little glass bottle she'd got from the tallyman the other week, sniffed it and poured it into a bowl, with a few strange-looking powders. She poured some water in and then started to mix vigorously while poor George shrank back in fear of what was to come. 'You can be off now, Annie,' she said, shooing her with a wave of her hand. 'This'll have him right as rain by later on.'

By the time Annie got to the laundry, her mother and the Missus were standing over a pile of sheets in the wash house, inspecting them closely.

'Oh, don't get your corsets caught in the mangle,' Bessie was saying. 'It'll come out in the wash.'

Annie's heart sank as she peered at the heap of sheets. They were flecked with blue stains.

'Some silly idiot's gone and forgotten to stir the bluing tub properly while the sheets were in it, and I want to know who it was!' said the Missus, folding her arms over her chest. Annie couldn't help but notice that the Missus' bosom almost reached the waistband of her skirt.

Mum was running her hands over the stains, assessing each one.

'We should be able to get them out, but they will need a good boiling to do it,' she said, holding a sheet up at the window.

'Well, it had better come out, or I'll have someone's guts for garters,' said the Missus. She spun around and eyed up her workers: 'Now, which one of you good-for-nothings did it?'

Annie swallowed hard. It must have happened when the headmistress knocked at the front door and she left the blue bag in the tub. But before she could speak up, Esther stepped forwards.

'It was me,' she said. 'It was my first day, see, and I forgot how to do it properly. I'm very sorry.' She looked at the floor.

Annie was about to say this wasn't true, but Vera grabbed her hand. 'Let her take the blame,' she whispered. 'She's got a guilty conscience, that's for sure.'

'Well, I will be docking you a shilling, but you're honest enough to own up, so you can keep your job,' said the Missus. 'Let this be the last time I have to talk to you about mistakes.' And she stalked off out of the wash house.

Esther flushed pink as Vera tutted at her on her way out to the sorting room to fetch some starch. Annie waited a moment before going over to Esther at the copper, where the water was bubbling away: 'You shouldn't have said it was you, when we both know it was my fault.'

Esther turned to her, looking downcast. 'It's all right Annie. Let's face it, I know I'm not liked here. It just seemed pointless for you to lose pay over it. I've seen how hard you work, and your mum has the baby on the way . . .'

'But you need the money too!' said Annie. 'I'm really grateful, Esther, truly I am, but I was hoping you'd be here long enough for us to be friends at least.'

'Friends?' said Esther, tucking a strand of hair behind her ear, her face lighting up in a smile.

'Yes,' said Annie, carefully pushing one of the stained sheets into the boiling water. 'Friends. I mean it.'

4

November 1918

The box mangle put the fear of God into Annie because if you made a mistake while you were running the sheets through it, your fingers would get crushed.

The bed-like contraption took pride of place in the middle of the wash house and the Missus would give it a little pat now and again when she bustled past. It was, quite simply, her pride and joy because her old hubby had had a big win on the horses one year and he went out and bought it for her as a present.

It had a big box filled with stones on the top, to press down on the sheets and blankets. You had to feed the sheets into it on a special roller, which was slipped under one end of the box, and then you turned the hand wheel and the box would move along, squishing the water out as it went. When it reached the end of the wooden frame, a chain action made the box reverse. You had to feed the sheets in carefully because sometimes that roller would slip and then you could end up with the whole weight of the box on top of your fingers. Annie had never seen it happen, but she'd been warned about it.

Apparently, there was one dozy laundrymaid who never

listened to Bessie or the Missus, and she had both hands as flat as pancakes now from getting her fingers caught in the box mangle and that would be no good when she came to get married because she wouldn't even get a wedding ring on her poor, squashed little fingers, silly girl. She worked at another laundry these days, but no one seemed to quite remember the name of it when Annie asked.

Bill was cranking the handle of the mangle to squeeze the water out of the sheets which hadn't been ruined by imperfect bluing. Bessie was dunking woollen socks, one by one, in lukewarm water in one of the washtubs and giving them a stir with a little stick. Then they had to be rinsed in another tub and the water gently squeezed out by hand.

There was a hand wringer for flannel nightshirts and the like, which you had to attach to the side of a wooden tub. Annie quite enjoyed doing it, but after a while your arms ached from turning the handle and, of course, the water spilled out and half of it went all over the floor and not in the tub where it was meant to go. All the flannels and the woollens then went into a basket to go upstairs to the drying and ironing room. Annie liked that best of all, because you got to put the socks over little wooden stays to reshape them.

Flannel vests and underclothes were put on stretching racks which stood behind a giant clothes horse in the ironing room. There were wires suspended across the ceiling in there too, to hang the sheets when it was raining.

Bessie slapped the first lot of woollens into the wicker basket on the table beside her. 'I'll take them up,' said

Annie, desperate to escape the boredom of the wash house, even for a moment, and to spend five minutes with her mum.

The Missus was writing in her ledger in the hallway as Annie made her way up the narrow staircase, which creaked in protest when you stepped on it. The dark varnish had worn off the middle of each stair from the endless trips up and down made by the women fetching and carrying. The walls were flecked with black mould spots where the dampness of hundreds of days of drying wet clothes indoors seemed to have seeped into the building, and at the top of the stairs the wallpaper was peeling right off.

The ironing room smelt nice, though, because the clothes were clean, but it was like a furnace in there, thanks to the black iron pagoda stove. The stove stood about five feet tall, with little ledges all the way around it, to put the irons on for heating. Its grille at the bottom was like a hungry little mouth which constantly needed feeding and that made Bill and the other laundry hands grumble as they lugged bucket after bucket of coke up and down the stairs, making sure that the stove was always piping hot.

On freezing cold days, you were grateful for it, but most of the time it was hotter than holy hell up there, at least that was what Bessie said, which was why she worked in the wash house. Some of the ironers told Annie that was a load of claptrap, and Bessie was just ham-fisted and the Missus wouldn't risk her scorching the customers' best linens with her cack-handed ironing.

The pressers thought they were a cut above the washer-women because, they would say, there was a skill and a certain way of doing things with ironing, whereas washing was just dunking stuff in the soapsuds. Annie hadn't repeated that to Bessie because then the fur would have really flown.

Annie's mum was the boss of the pressers, of course, but her mum's sister, Aunt Clara, worked there too. Aunt Clara helped Nanny Chick out at home in the early part of the week and then would come in for ironing and packing, usually from Wednesdays onwards. She only lived around the corner from Annie in a couple of rooms in Steele Road, and sometimes, when Annie didn't want to go home to find Bill hogging the best seat in the scullery, she might find some excuse to pop in on her aunt, who always had a ready smile and the kettle on.

Annie peered around the door to the ironing room. Her mother was already hard at work at the long padded board which ran the length of the wall under the window, while the rough ironers were pressing sheets on the table in the middle of the room, using the heaviest 'sad' irons, which weighed about ten pounds each. Annie used to wonder why they were called 'sad', and nobody really knew, but Nanny Chick said it was probably an old-fashioned word for how solid they were. The irons all had padding around the handles because they got red hot and Annie was always amazed by how the women held the irons near to their faces to check the heat before pressing down on the cloth. When one iron got too cool, it was placed back on one of the ledges around the stove and another one was taken off. Each ironer had a tin bottle with a sprinkler head, to douse the clothes with lavender water as they ironed out the creases. The smell when the steam rose was quite delicious.

Mum was humming to herself, working briskly with the smaller polishing irons on some collars. She'd shown Annie how to bring them up nicely. Mum passed the iron quickly over the wrong side of the collar, at the same time curving the collar after the iron. Once she'd reached the end of the collar, she repeated the process twice more. There was not a wrinkle in sight by the time she'd done.

Her hair was pinned up in a bun, the way she always wore it, and her hips swayed a little as she ironed. There was no time for chit-chat in the ironing room, Mum made sure of that, but Annie liked to see her working when she got the chance. Her favourite thing was when Mum was goffering, doing the special wave on the edges of pinafores and baby bonnets. She used a pair of tongs which were heated on the pagoda stove, and she was so nimble, she never once burned her fingers on them.

Mum's features were fuller these days, because of the baby, but with her curled fringe framing her face, Annie thought – no, she was sure – her mum was the most beautiful laundress in the whole of Soapsud Island. She wished they looked more alike. Their hair was the same shade of glossy dark brown, like the shell of a chestnut at Christmas, but Mum's had curls whereas Annie's was straight. There was a roundness to Annie's features which Mum didn't share, especially her eyes. Annie often wondered if she'd got that from her dad because even though George's hair was darker still, he had the same little round eyes but his were green. Her own eyes reminded her of two plain little coat buttons, but Mum's had a life and a light and a sort of almond shape to them. Plus, Annie's nose wrinkled when she laughed, which she hated.

There were no pictures of her father anywhere in the house, so she couldn't be sure if she took after him. Annie once tried asking Mum and Nanny Chick what her daddy looked like, but they always had things to do and dismissed her with a wave of their hands. Then Bill came along and the subject was as closed as his fist banging on the kitchen table.

'Hello, love, what've you got there?' said Mum, gesturing to the basket in Annie's arms and wiping a bead of sweat from her brow.

'Just some socks for the stretchers,' said Annie. 'Then I'm off to help Vera with the starching.' She needed to make sure that Vera got the quantities of starch to water right; too little and it wouldn't stiffen anything and too much and it would end up all lumpy, like a bowl of Nanny Chick's custard. All the shirts would be starched by hand, but the collars and cuffs and handkerchiefs were netted up and dunked in a big vat of the stuff.

Annie was just making her way back down the stairs when there was a loud knock at the door.

'Oh, not again!' muttered the Missus, heaving herself out of the rocking chair and waddling down the hall, her stockings wrinkling around her fat ankles as she went.

The knocking grew more insistent. 'All right! All right! I'm coming!'

Bill's face appeared around the door of the wash house. The Missus turned and gave him a little nod and he nodded back. There were no underage girls in today because she'd told them all to stay home and the only dopey-drawers who'd forgotten and turned up for work this morning had just slipped out of the back door and was, at that very moment, skipping away down Antrobus Road.

She pulled open the front door with a 'Yes?'

A man was standing there, wearing a bowler hat and a very smart woollen overcoat. It was not the sort of thing you saw around Soapsud Island, to be honest. He had a clipboard tucked under one arm and a very tidy little moustache. He tipped his hat and revealed a few wisps of hair on a bald pate.

'Good morning, I'm Mr Timms, from the council. I believe this establishment may be in serious breach of the Factory Act. May I come in?'

It wasn't really a question, as he already had a foot over the threshold. He was no taller than the Missus; in fact, he must have been about half her body weight, but there was something about his officious manner which seemed to have struck her dumb and she stepped backwards down the hallway to allow him in.

He looked askance at the peeling wallpaper and caught sight of Annie peering over the banisters.

'I believe, madam, you have several underage girls in your employ.'

'No, that's a lie!' said the Missus, clasping a hand to her

chest. 'A vicious smear. Some of my girls may look young but they are all over the age of fourteen, I can assure you.'

He sniffed and ran a finger over his moustache. 'And I also understand you are employing a woman in the very late stages of pregnancy, which may be injurious to her health and that of her unborn child.'

'Oh, Lord!' cried the Missus, throwing her hands up. 'Never! I would never do anything to harm a littl'un. What a lot of tripe!'

He raised an eyebrow and she added hastily, 'If you don't mind my saying so, Mr Timms.'

'Well, perhaps you won't mind if I carry out an inspection?' He pulled out his clipboard. 'I have an authority here from the council and you know the Board of Trade are very keen to ensure that the working hours do not exceed the recommended fifty-four per week, and the council will take a very dim view of any hand laundries found to be flouting health and safety . . .'

'Yes, no, well, of course. We have nothing to hide here at Hope Cottage! No women about to give birth here and no schoolchildren, are there, Bill?' Bill had made his way along the hallway and was standing next to her, his thumbs tucked into his belt loops and the most sickly-looking grin on his face. He reminded Annie of one of the clowns at the funfair on Acton Green last summer.

'No, all above board and shipshape, Mrs Blythe,' he chirped.

'Perhaps I could interest you in a nice, reviving cup of tea first?' said the Missus, catching sight of Annie at the top of the stairs. The note of desperation in her voice was as clear as day. She needed to distract this council fella to give Emma a chance to get down the stairs and out of the front door, sharpish.

'Most kind, but no, thank you,' said Mr Timms, his moustache twitching, 'I must press on. Let's start with the upstairs rooms, shall we?'

Annie got a bird's-eye view of his bald head as he climbed the stairs. Her palms were sticky with sweat and she could feel her face was flushed too. She looked so guilty, it was bound to give the game away. When he went into the ironing room and caught sight of her mother, they would be done for.

'And how old are you, young lady?' He gave her a little smile and flashed very white teeth as he did so. Perhaps they were false; Bill's teeth were yellow in comparison.

'Fourteen,' said Annie. He raised an eyebrow. 'And a half,' she added for good measure. 'I'm small for my age, that's all.'

'What's your name?'

'Annie Austin,' she said.

He gave a little 'Hmph' and jotted something on his clipboard. The Missus showed him another one of the drying and stretching rooms at the back, overlooking the yard, where some fancy lacework was pinned out to dry on the table and flannels were held in wooden stretching frames to stop them shrinking.

'Very nice,' he said, 'but I want to see your workers.'

He turned to Annie. 'Why don't you show me what's in this room?'

She stood rooted to the spot, unable to move or speak.

He stepped past her and pushed open the door to the ironing room and she followed, her heart in her mouth, with the Missus hot on his heels, like a little lapdog. Two of the rough ironers had turned their irons out and stood idle at the table. A third was even toasting a piece of bread with her iron but Mum was nowhere to be seen.

'Just having our elevenses, Mrs Blythe, like we always do,' said one of the rough ironers, brightly.

'Yes,' said the Missus. 'I do make sure my girls always have a tea break mid-morning, mid-afternoon and not forgetting lunch!' She made it sound like a restaurant rather than a hand laundry. Annie's stomach rumbled at the thought of so much food.

Mr Timms walked over to the ironing table, which was covered by a long tablecloth, and flipped the cloth up, peering underneath. He stroked his moustache. You could have heard a pin drop.

'Well, the ventilation in this room is inadequate, Mrs Blythe, but you could remedy that by opening a window,' he said, eventually. 'Particularly if your workers are eating at their work stations, which is something we don't encourage.'

He walked over to one of the ancient sash windows and yanked it upwards, letting a blast of cold November air into the room. The sheets, which were suspended on wires criss-crossing the room above their heads, started swaying to and fro.

'Of course,' said Mrs Blythe, grimacing at the thought of all the heat escaping. 'Fresh air does everyone good, don't it, girls?'

The pressers nodded in agreement.

'And how many women do you typically have working here in this room?'

'Early on in the week, probably four, or perhaps three, like today,' said Mrs Blythe, casting her eyes around the room, wondering where on earth Emma was. 'End of the week maybe seven.'

'I see,' said Mr Timms. 'Let's go and look at the wash house, shall we? How many women down there at the washtubs?'

'Half a dozen,' said Mrs Blythe, 'not counting my three laundrymaids.'

'I see,' he said, his little moustache twitching a bit, 'I'm interested to see the state of the floor. Loose tiling can be a health hazard and a breeding ground for disease, especially if the drainage is poor.' He sighed. 'As it so often is in these cases.'

The ironers waited until the stairs had stopped creaking, so that they were sure the factory inspector had gone off into the wash house downstairs, before pulling back a little makeshift pair of curtains underneath a wire sorting rack, where the freshly ironed clothes were placed. Emma had crawled under it to hide and had to be hauled to her feet, as she was almost bent double.

'Oh my Gawd,' she said. 'I think I've lost the feeling in me legs, girls! It was like trying to conceal a blooming elephant, hiding me in there!'

Annie rushed over and hugged her mum.

'Are you all right, is the baby safe?' said Annie.

'Don't worry, chicken, it's all all right and it will take

more than some fussy little bloke from the council to stop me working,' she said, stroking Annie's hair and holding her close. 'We are laundry girls, ain't we, and without the likes of us, where would the posh men be?'

The gas lamps in Antrobus Road were lit by four o'clock in the early winter afternoons, casting a yellow glow through the smoke from the coal fires, which rose above the houses in Soapsud Island.

It was on one of those cold November days, when the smog caught you in the back of your throat, when Jack, the laundry errand boy, came running down the street in the failing light with news which would change everyone's life.

'The war is over! The war is over!' he yelled, flapping a copy of a newspaper.

There was a near-stampede on the stairs as the pressers came charging down to read the headlines and Bill nearly put his back out picking Mum up and spinning her around. Aunt Clara and her friend Dora stopped folding clothes into hampers in the front room and came out to see what the fuss was about, and the washerwomen joined Annie and the laundrymaids in the yard outside, as shouts went up the length of the street.

Annie peered out of the gates of Hope Cottage to see workers from the other laundries streaming out into the road, hugging each other. Some of the women were wiping their eyes on their aprons while the laundrymen threw their caps in the air.

One of the fellas from the Sweet Lavender Laundry

came running along, shouting: 'Everyone round to the Railway Tavern! It's a knees-up!'

A gaggle of women and men had gathered at the front of Hope Cottage and the Missus stood on the front step with her arms folded. 'I don't care if Kaiser Bill himself is riding on the top of my delivery cart down Acton Lane!' she shouted. 'Get back to work, or I'll dock your pay!' But her protests fell on deaf ears. Bill was already leading the men from the other Soapsud Island laundries off for a celebratory pint or three around the corner, to the pub on Bollo Lane, and the women were following, even Mum, swaying from side to side as she walked, arm in arm, with Aunt Clara and Dora and the ironers. They were spread right across the road, laughing as they went.

Jack the errand boy grabbed Annie and kissed her on the cheek. He was a good year younger than her but it still made her blush. 'Oh, you should have seen them up on the High Street, Annie!' he cried. 'There's people hanging off the buses and the trams and they're selling flags and people are singing.'

Annie looked back into the wash house and saw one figure, dressed all in black, still determinedly scrubbing away at her washboard. It was Bessie.

'Come on, Bessie,' said Annie, gently, walking towards her. 'Everyone's going for a knees-up! It's the end of the war and Jack said there's flags and everything.' It sounded pathetic once she'd said it, but she was desperate for Bessie to come along.

Bessie looked up at her, and Annie could see that there were tears in her eyes. 'I won't be buying no flags, Annie,' she said. 'I ain't got anything much to celebrate. But you run along now.'

The church bells at All Saints started to ring out, pealing the news far and wide.

Jack stuck his head around the wash house door. 'Come on, Annie! Esther and the others are waiting for you.'

'Go, on,' said Bessie, with a weak smile. 'Go and enjoy yourself. I'll mind the laundry and keep the Missus happy.'

Annie found herself swept along with all the laundresses and laundrymen, as London's Washtub came out to raise a glass to the end of four long years of fighting. She wasn't sure how many laundries there were in Soapsud Island but there must have been dozens because every corner they turned brought another crowd of jubilant people, smiling and laughing in a way Annie had never seen before. She should have been happy, but she couldn't get the thought of Bessie out of her head, all alone and grieving for her son, lost at the Western Front. And there was something else; she tried to push it to the back of her mind, but she knew that if the war hadn't happened her life would have been very different. She'd have a father. Her real father would be here in Acton with her.

By the time they reached the pub, the hurdy-gurdy man was there. He pushed his barrel organ on top of a pram, on account of his limp, and Annie noticed that, despite the party atmosphere, the laundrymen turned their backs on him when he arrived.

Jack emerged from the pub with two bottles of ginger beer and handed one to Annie.

'He's that coward who shot himself in the foot, ain't he?' he said.

The hurdy-gurdy man was still wearing the blue flannel suit and red tie he was given by the soldiers' hospital up in Edmonton where his foot was treated, but the suit was filthy now and he wore a patched greatcoat over it, against the cold.

Annie shrugged her shoulders. She'd heard that rumour too, but by the time the hurdy-gurdy man got home, his missus had gone off with a fella from the munitions factory in any case, and now he was left with just his blind mother for company. Could anyone blame him for trying to get back from the trenches? If Bessie's son had done that, would everyone hate him too? Perhaps they would, but at least Bessie wouldn't be alone and still working in the laundry while the rest of London had a party.

The hurdy-gurdy man doffed his cap and started working his way around the crowd outside the pub, asking for pennies to play a tune. A woman who was all hips under her laundry apron, with barely a tooth in her head, earned a few cheers by jeering at him: 'Why dontcha play "I've Got a Blighty One", then? 'Cos you'll know all about that.'

She did a funny little jig and hopped on one foot as she sang: 'When I think about me dugout, where I dare not stick me mug out, I'm glad I've got a bit of a Blighty one.' A few of the rough women from around Stirling Road cackled with laughter but he ignored them and started to turn the handle of the barrel organ and it played 'It's a

Long Way to Tipperary', the notes chiming out across the late afternoon air.

Some of the laundry women relented and chucked a few pennies in the hat and started singing along: '. . . it's a long way to go. It's a long way to Tipperary, and the sweetest girl I know . . .' and before anyone knew what was happening, the whole pub seemed to have joined in.

The laundrymaids linked arms in two lines across the street and started moving towards each other and away again, tapping as they went. A few started some kicks and Vera lifted the hem of her apron with a whoop: 'Me dad's beaten the Hun! He's coming home!'

The two lines set a rhythm, forwards and back, forwards and back. Vera pointedly refused to link arms with Esther, so Annie went over and joined in, allowing Esther to link on the end of the line beside her.

'Farewell, Piccadilly, goodbye Leicester Square . . .'

Annie danced but her feet felt like lead. She was dancing on her father's grave, every step on the cobbles pounding his bones deeper into the mud. The mud in those trenches was terrible. She knew that because she'd overheard Bessie and some of the ironers talking about it when their boys came home on leave. Some of them never came home to Acton again after that, poor souls. Poor souls, because they died going 'over the top, boys'.

The war was over, but her father was never coming home.

5

May 1919

The laundry was full to bursting with whites in the run-up to Empire Day.

The Missus at Hope Cottage had taken in extra work from the streets of Soapsud Island, so that every little girl who needed a pristine dress to dance around the maypole in would have one. It was a constant source of wonder to Annie that families like hers, which struggled even to put shoes on their kids' feet, could find the money for such pretty frocks. Her mum and the other women made sure they paid into the boot club at the laundry at a penny a week to save for shoes. But expensive dresses seemed to appear as if by magic on such occasions, and they were always sent to be washed and pressed so that they were sparkling white.

Mothers might go hungry and the drapers up on the High Street would be owed a few quid, but the little girls always had something nice to dance in. It was a shame on a family not to dress up the children and be spotlessly clean. Everyone knew who the grubby kids without a nice frock were and no one wanted to be seen with them as they tagged along at the back of the procession. Mostly, their mothers would stay indoors anyway, so they didn't have to see people pointing and staring. Annie didn't like to get involved in all that tittle-tattle, but it was just the way things were.

Nanny Chick had sewed up a little dress for Ivy, altering of one of Annie's old petticoats. It had some nice lace on the bottom and that had been pressed into service to make a bit of detail for the hem and the cuffs, which was pretty. She was such an easy baby, sturdy as anything, just like Bill, and she seemed to shrug off coughs and colds with a wave of her chubby little hand. She slept like a log, tucked up in the fruit crate at the foot of Annie and George's single bed. Mum said having her was just like shelling peas; she was back at her ironing board barely a fortnight after giving birth, just as the Missus had hoped. There had been a scare, of course, with the terrible flu that winter. Mum made sure that Ivy didn't even leave the house when it was at its worst, even though it meant Nanny Chick was climbing the walls having the baby under her feet all day.

Nanny Chick wasn't managing as well as she used to, but Mum didn't want to put the baby in the nursery that the council had built on Bollo Bridge Road, which some of the other laundresses put their babies in, and so Annie had to stay off work too. 'A few of those poor little mites got the flu and now their poor mothers are grieving,' said Mum, her hands wringing the edges of her apron. 'I can't risk her catching it, Annie. And if the Missus complains, then she'll have to deal with me,' she said. She kept George off school too and so Annie had to play endless games of hide and seek under the table in the scullery with him and Ivy to keep them entertained.

As it was, the Missus herself was laid up in bed for two weeks, saying she was dying. She wasn't, of course; she had the constitution of an elephant, but when Easter arrived she was still bending Bill's ear about the terrible night sweats she'd suffered and the aches all over her body, so bad she knew how our good Lord Jesus must have felt.

Then the first blossom started to appear on the trees and the nights began to get lighter. The whole neighbourhood seemed alive with the excitement of the impending Empire Day parade. Annie smiled to herself on the way home from work in the evening as she overheard the little girls from down her street making up songs about their new dresses as they played with a skipping rope, which they stretched from one side of the road to the other, calling on each other to 'jump in'. Their brothers were too busy building carts out of bits of wood and old pram wheels to care, of course, and some poked sticks at each other, like pretend rifles. It was six months since the guns had fallen silent at the end of the Great War, and with so many injured soldiers home, it was going to be a Peace Day celebration with a brass band too, helping to raise some money for the local hospital.

Annie wouldn't have a new white dress for Empire Day, of course. She was too old for that now, as a working girl, and she was content just to be involved in helping to get everyone else looking spick and span. But she was hoping the Missus would give her an hour or so off in the afternoon to join in the celebrations.

Every spare scrap of material was being pressed into service to make fancy dress costumes for the children the length of Fletcher Road. Mothers knocked on each other's doors when they ran short of thread or needed a bit of ribbon for trimmings. George had been picked to dance around the maypole with some of the other children from Rothschild Road School and he would have to wear a perfect blue and white sailor suit; he wasn't very happy about that. George wanted to be a little soldier, and so to keep the peace at home Bill had carved him a gun in the back yard, with much cursing about splinters in his fingers. But he did George proud with it and George now spent all his time marching around the house, the wooden gun slung over his shoulder, pleased as Punch.

Annie couldn't help but notice that her little brother's cough was as bad as ever, despite it almost being summer. And when Nanny Chick came to make him a pair of white shorts from one of Bill's old shirts, she had to take the waist in twice.

Annie took them with her to the laundry to be starched, with his sailor suit top. Its collar was the colour of a robin's egg, a beautiful pale blue, and Mum would make sure George looked handsome by pressing it just right.

Starching clothes took ages, but Annie preferred it to washing. The Missus had her own recipe for starching and Annie had learned it off by heart. For the trimmings: half a tablespoon of starch, a quarter teaspoon of lard, half a cup of cold water and one teaspoon of borax and a quarter of a pint of boiling water. The lard really made the clothes shine. For the body of the clothes she was to use five tablespoons of starch, so the petticoats would be nice and stiff. The mixture had to be stirred with the cold water first and Annie slowly added boiling water, stirring constantly, to remove any lumps. The starch had to be cooked on the stove for half an hour and then strained. She'd add more water with Dolly Blue to the mix, to bring out the white-ness of the clothes. Annie had to put the starch on the dresses while it was still hot and rub it in with her fingers; it came out looking a bit like jelly but it was so warm that it sometimes burned her. She wiped off any excess with a clean, damp cloth.

The little white dresses were hung to dry and then dampened again, ready for ironing, each one rolled up and placed neatly in a wicker basket to go upstairs. Annie was just picking up the next load to take up to the ironing room when the Missus came running into the wash house.

'I've lost another one of my best pressers to that new power laundry in Packington Road,' she cried. 'That ungrateful wretch. I saw her and her daughter through the war and this is how she repays me. It's all "steam power" this and "gas iron" that these days. Well, she won't know how to work any of it, and I shan't have her back!'

She looked around at the assembled washerwomen and laundrymaids, who had stopped scrubbing and starching. There were two patches of high colour on Mrs Blythe's cheeks as she stood, with her hands on her hips, shouting to the whole room: 'Don't any of you lot even think about leaving! I won't stand for it. Now, Annie, stop gawping, girl, and get those dresses upstairs.

'Esther and Vera, you go with her. You know how to iron, don't you?'

Bessie harrumphed to herself and got back to her washboard; she had no intention of going anywhere – better the devil you know, that was her motto. The laundrymaids nodded and traipsed after Mrs Blythe. The youngsters from the packing room, who were still on sweeping-up and laundry-marking duties, found themselves shunted into the wash house to help Bessie, who clucked round them like a mother hen.

Vera whispered to Annie on the way up the stairs: 'I heard the pressers at that new place, Miss Toomey's, are getting six shillings a day for ironing! And they get proper breaks an' all.'

'The rules are they can only work fifty-four hours a week too,' said Esther, turning around on the top step to join in the gossip. 'Sounds like a dream.'

'I wasn't talking to you!' Vera cut in. 'Mind your own beeswax, Esther.'

Poor Esther looked away and trudged off into the ironing room. Vera was still so mean to her; Annie couldn't see the point of it. The war was over.

'But my mum only gets six shillings and sixpence a day and she's the top ironer,' Annie whispered, in case the Missus overheard – she wouldn't have her girls discussing wages. 'It can't be true.'

'Well, I heard it *is* true, so there!' said Vera, with a note of triumph in her voice. 'Might think of going there myself!' She tossed her blonde curls over her shoulders. As she did so, Annie couldn't help but notice some bruises on the side of Vera's neck. They looked like finger marks.

Mum appeared in the doorway. 'Now, girls, you know I won't have idle chatting. Come along.' She wasn't a big woman like the Missus but she didn't need to raise her voice to them because she just had a way about her, a way that made you listen.

'Sorry, Mrs Pett,' they chorused.

It seemed strange calling her Mrs Pett instead of Mum but that was the rule when Annie was at work; she wasn't treated any differently from the other laundrymaids. In any case, she wasn't a Pett, she was an Austin and so was George. It was a small comfort to her that she didn't share Bill's name, even if he did rule the roost.

Annie plonked the wicker basket down by the ironing board. The rough pressers would usually be working on sheets, napkins and pillowslips, but today everyone had been promoted to the role of best presser to get the Empire Day dresses done. Aunt Clara and Dora from the packing room were working away at the centre table, along with another two women, each taking a corner of the table to iron on. Annie spotted that Aunt Clara was ironing George's little sailor suit. She worked so quickly and then it was on to the next piece. All the women were paid per piece and seemed to work at lightning speed with searing-hot irons. Annie didn't think she'd ever be as good as that.

'Right, girls,' said Emma. 'Get a dress each and unroll it, please.'

Emma, Vera and Esther found a space each on the long ironing board under the window and carefully unrolled a white dress each. Some had delicate lace trims while others had embroidered panels down the front. They were all beautiful. Annie had never worn anything like this when she was little, but she felt a sense of pride at being able to make other people look nice.

'First, you girls will watch me and then you can start on your own dresses,' said Mum.

She doused the dress with lavender water and pulled it, inside out, over the bosom board attached to either end of the long ironing board – this was a small board, about half the width of the other one, and perfect for getting the front and the back of the dress smooth. She picked up one of the plain, heavy 'sad' irons from the stove and held it an inch away from her face to test the heat. 'You see, girls, it ain't burning me, so it ain't going to burn the frock.' She pressed the yoke, the front panel and the waist, before moving down to the skirt. 'Once you have done the body you can get it off the bosom board and move down the line, so we all have a bit of space.' Emma then turned the dress so that the embroidery on the front was facing the right way out. She dampened it and then covered it with a clean white cloth before choosing one of the smaller, lighter, polishing irons.

'Now, girls, remember to iron straight across the embroidered bit, rather than going around it in a circle, because that will only make the middle puff up,' she said. 'If you need to, you can help each other out. One of you can hold the dress straight while the other one irons it. The same goes for lacework. It is delicate, so go gently, and you need to damp that down a fair bit before you start pressing.'

Vera rolled her eyes. It was clear that she didn't want Esther helping her out. She shook out the dress she was going to work on and stalked off to the pagoda stove to get an iron.

Annie pulled the dress she was working on over the bosom board, as Esther whispered, 'I don't know what's got into Vera, lately.'

'Just ignore her,' said Annie. 'She's just in one of her moods.'

Vera positioned herself at the end of the long ironing board, as far away from Esther as possible, and started pressing briskly.

When she was finished with the bosom board, she shifted along and Esther put her frock on the board, inside out.

The Missus came into the room and Aunt Clara made the mistake of wondering, out loud, how much she'd earned this week with all the extra dresses she'd pressed. The Missus shot her a filthy look and tutted in her general direction before bustling over to Mum.

'I don't know what I'm going to do, Em,' she confided. 'It's getting harder to find decent workers and if I take any more young'uns on, it's going to look more like a blooming schoolroom in here than a laundry.'

Annie and Esther exchanged glances and suppressed a fit of giggles. To cover up their laughing, they nipped over to the shelf by the sorting rack, pretending they had run out of lavender water and needed to refill their shakers.

'I'll get Bill to put the word out around the Railway Tavern,' said Mum, shaking out another dress. 'I heard people were being laid off at the munitions factories now, in any case, with the war being done, so people are bound to need work.'

'Tell 'em we are a hand laundry, a *careful* laundry,' said the Missus. 'It's tradition. That's got to mean something, ain't it? It's just people's heads getting turned with all that new-fangled machinery in the power laundries. It can't be good for the clothes.'

Annie glanced over at Esther again. The colour had drained from her friend's face.

'What's the matter?' Annie whispered.

There, right on the front panel of the white dress Esther was working on, was the unmistakable 'V' mark of a searing-hot iron. The horrible black scorch glared up at them. 'I don't know how it happened, I swear,' said Esther, tears pricking her eyes. 'I tested the iron next to my face and everything. I must have pressed it too hard.'

Vera was working away at the end of the board and suddenly piped up: 'Oh, dear, Esther, you clumsy clot, what's that mark there?'

Mum came rushing over. 'Ye gods and little fishes, girl!' she cried. 'What have you done?'

Annie had never heard her mother swear but this was as close to it as she ever got. She wasn't angry with Esther, it was more sheer exasperation and disbelief. Mum was shaking her head, as if she might look again and the scorch mark would be gone. But it wasn't. It was still right there, slap bang on the front of some little girl's best Empire Day dress.

Esther stood there, wringing her hands. Annie put her arms around her to try to comfort her in some small way. Vera just carried on ironing, regardless. 'Well, there's work to be done. I'm not losing pay for slacking, that's for sure,' she said, under her breath.

The Missus was beside them in a heartbeat, as Emma held the dress up to the light. Esther was crying now, big, fat tears rolling down her face. Her nose was all snotty and she was gulping for air. 'I'm so sorry! I didn't mean it to happen, I don't even remember doing it!'

'Oh, for the love of everything that is holy!' shouted the Missus, her eyes bulging behind her dirty glasses. 'Esther, my girl, you have gone and done it now. I can't put up with this level of incompetence! First it was the sheets and now this. Whatever next?'

Esther couldn't speak and began to quake in her boots as the Missus yelled in her face: 'Now, get your coat and get out of my laundry. You're fired!'

Annie made to follow Esther, to say she was sorry to see her go, but the Missus grabbed hold of her. 'And where do you think you are going?' she hissed, so Annie had to stay there, pressing more dresses, watching from the window as her friend left Hope Cottage for the last time, her shoulders drooping in defeat as she made her way down Antrobus Road.

News of Esther's sacking spread through the laundry like wildfire and Bessie couldn't wait to get the full story of the dress disaster from Annie when she came back down to the wash house that afternoon.

Word was that the Missus had gone around and paid a pound to the family of the little girl to hush up what had happened to the dress at Hope Cottage. She then sent the delivery cart up to Derry and Tom's in Kensington High Street to buy a replacement dress, all out of her own pocket.

Annie couldn't prove it, of course, but she couldn't help thinking Vera might have had something to do with it because she'd perked right up, the moment Esther left. In fact, she'd been humming to herself all afternoon and even linked arms with Annie, nattering all the way up Bollo Lane and across the railway tracks, after the Missus let them out early. Vera had a funny, tottering sort of walk because her boots were a size too small and she couldn't afford new ones. Every now and again she'd stop and say, 'Oh, Annie, me feet are killing me!' so it became a bit of a joke between them by the time they'd got up to the park on Bollo Bridge Road.

The bandstand was festooned with flowers as white as the little girls' frothy dresses, and Annie felt the boom of the big bass drum right in her chest as the musicians struck up a marching tune. The Mayor and lots of very well-to-do people, including the vicar, were sitting on a special stage which had a tarpaulin over it for a roof. There were two great big swags of foliage slung across either side, with more flowers and greenery tied with ribbons across the front, and Union Jack bunting.

At either side of the stage, on chairs lined up on the

grass, were wounded soldiers wearing the soft, blue flannel suits given to them by the hospital. Some of them had crutches beside them and their arms or legs were bandaged; others wore eyepatches and one had half his head wrapped up so that just a little tuft of hair was visible. Annie didn't want to stare, but one soldier had skin which looked so red and bumpy all down one side of his face, it was as if he had been left in front of the pagoda stove in the laundry for too long and melted. Some other soldiers had arms or legs missing. Those were in wheelchairs near the front, with pretty nurses in starched uniforms, smiling behind them. Their trousers and jackets were folded up and pinned so that the spare bit of material where their limbs should have been didn't flap about. They all looked young, so young, compared to the Mayor, whose thinning salt-and-pepper hair lifted in the breeze as he stood, proud and tall, and addressed the crowd.

In front of the stage was a maypole with a garland of white roses on the very top and a gaggle of excited girls and boys holding their ribbons, waiting for their head-teacher, Miss Frobel, to give them the orders to start skipping about on their eager little legs.

A crowd had already gathered to see the dance and the fancy dress Peace Parade, but first the Mayor spoke: 'My lords, ladies, and gentlemen, on behalf of the borough, may I extend the warmest welcome to our returning heroes at this, our celebration of our most glorious Empire and our victory in the war to end all wars.'

Some important people on the podium clapped loudly at that bit and the vicar tightened his grip on his Bible. A nurse leaned forwards and helped a soldier light a cigarette. His hands were shaking.

'Acton welcomes you all home. We are grateful for your sacrifice and the borough is pleased to announce we will soon be building Homes Fit for Heroes, new homes, right here in Acton.'

There was polite applause from the crowd, the majority of whom didn't care too much about the new council homes because *they'd* still be crammed into a couple of rooms off Bollo Bridge Road and sharing an outside lav with a family upstairs, regardless. They really wanted to see the children dance around the maypole, which was being held steady by four little boys, seated at the base, one of whom was picking his nose in a quite determined way.

'Without further ado . . .'

But the Mayor was drowned out by the arrival of the fancy dress parade led by three rows of boys in short trousers and jackets, bugling with all their might, creating such a din that Annie and Vera had to stick their fingers in their ears. Behind them came children dressed as farmers, nurses, sailors, soldiers and firemen. There was even a Lord Nelson and a Britannia, with a huge red plume of feathers sticking out of the top of her helmet. She was followed by the Angel of Peace – that annoying Nancy from around the corner in Beaumont Road, wearing a sheet, with a white dove on a wire fixed to the back of her head. It was a source of amazement to both Vera and Annie that she had managed to get that role for herself, because she spent half the week washing shirts in the

Cambrian instead of going to school. Nancy was the tallest girl in Soapsud Island, so she certainly did make a striking angel, though.

'And that is lovely and quite enough, thank you, boys!' trilled Miss Frobel above the racket, smoothing the folds of her dress, which had been bleached to a dazzling shade of white.

The bandmaster, his belly just about contained in a little bum-freezer of a jacket, turned and gave her a bow, before raising his baton, and the band struck up a rousing rendition of 'Rule Britannia'. Miss Frobel, for reasons best known to herself, started waving her arms in time to the music to conduct the children dancing. The boys and girls set off, skipping and bobbing around the maypole, clutching their ribbons for dear life. Annie caught sight of George, pale as a ghost, weaving in and out. Some of the laundrymen joined in the chorus, 'Britons never, never, never, shall be slaves', and everyone clapped and cheered at the end.

One fella went a bit over the top and carried on singing, long after everyone else had finished. He was swaying from side to side, with a bottle of beer in his hand. 'Rule Britannia, that's right, Rule bleeding Britannia . . .'

'Oh, look, some old drunk,' said Annie, nudging Vera in the ribs, as the band played on to try and drown him out. He was unshaven and his shirt was untucked. He staggered and bumped into a crowd of laundresses, who shoved him back. Two coppers grabbed hold of him and there was a bit of a tussle before they took hold of an arm each and marched him off out of the park, sharpish.

Vera turned to Annie and said, almost in a whisper, 'That's my dad.'

She slunk back into the crowd, looking for somewhere to hide, in case people had overheard her.

Annie followed, catching hold of her hand. 'I'm so sorry, Vera, I had no idea . . .'

Vera spun around, the shame of such a public humiliation etched on her face. 'He says the war was all for nothing, all the talk of sacrifice. He saw his friends blown to bits next to him in the trench and others burned with mustard gas and then he came home, it was like nothing had changed except life got harder because there wasn't so much work and then he didn't want to work no more.'

'I thought he had a job at the Du Cros factory.' Annie's little brother was obsessed with motor cars and loved seeing the Du Cros cars when they came gliding down the High Street from the factory on Acton Vale. 'How on earth are you managing without his wages?'

Vera was crying now: 'There's eight of us, Annie, eight of us in two rooms and me and Mum are bringing in the most with the laundry work. My brother – the one who is just a year younger than me – is a bootblack up at the station and the next one is a stable boy down at King Street and the others are supposed to be in school, except the baby of course, but half the time they are taking in bits of laundry at home, 'cos I showed them how to do it with a washboard and that. Just for pennies.'

'Is that why you are still so angry with Esther?' asked Annie, touching Vera's arm. She could feel that her friend was trembling.

'It wasn't like the war hurt her or her family at all.' Vera pulled away. 'Doesn't seem fair.'

'That's not true,' said Annie, softly. 'The family lost their shoe shop because of people lobbing bricks through their windows all the time.'

Vera bit her lip. 'I know, but it's not the same as for the rest of us. My dad has lost his marbles, Annie, and I don't think he is ever going to get them back.'

'Is that why you did it?'

'Did what?'

'Burned the dress.'

'I never did, and you can't prove it!' shouted Vera, colouring up. 'That's a stinking lie.'

'But you would have had time, when Esther and me were over by the sorting racks, wouldn't you?' said Annie, as Vera avoided looking at her. 'But it doesn't matter now anyway, because Esther has lost her job, so it's too late. But what I am trying to say is that it isn't fair to blame her any more than it is to blame the likes of me.'

Vera gazed into the distance.

'He comes into my room at night, shuts the door, when the little ones are sleeping beside me and Mum is washing up in the scullery,' she said. 'He kneels down beside the bed and then he strokes my hair and says I'm the prettiest of them all and then he starts crying.'

'I'm sorry,' said Annie, who really didn't know what to say.

'He talks about the trenches sometimes, the mud and the rattles going off to warn of the gas attacks, and men dying like they were drowning, all frothing at the mouth.

He still has nightmares about the Hun, with their helmets like coal scuttles, charging in on top of them in their dugout, with their bayonets. It all sounds so blooming scary, Annie, it chills me to the bone to think about it. Mostly he just cries and strokes my hair. I told him I needed to sleep the other night, I was so tired, and he got angry and called me a name.'

'What kind of a name?' said Annie, who had overheard some choice language from the laundry hands but wasn't sure what any of it really meant.

'He said I was an ungrateful bitch and put his hands around my throat,' said Vera.

Her fingers touched the bruises on her neck. 'Mum came in and stopped him and then he slapped her one. I don't think he wanted to hurt me, Annie, truly I don't. When he isn't sitting at the table staring at the wall or crying by my bed, he is down the pub.'

'Can't someone help him?' said Annie.

'No,' said Vera, with a sigh. 'People see the injured soldiers in their blue uniforms and they feel sorry for them, but who feels sorry for my dad? He has all his arms and legs working just fine; it's just his mind's gone strange. Now everyone will think he's just a useless drunkard . . .'

Annie looked around her. Bill and the other laundry-men were playing hoopla and joshing with each other about who was going to knock the most coconuts off the shy, while nurses tried to cajole them into shelling out a ha'penny on another little flag for the hospital.

Mum and Aunt Clara were sitting on the grass with Ivy, sharing a piece of cake, as the Mayor started handing out prizes of a penny each for the best dancers and the best costumes and so on. The Union Jacks at the front of the stage fluttered in the breeze. This was what people wanted: the kids turned out nicely and the music playing and the Mayor making a good speech, to say that everything was going to get better. They didn't want drunks spoiling it, even if they were only drunk because they were trying to blot out what they saw at the Western Front.

The two girls wandered around the park for a while, arm in arm.

Eventually Vera said: 'You know, you're a proper pal, Annie, just to listen to me.'

'I'm sorry I can't make it better,' said Annie, who couldn't help wondering what would have happened if her father had survived the war. Would he have come home and cried by her bed and called her rude names or slapped Mum?

Annie glanced around for George but couldn't see him anywhere. Then she noticed that some of the nurses had rushed over to the maypole and one was saying: 'Stand back, children, give him some air.'

Her mum saw them too and handed the baby to Aunt Clara before picking up her skirts and running across the grass to where a small crowd had gathered. She screamed as she realized that the little boy lying on the ground, clutching his chest, was hers.

'Make way,' shouted a tall gentleman carrying a black bag. He ruffled George's hair and sat him up, before pulling a stethoscope out of his bag.

George's breathing was shallow and wheezy as the

doctor listened to his chest. Vera was standing right beside her: 'Gawd, he don't look too clever, Annie.'

Annie flew to her brother's side. She knelt down next to Mum and held his hand. He coughed and she instinctively put her best white handkerchief to his mouth, for him to spit in, because it helped to get that muck off his chest with all that coughing. She folded the hankie and was about to pop it back into her pocket, but the doctor stopped her. 'Let me see,' he said. She opened the folds of material. It was spotted with blood.

'How long has he been having these symptoms?' the doctor asked, the concern on his face plain for all to see. Other mothers started pulling their children away and one said, 'Let's hope it ain't catching.'

'He's always had a bit of a weak chest, but I have never seen anything like that before,' said Mum, almost by way of apology. 'I thought it was getting better, now the winter has gone. It must be that he has worn himself out with all that gallivanting around the maypole.' She gave a weak smile and then clutched George to her and he started to cry. 'Will he be all right, doctor?'

The doctor stood up and Mum followed suit. They put their heads together. 'I'd like to see him up at the hospital as soon as possible, this afternoon,' he said, lowering his voice to a whisper. 'And keep contact with other children to a minimum for now.'

Then he turned to George: 'No more gadding about today, young man.'

Bill appeared at Mum's side, as Annie took off her cardigan and wrapped it around George's shoulders. Annie picked her little brother up. He really was light as a feather, it would be no bother for her to carry him all the way home to Fletcher Road. But Bill took him and popped him on his shoulders instead, making George laugh by jigging him up and down a bit.

'Oh, Annie, I will never forgive myself if there's something seriously wrong with him,' Mum whispered, as they walked along, with people pointing and staring at them. Aunt Clara followed with Ivy. 'Lots of littl'uns have a cough in the winter that won't shift until the summer, don't they?'

Annie mumbled her agreement, but she couldn't help wondering whether poor George had just been overlooked, with all the fuss over the new baby and everything else going on at the laundry. And she could have sworn she overhead Bill muttering under his breath: 'Doctors' bills, that's all we blinking need,' as they were leaving the park.

6

July 1919

George was in the isolation hospital up Willesden Lane for six weeks before he was allowed home.

The doctors had to collapse his left lung to give it the best chance of healing after an X-ray showed he had tuberculosis. Mum said that the doctors had a funny little wooden box with a contraption in it, which looked like a bicycle pump, and George had to lie on his side on a trolley and he screamed when the needle went into his chest.

She cried when she told Annie and Nanny Chick about it, she felt so guilty, and then she stopped eating for a few days. Nanny Chick gave her what for and told her to pull herself together because there was no good her going to an early grave and leaving three littl'uns without a mother.

TB, the White Death – there was no cure for it, Annie knew that only too well. She'd learned in the laundry to avoid the washers and the packers who were always coughing, because Mum said they might spread germs. They were the ones who looked like ghosts and were thin as rakes, no matter what they ate for elevenses.

But it had never crossed anyone's mind that George could have it, although the doctors said just playing out with the other kids in the street would be enough to catch it, and he had spent some time in the day nursery at Bollo Bridge Road too, which Mum felt sure was to blame.

The doctors said George was a strong little boy because he must have been infected with TB for over a year, judging by the state of his lung. Every Saturday afternoon, when Annie went up to visit him, there seemed to be a little bit more to him, which gave her hope. Mum went twice in the week, leaving work early, but she was pregnant again and was starting to get so tired. She'd been nearly thirty-five when she popped Ivy out and had been surprised to find herself pregnant again so quickly. It seemed she was destined never to get a moment's peace in the house, what with Nanny's legs not being what they were, so she couldn't do as much, and then there was Bill to be waited on hand and foot.

George didn't seem to mind that he was on his own a lot at the hospital. He sat tucked up in bed with sheets starched so stiff he could barely move and he smiled in a way that Annie hadn't seen in ages.

'It was beef stew again today, Annie,' he said, as she smoothed his hair back from his forehead. His eyes still seemed to be eating up his face but there was a plumpness to his cheeks now. 'And I get cocoa and biscuits too.' She couldn't hug or kiss him, in case of catching the infection, which seemed silly to her because she'd shared a bed for long enough and not picked it up, but rules were rules. The nurses were absolute sticklers, with a 'don't sit there' and a 'don't touch that', but George didn't seem to mind being bossed about.

The ward had a huge balcony so that the nurses could wheel the children outside to get fresh air in their beds and they usually spent the mornings out there. George had got chatting to a scrawny little boy in the next bed who came from Hanwell and they talked about all the games they were going to play in the street when they got out, but the boy disappeared after a week or so and didn't come back.

'Has Charlie gone home?' Annie asked a nurse, but she didn't answer and looked away, busying herself arranging the flowers which stood on the table in the centre of the room. Annie didn't ask again. She had guessed the truth and it was too awful to speak out loud.

Doctors said the best hope for George was that his lung would heal and then the TB would just be sleeping inside his body, but George would always have a weak chest. It could spread to his bones and cause him pain, or it could develop in his lungs again – but nobody could be certain. Nobody talked about the worst happening, but that thought hovered, like some ghostly faceless figure, in Annie's dreams every night. Annie knew she'd have to take extra care to give him whatever food she could and make sure he was warm at home, no matter that she'd go hungry herself. She just wanted her little brother to come back, and the run-up to him leaving hospital was like counting down to Christmas – except for the fact that Bill kept moaning about how the payments for their health insurances would go up now that George needed to see the doctor more often. It was already five shillings and fivepence quarterly for the family, but that was going to go up to six shillings and sixpence to cover the extra check-ups and care that George would need.

Annie was going to say she'd do extra hours to cover it and she'd been planning to mention it at teatime, but Bill was busy complaining that the corned beef they'd had was giving him terrible indigestion.

The pretty pink geranium pot plant that Annie had been tending on the window ledge, so that George would have something nice to look at when he came home, seemed to have wilted under the weight of Bill's misery. Either that or he'd been chucking the dregs of his tea into it when Annie wasn't watching, which was the most likely explanation.

Annie was washing up in the scullery and Mum was darning socks at the kitchen table when Bill turned to her and said: 'We'd best keep him away from our Ivy, and with you being in the family way, I can't have the baby or you catching it.'

'What are you saying?' said Mum, plonking her work down in front of her.

Bill lowered his voice and Annie had to strain to listen in, but she caught enough of it to hear the words 'Suffolk' and 'fresh air'.

'I won't do it, Bill, I won't!' Mum cried. 'You promised me he would always be with us, no matter what, and I won't send him away. Not now, not when he might not . . .'

'I suppose I will have to put another penny on the burial insurances, if he's staying,' Bill cut in, matter-of-factly.

Mum collapsed onto the table and started to cry, huge great sobs. 'Don't say that, Bill! No, I can't bear it!'

Annie rushed to comfort her, but Bill blocked her path: 'You stay out of it!' His hands were calloused from years of hard graft in the laundry and Annie knew all too well how it felt when they clattered against the side of her head, but she stood her ground.

'No,' she said. 'I'm not going to stay out of it. He is my brother.'

'You need to learn some manners,' spat Bill, his eyes flashing with a look approaching malice. 'This is grown-up talk.'

Mum looked up, imploringly. 'Please, Annie, don't . . .'

Annie felt the rush of air and then searing pain as the flat of his palm struck her ear, making it throb, but she willed herself not to move an inch.

'Oh, you want more, do you?' He raised his other hand and made to strike her, but Mum screamed, 'No!' and grabbed his arm. He shook her off, like she was nothing more than a little sheet blowing in the breeze, and she sat back down at the table.

Upstairs, Ivy started crying for her mother.

Nanny Chick hobbled into the room to see what all the fuss was about. She had a shawl drawn around her shoulders and wore the same high-necked black blouse she always did, with a heavy gold locket fastened at the neck. Her silver hair was parted straight down the middle and pulled back into a low bun and her cheeks were a mass of lines and creases, but there was a kind of fire behind her piercing blue eyes which defied her years. She had her knitting with her; she was always clicking away with her needles, working on a new dress for Ivy.

'*You* can stay out of it an' all,' said Bill, his mouth twisting into a leer. It was as if all the unpleasantness, which Annie knew was cooped up inside him all day long as he toiled in the wash house, was there on his face for all to see. 'This is about what's best for the family.'

'Don't you dare lecture me about family, not until you've lived as long as I have,' said Nanny Chick, ambling towards him, to his utter astonishment. She brandished her knitting needle. 'Don't think I won't use it!' she said poking it towards Bill's pudgy face. 'Who do you think you are, getting handy with my girls?'

He recoiled as the pointy end of the needle skimmed past his cheek.

'Oh, you'd better believe it,' said Nanny. 'I've fought worse than you.'

'You're stark raving mad, woman!' he said, throwing his hands up and turning his back on her. 'Can't a man speak his mind in his own house?'

But Nanny Chick was just getting into her stride: 'I'm paying half the rent here and don't you forget it.' She prodded him in the paunch over the top of his trousers. 'I won't be told what to do by a bleeding *dollyman*. This is my house just as much as yours.'

Bill scowled at her. He was just a laundry hand and he hated to be reminded of it because the ironers out-earned him two to one and they were all women. Without Nanny Chick's savings to top up their income they'd be squished into two rooms down one of those rough-and-tumble streets, like Stirling Road, because he only earned about a pound a week. The fact that he didn't bring in enough to keep his wife rankled with him something chronic. He slunk off towards the sink and they all knew he was defeated.

'My grandson is coming home, and he can have my bed,' said Nanny Chick, turning on her heel. 'I can sleep in the rocking chair and shame on you for saying otherwise.'

Tears seemed to come from nowhere and Annie heard herself crying. Her ear suddenly felt huge on the side of her head where Bill had thwacked it. But she knew she wasn't crying about that. She was crying for George, poor George, who had consumption and who wasn't even wanted in his own home. And for her mother, who just seemed frozen at the kitchen table, unable to speak up to protect him.

Nanny turned around and barked at them: 'Annie, stop snivelling, girl, and don't cheek your elders or you will come a cropper. Emma, that baby of yours needs seeing to, there's no use sitting there crying. I have never seen anything like it in all my born days . . .' And she shuffled back off into her room, chuntering to herself as she went.

Ivy was wailing her head off upstairs and Mum sighed as she went to see to her. Annie heard her mother humming 'Rock-a-bye Baby' to get her back to sleep.

Bill glowered at Annie across the scullery. She grabbed her cardigan and bolted for the front door before he could take another swipe at her.

The net curtains in the other houses were twitching as

she made her way up the street. You could tell which families worked in the laundry because their curtains were starched and blued to look pristine, but the fingers clasping them were every bit as desperate for gossip as those in houses where the windows were just covered in newspaper or a tatty old blanket. The walls were thin enough that the neighbours on both sides must have heard the raised voices, and Annie probably hadn't helped by banging the door shut on its hinges as she left.

It was a warm evening and several people had brought chairs out from their sculleries to sit in the street while the kids played hopscotch and kick the can. A couple of women in their aprons, with arms folded, put their heads together as she walked briskly past, realizing that her family had just provided the evening's entertainment.

She wandered aimlessly up Acton Lane and on to the High Street, past the carts which the costermongers had parked up for the night. The shops were all shut now, their blinds down. Annie turned into Churchfield Road, past Ravilious, the draper's, where she sometimes liked to look at all the beautiful ribbons displayed in the windows and dream about putting some fancy trimmings on her blouse. She walked along to where Esther's family's shoe shop used to be. It was a penny bazaar now. A painted sign on the front said, 'All items 1d, inspection invited, step inside'. Nanny Chick would call it a 'diddle 'em' shop because it sold a lot of tat and when it all fell apart, the person running the shop had usually moved on, like some fly-by-night, so you might as well throw your penny down the drain.

There was a front door to the side of the shop, with brown paint peeling off it. Annie had been meaning to try to find out how Esther was, after losing her job, and then with George being so sick and her working all hours at the laundry, she just hadn't had the time. Before she knew what she was doing, she had rapped at the door.

It creaked open a little way and a small, grey-haired man, wearing half-moon glasses, peered out at her: 'What do you want?' He almost sighed as he said it, as if he were used to people hammering at his door in the evenings for no good reason, and he spoke with a heavy accent, so it sounded as if he was saying 'Vot do you vont?' Annie realized she must be speaking to Esther's grandad.

'I'm a friend of Esther's,' said Annie, buttoning her cardigan to make herself a bit more presentable. 'Does she live here?'

'Yes,' said the man. He stepped forwards and glanced nervously along the street. There was a sudden footfall on the stairs and Esther's eager little face appeared behind him in the hallway: 'Annie!' she cried, pushing past him. 'Come in!'

The smell of cooking filled Annie's nostrils as she made her way up the narrow staircase to Esther's home.

The walls were damp to the touch when she put out her hands to steady herself, but once she was through the door into the living room, the warmth of their home seemed to seep into her pores. There was a cracked blue and white china jug on the table filled with flowers and a pot was bubbling away on the stove, which sent the scent of cooking wafting across the room. The table was laid for dinner but there were only two places set. There was no carpet, just bare boards, but there were homely touches: old photographs and some paintings of horses, two brass candlesticks and an engraved brass goblet on the mantelpiece – a bit like the one Annie had seen in church.

'Where's your mum?' asked Annie.

'She's cleaning up at the hospital in the evenings now,' said Esther. 'It's bringing in a bit extra, which is good.'

Annie swallowed hard. It didn't seem fair that Esther's mother should have to go out and work evenings, just because of something that Vera had done.

Esther's grandad motioned for Annie to sit down and she pulled out a chair, which squeaked on the boards. Esther sat opposite her and he perched on a sofa which was covered in a beautiful patchwork quilt. Some of the squares were embroidered with woodland animals and flowers in reds, greens and gold thread.

'You like it?' he asked. 'From my home country, my grandmother made it a long time ago.'

'It's very pretty,' said Annie. 'It must have taken her ages.'

'So, I have got myself another job,' said Esther, brightly. 'It's up at Eastman's, the dyeing place. I start next week.'

'Oh, that is wonderful news!' said Annie, who knew that working for Eastman's was a bit of a comedown for any girl from Soapsud Island. If there was a laundry tradition in the family, that was where you were supposed to stay, not work in the dyeing factory. It was a bit different for Esther, of course, and she was looking for a fresh start.

'And the best thing is I have time enough to go to some night classes that the council are laying on for us factory girls,' added Esther.

'Like extra learning?' said Annie, who was fiddling with the hole in her left shoe, to stop her stocking from poking through where the leather had worn out.

'Yes, it's learning about how to be a manager, how to keep books and that,' said Esther.

Esther's grandad was watching Annie's feet with interest. She felt herself blushing as she realized that he too had spotted the hole in her shoe.

'Take it off, I fix this,' he said, motioning to her foot.

'No, honestly, it's nothing,' she said, wanting the ground to swallow her up. Annie tucked the offending shoe behind her right calf, to hide it from view. She barely knew him, and it was just not right that he should be repairing her shoes for her. Besides, she didn't have any money to pay for it – which was why the hole was there in the first place.

'Come, come.' He waved his hands around. 'Give it.'

Esther laughed: 'It's no good, Annie, you'll have to let him mend your shoe or he will keep going on about it.' She stood up and took another bowl from the draining board by the tiny sink as Annie took her shoe off and handed it to him. He examined it carefully and then picked up a leather apron from a little wooden crate by the side of the sofa. The crate had all sorts of bits and pieces in it – leather, hammers, tools that Annie had never seen the like of before.

'Come on, you can stay and have some chicken soup,' said Esther.

'But I've already eaten! I couldn't take food from you, it wouldn't be right,' said Annie, who realized that money was even shorter for Esther than it was for her family.

Esther's grandad was working away on the repair, tap-tapping softly. He picked up what looked like a little horseshoe and some nails and fitted it to the front of the sole and then motioned for Annie to give him the shoe from her right foot, so he could do the same on that one.

'Please eat,' he said, pointing to the soup.

It seemed rude not to, so Annie tried the soup. It was the most delicious thing she had ever tasted, but then again, that was compared to Nanny Chick's pies, which were a bit hit and miss, to say the least.

Annie gave her friend all her news, which was mostly about George's illness, and promised to keep in touch more. 'I'll come and see you too,' said Esther. 'I don't want to lose our friendship, Annie.'

'Me neither,' replied Annie. She'd known Vera since she started work, so they were friends, but there was something kind about Esther. It was as if she had chosen to be Annie's friend, which made it special.

Night had fallen by the time Annie got home to Fletcher Road, tapping her shoes along the pavement as she went, to amuse herself. But she got that horrible twisty feeling of butterflies in her stomach as she lifted the latch, in case

Bill was still up, squatting in the kitchen like some toad waiting to catch a fly.

Thankfully, the kitchen was silent, save for the scratching of the mice skittering over the red and black linoleum in their nightly dance. They were making the most of being able to scavenge without Mum's broom chasing them out of the place.

As Annie climbed the stairs, the only noise she heard was the creaking of bedsprings and the familiar, animal grunts that she knew came from her stepfather. Once he was snoring, a different sound carried through the thin walls that separated their bedrooms; it was her mother, sobbing.

Annie promised herself then, that if she ever got married it would bring happiness; if it couldn't, then she'd be better off alone.

7

August 1919

It was raining cats and dogs one evening when there was a hammering on the front door.

Mum was at the top of the stairs, grumbling about who'd be calling this late and didn't they know they'd woken the baby up? Annie went to answer it.

There was a fella standing there, completely soaked through, dressed in one of those blue uniforms she'd seen the soldiers from the hospital wearing at the Empire Day parade, with medals on his chest and an army cap on his head. His neatly clipped little moustache twitched a bit as he spoke but he kept looking past her, into the house: 'Emma?'

He had a kitbag at his feet, and Annie couldn't help noticing that there was something unnaturally rigid about the way he was standing, as if he had a broomstick stuck down the back of his jacket, and his fingers were rubbing against each other, like a kind of itch on both hands that he couldn't scratch.

'Who is it?' called Mum, making her way down the stairs. She was six months pregnant with her next and she had to steady herself with one hand on the wall as she descended, in case she tripped.

Annie didn't know what to say, so she pushed the door open wide; she didn't want to be rude because the visitor knew her mum's name. The man stood there, perfectly still and straight, his eyes staring through her, the rain running down his face. His fingers seemed to have developed a life of their own, rubbing frantically, so that his hands appeared to shake.

Mum had reached the foot of the stairs now and a half-strangled sound came from the back of her throat as she looked at him and then she gasped: 'Arthur!'

Nanny Chick appeared in the hallway and she pushed Annie behind her skirts, before looking him up and down: 'I suppose you'd better come in.'

Annie was shooed away upstairs and the scullery door was firmly closed but she sneaked back out of her bedroom, straining to hear what was happening.

There was the sound of plates being laid on the table and then the man started talking, his voice carrying up through the floorboards, so she could make out the odd word or two. He spoke about 'trenches' and 'gas attacks' and then there was the unmistakable sound of sobbing. It wasn't a woman crying, it was a man's voice, which shocked her, because she'd never heard a man cry. There were great, heaving sobs, and they made him cough, which seemed to shake the whole house.

Mum was saying, 'Shhh', and 'Don't upset yourself no more', and then the scullery door opened and Annie had to crouch down low in case she was spotted. She heard footsteps and saw Nanny Chick pulling on her shawl and disappearing through the front door.

The crying downstairs was more like a wailing sound now. Annie sneaked downstairs, one step at a time, avoiding the creakiest stairs, and stole along the hallway. Nanny had left the scullery door ajar and she peered through, to see the man slumped forwards onto the table and Mum with her arms around him, stroking his hair, saying, 'It's all right now, they can't hurt you.'

She held her breath, watching her mother tenderly holding the man and his hands were on her belly, and he was saying: 'Oh, Emma, Emma, God forgive me, God help me.'

Annie scampered away, back up the stairs to her hiding place on the landing, and waited for the crying to subside. It couldn't have been more than half an hour later when Nanny reappeared, with Aunt Clara at her side, talking together in low whispers.

Another ten minutes or so passed, and Annie's toes started to tingle from being crouched down for so long, but she was rooted to the spot by the presence of this stranger in the house. Part of her wanted to see what Bill would have to say about it when he got back from the pub later, but she knew she'd be for it if he caught her out of bed. Then Aunt Clara came out of the scullery with the man beside her, with his cap in one hand and his bag in the other, as she bustled him off down the hallway and out through the front door.

*

Bill eyed her carefully as he chewed his toast at breakfast the next morning.

'Now, Annie,' he said. 'Your mother and me need to tell you something about the man who came here last night. It's your Uncle Arthur.'

Mum sat down beside her. Had Mum told Bill about how she'd been hugging Uncle Arthur? Annie couldn't help wondering.

Bill went on: 'He'll be staying with Aunt Clara for a while. He's had a rough time of it in the war, so you're not to bother him, do you understand?'

For some reason, Annie felt tears prick her eyes then, as if it was all her fault that Uncle Arthur had got upset. 'I only opened the door because he knocked on it.'

'Don't be smart with me,' said Bill. 'The man is not well in the head and he doesn't need you . . .'

Nanny Chick came over from the sink, where she'd been washing up, and cut him short. 'I'll handle this,' she said, firmly. 'He's seen things, terrible things, in the war and he just needs peace and quiet, which is why he's at Aunt Clara's for now. But it's best to stay out of his way, that's all. Do you promise me?'

'I promise,' said Annie, not really understanding what she was promising to do or why; but she thought of Vera's dad putting his hands around his own daughter's throat, and she was very glad that Uncle Arthur was not staying under their roof.

Life carried on, with Mum getting bigger with every passing week, and Annie stopped popping in to see her Aunt

Clara on the way home from work, in case she bumped into her strange Uncle Arthur. Nobody spoke about him in front of her but she overheard Mum and Nanny talking often enough.

'He barely utters a word,' said Nanny Chick, tutting to herself. 'Not even to say "please" and "thank you" to Clara!'

'It can't be helped,' Mum replied. 'His nerves are shattered and the gas has ruined his lungs. We need to be kind.'

'But what about Clara? She's barely slept a wink because he keeps getting up in the night and shouting and walking up and down the hallway. The neighbours upstairs will complain if it keeps up. And Dora told me he takes all his meals in his room and he doesn't wash for days on end. And when she went in there to change his sheets, the bed hadn't been slept in – he'd been lying down on the bare boards underneath it, with his kitbag for a pillow, if you please!'

'Mum,' said Emma, with a sigh. 'We can't possibly imagine what he's been through, and he's still family . . .'

'He's no blood relative of mine,' said Nanny curtly, but then the conversation stopped because Mum called out: 'Annie is that you?' And she had to run back up the hallway and pretend she hadn't been eavesdropping.

Having this stranger lurking around the fringes of her family made things even more tense than usual in the house, particularly with Bill, who could barely hear Uncle Arthur's name mentioned without throwing down his newspaper and storming off to the lavvy. So, Annie took refuge in the bustle of work, and all the excitement about the new steam-powered calender press which the Missus was having installed.

The Missus had employed a couple of sweary brick-layers from Stirling Road to build a new boiler house, and by that autumn, Hope Cottage was more like a building site than a laundry. To make matters worse, Bill had been put in charge of overseeing the whole project, as well as maintaining the new machinery, which made him strut about with an air of self-importance.

He'd even taken to sporting a pristine handkerchief in the breast pocket of his waistcoat, like a proper gentle-man, and Annie had overheard him trying to speak posh when he took delivery of the new boiler from Townend's Machinery Company.

Annie had got her impersonation of him down to a T, much to Vera's amusement. Whenever they had to shake a few nets of hankies out of the washtubs, Annie would snatch a handkerchief and waft it about in the air as she strutted across the wash house floor: 'Hi say, my good fella, put that new boil-ahh over theyah and h'I'll be orf to have my tea!'

Even Bessie got in on the act, innocently asking Bill how the new 'boil-ahh' was doing, while giving Annie and Vera a wink, setting them off in fits of giggles.

'What are you dozy moos laughing about now?' Bill would mutter to himself as he swaggered off to do more important managerial tasks, such as checking the level of the beer in the barrel under the stairs.

The calender press itself was a sight to behold. It was

driven by pulleys which were steam-powered through a series of rods feeding through into the boiler house next door. It took a bit of getting used to, and the dangers were similar to the box mangle, in that Annie had to 'feed' the sheets through the large heated rollers to press them. As she did so, each sheet would give off a great swoosh of steam. It had the advantage of getting the sheets dry enough for ironing, which was a real bonus on rainy days.

Annie was carefully pushing some sheets through the press on one of those autumn days when the rain was coming down like stair-rods, when Vera ran in and said there was a bit of a kerfuffle upstairs in the ironing room.

'It's your ma,' she gasped. 'She says she's having the baby!'

The Missus came running in: 'Your mum says you are to go and fetch your Aunt Clara and meet her back at home. With any luck, it'll be just like shelling peas with this one and she'll be back at work nice and quickly.' She gave Annie's shoulder a little squeeze: 'Good luck to her, but don't you be too long on your errand. I want you back here finishing them sheets off. Your Aunt Clara and your nan will see she's all right.'

Annie nodded and ran, as fast as she could, down Antrobus Road, avoiding the worst of the potholes, which were filling up with rainwater. She was drenched by the time she got to Aunt Clara's house but she hesitated outside the front door. In the past, she'd just push it open and walk in but now, with Uncle Arthur staying, she didn't dare. She knocked timidly.

There was the sound of someone shuffling down the

hallway and then the door opened. He was standing behind it, unshaven, in a nightshirt, his moustache all overgrown
and his cheeks sallow from lack of daylight.

He stared at her and started rubbing with his fingers,
so he looked as if he was itching on the inside.

'Is Aunt Clara there?' said Annie, doing her level best to
be polite. His legs were all hairy, sticking out of the bottom
of his nightshirt, and she'd never seen a man dressed like
that before. Nanny would say it wasn't decent. 'It's Mum,
she's having the baby.'

'Baby?' he said. His head started to shake and his arms
went rigid. 'No, no. It's not safe. What time is it?' He
looked wildly around him, as if someone had just tapped
him on the shoulder.

'It's not lunchtime yet. Where's Aunt Clara?' said Annie.
'Please?'

'No, it's not safe. She's out,' he said. 'Go away.' He
slammed the door in her face and let out a yell, which
made her jump out of her skin, sending her running away
down the road, as fast as her legs would carry her.

Panic was rising in her chest. She couldn't go home
without Aunt Clara, so she ran up Acton Lane to see if
she could find her in any of the shops. Her palms were
sweating despite the chill of the damp air, and she'd
almost given up hope, running up and down, peering in
shop windows, when she bumped into her aunt coming
out of the butcher's.

Annie almost fell into her arms: 'Mum's having the
baby, I tried to find you and I think I might have upset
Uncle Arthur,' she said. 'But I didn't mean to, I'm sorry.'

'Slow down, Annie,' said Aunt Clara, smoothing Annie's soaking wet hair out of her face. 'I'm sure you haven't done anything wrong. Let's get home to your mum and you can tell me about it on the way.'

As they walked back down Acton Lane, Annie started to calm down. 'He seemed upset that I'd disturbed him, that's all,' she said. 'I was just trying to find you because the baby is coming and Mum needs you and I'll be for it if I don't get back to work too.'

Her aunt turned to her: 'There's no harm done. Arthur is still very jumpy about loud noises because of the shelling at the Front during the war. But deep down, he loves you because he is your uncle, so you must forgive him if his behaviour seems strange. He will get better in time, I'm sure of it.'

By the time they got home, the cries of a newborn baby filled the house and Annie rushed upstairs to see her little sister Elsie for the first time. She was all pink with a perfectly pudgy little baby face.

As Nanny Chick fussed around Mum, who was resting in bed, Annie held the baby and pushed all the thoughts about the man a few streets away, still stuck in the horrors of the war, to the back of her mind.

8

November 1925

'You'll catch your death of cold going out like that!'

Annie had spent ages painstakingly taking up the hem of her skirt, so that it hung just below her knees, like the women she'd seen in the cinema up at Shepherd's Bush the other weekend. Nanny Chick was not impressed. In fact, it was fair to say, she was scandalized: 'It ain't decent flashing that much leg, Annie! You'll give fellas the wrong idea.'

'All the girls at the laundry are wearing their hems this short now, Nan,' said Annie, smoothing it down, feeling a bit daring, as she stepped out of the front door to go to work.

Mum didn't mind but she had drawn the line at Annie getting herself a corselette, like the film stars wore, to flatten her bust. Besides, she didn't really have much of a bust to flatten; she still wore a cotton chemise with a liberty bodice over the top. Mum wouldn't be parted from her whalebone corset, which nipped her in at the waist, even after four kids. Nanny Chick was the same; it was something that all the older ladies still saw as part of the ritual of getting dressed.

Vera said she was saving up for a corselette like she'd seen in Derry and Tom's down on Kensington High Street, and a drop-waisted dress too. Annie was secretly envious of her friend's curves; she'd seen the way that some of the laundry hands looked at Vera these days. She was more striking than ever, tall and fair, with her hair cut into a fashionable bob which seemed to have given it bounce and curl, as if it had a life of its own. The Missus wouldn't stand for any nonsense, but old Chas had been known to throw a sheet on the floor of the sorting room and call out to Vera to 'come on in here and get a cuddle'. The girls laughed themselves silly about that because Chas only had one good eye; the other one had a terrible squint. 'I was in there earlier, Chas,' Vera would yell back to him. 'You didn't even bleeding well see me!'

It was a fine late autumn day, with a nice breeze blowing, so by the time Annie got to Hope Cottage, Mum was training up a new intake of laundry girls how to peg clothes out properly in the back yard.

As she got on with sorting through the latest batch of dirty clothes, Annie could hear her mum explaining things to them out in the back yard: 'Right, girls, you hang the clothes wrong side out and with the wind. Nightdresses go by one side of the lower hem, and corset covers can be thrown over the line and pinned at the middle seam at the back.'

No matter that she had got her hands full at home with little Elsie and Ivy, who were a right pair of pickles, and George, as well as Nanny Chick, who was getting doddery; Mum still found it in her to be kind to the new laundrymaids, even if some of them couldn't tell their left from their right.

Annie sighed to herself as she picked up a pile of under-clothes from the big houses up in Holland Park and began to sort through them. A slip of the finest cream silk slid between her fingers. She couldn't imagine wearing something like that, it was so soft. There were silk bloomers too, but when Annie checked them, they were stained with blood. Posh women bled every month, just like she did, but she didn't have anyone to get the stains out of her drawers. Mum kept a bucket with a lid on under the sink in the scullery and she put rags in there to soak when she had her time of the month. No one spoke about it, she just got on with it, and on washdays at home she'd bung them in the copper after everything else had been boiled. Annie put the knickers into a zinc bath of cold water and tipped some salt on the top and began to work it into the blood-stain. The water started to turn reddish brown as the blood started to come out, which was a relief. It wasn't that she hated dealing with bloodstains, it was just the responsibility of getting them out of such beautiful clothes. She held the bloomers up to the light, to be sure they were clean.

'They've got some fancy drawers, those Kensington girls, don't they?'

Annie spun around. Ed the carman was leaning on the wash house door, watching her intently. He held a roll-up cigarette between his long fingers and there was something about the way he smiled at her which made Annie's knees go weak.

'Don't be so daft,' she managed, her voice quavering as she felt herself blushing scarlet. 'Shouldn't you be out collecting, in any case?'

Things had got quite busy at the laundry, and that meant Hope Cottage took two deliveries of dirty clothes in, on a Monday and Wednesday, and deliveries went out Fridays and Saturdays. Ed the carman, with his sandy-blond hair and wolfish grin, was around a lot more these days. He still stood there, hands in his pockets, ciggie dangling from the corner of his lips, but he had grown taller and he wasn't just a teenage boy doing a man's job any more. Annie still managed to sneak out to feed Moses the horse as he stood patiently outside in the street, but she'd started to look forward to the chats with Ed a bit more than she'd let on to anybody. She hoped he hadn't noticed.

'I'm a man down this week, Annie,' he said. 'Jack's off with the measles, which is going to make getting the laundry in a bit of a poser. I need someone to mind the horse and cart for me who isn't going to run off screaming like some scaredy-cat every time he whinnies.' Bill glanced up from the washtub, where he was possing some blankets half to death, by the look of it, with a big stick.

'Or nip off into the pub to wet his whistle every five minutes,' whispered Ed.

The time Bill used to drive the horse and cart had become something of a laundry legend. The Missus got suspicious about why the deliveries were taking so long, so one day she'd gone along too. 'And blow me down,' she told Mum when she got back to Hope Cottage, 'if that damn horse didn't stop at every pub between here and Shepherd's Bush along the way.' And that was the end of that little jaunt for Bill.

The Missus bustled in. Anyone would think she'd been eavesdropping.

'She ain't going anywhere, I need her here,' she said.

'Well, I suppose the customers won't mind too much if one of their hampers goes missing, will they?' said Ed, his eyes narrowing as he drew on his ciggie. The story was that the Cambrian had lost an entire hamper the other week when some light-fingered urchins from Notting Hill made off with it.

'Oh, all right,' said the Missus, folding her arms. 'But you will have to scrub the wash house floor when you get back, Annie. I'm not paying you to sit up there like Lady Godiva on my wages.'

'Annie as Lady Godiva,' said Ed, with a wink, as Annie turned away so he couldn't see her turning beetroot, 'now that would be a sight for sore eyes.'

Moses the horse was chomping away at his nosebag as Ed smartened himself up for the laundry run; the Missus wouldn't have her driver looking like a scruffbag – she'd told him as much on several occasions. Annie watched transfixed as he did up his top button and tied his tie before pulling on his jacket and putting on his cap to complete his uniform.

As he settled himself in the driver's seat, he glanced down at her and caught her staring, so she busied herself taking the nosebag off the horse, bringing it over to the footwell. It was a cold day and she let the horse's breath warm her frozen fingers for a moment before patting his soft muzzle. Moses nodded appreciatively, looking for more food. 'I'm sorry, boy,' said Annie. 'I haven't got anything for you today, we've got work to do.'

'Come on, Annie,' said Ed, offering her his hand. 'We haven't got all day for you to be petting the horse.' He pulled her up to sit beside him. Annie felt a little fluttering in her stomach at the thought of spending so much time with Ed – they'd only had snatched conversations in the past, but if the truth be told, she'd always wanted the chance to get to know him a bit better. There'd been a few evenings down the pub at Christmas time and on bank holidays, but the men tended to drink in one bar and the women stayed in the other with a glass of sherry, and that was the way it was.

Ed picked up the reins and geed Moses into a walk. It was a bit bumpy up there on the driver's seat and Annie found herself being shuffled closer to Ed with every step the horse took. Their thighs were almost touching. Ed didn't seem to mind but Annie clasped the seat edge to try to steady herself.

'It takes a bit of getting used to, don't it?' Ed said. 'Everyone feels like that the first time.'

She nodded.

'We'll wet the wagon's wheels a bit,' he said, flashing her one of his smiles. 'Moses can have a drink too.'

They plodded up Bollo Lane towards Baronsmede Pond on Gunnersbury Lane, where Annie had seen lots of carts driving through the shallows before. Some schoolboys were chucking sticks into the murky water and gawping at the horse and cart as they clip-clopped through. As they drew nearer, Annie realized that one of them was her brother, George. 'Get yourself back to school, George Austin, or I'll tell Mum!' Annie shouted, reddening with anger. He wasn't usually one to play hooky, in fact all the teachers said he was one of the brightest, but lately he'd made friends with Vera's brother Alf, from Stirling Road, and seemed to be getting up to all sorts. Annie didn't like that, not least because it wasn't good for George's chest for him to be gadding about all over the town instead of sitting calmly in class. Annie would never be rude to Vera, but Mum always muttered about those 'rough types from Stirling Road' and she didn't want George falling in with the wrong crowd. He'd made a good recovery from the TB, the doctors said, but he got wheezy whenever he ran about, and winters were always a worry. At the first sign of a cold, it went right onto his chest.

Anyway, he'd come home with a bicycle the other week and couldn't say where he'd got it. Bill threatened to beat it out of him until George finally admitted he'd won it in a game of marbles from Alf. 'A likely story,' said Bill, and he marched right round to Vera's house to have words with her parents, but Vera's mum backed George up, while Alf stood there smirking in the background, so that was that. Vera's dad, of course, was three sheets to the wind down the boozer and couldn't have cared less where the bike came from, so there was no point in asking him.

George scarpered off with Alf, who turned and poked his tongue out. Ed turned to Annie: 'You're like a little mother hen with that brother of yours, aren't you?' She couldn't help noticing that his eyelashes were dark and long and they fluttered against his cheeks when he looked down at the reins.

'Well, I'm his big sister, so that is my job, I suppose.'

'I'd like to have someone looking after me like that,' said Ed, turning to her so that she was looking straight into his eyes, which were dark grey, like charcoal. 'I think that is a nice thing, for a girl to care about her bloke.'

Annie fumbled with the edge of her apron. Was he talking about her being his girlfriend? She couldn't answer him.

They clip-clopped along Acton High Street, past the Globe Cinema, which Annie liked to visit on Saturday afternoons sometimes, especially if it was a Charlie Chaplin film showing. They even had an orchestra playing in the interval.

'Do you ever go to the cinema?' he asked, casually, tucking a strand of his fringe back under his cap, so that all Annie could think about was how very good-looking he was. Moses swished his tail as they went along.

'Sometimes,' Annie murmured. 'I come up with my mate Esther, who works at Eastman's, the dyeing place.' Esther was doing well at work and was taking some exams soon in book-keeping. She kept trying to persuade Annie to come along to evening classes at the library, but Bill wasn't having any of it: 'What do you need to do that for? Waste of time and money! Your mother needs help with the girls at home and Nanny can't be left in the evenings, you know that.'

'I prefer going to the Crown,' said Ed, watching her closely. 'You know, the one with the double seats in the back row. Much more fun.'

Annie knew exactly what he meant. The girls at work all called it the 'fleapit' and there was a lot of gossip about what went on in those double seats, although the usherette was well known for coming around with her flashlight to make sure people didn't get too carried away.

'Perhaps we could go and see a show there sometime,' he ventured.

'Well, I'm not sure what my mum would say,' said Annie. Then she felt foolish for having said that. She wasn't of age yet, but she was twenty and she'd never been out with anyone. There just didn't seem to be time and the only person she was interested in was Ed and now he was asking her out and it made her hands go all clammy and her insides felt all messed up. The words had come out all wrong.

'Suit yourself,' he said, with a laugh. 'You're missing out on a nice evening, that's all.'

'I didn't mean that I wasn't interested,' said Annie, back-pedalling. 'It's just with my nan not being so well lately and my little sisters needing looking after, I just have to find the time, that's all.'

'I'm only teasing,' said Ed, geeing Moses into a little trot with a flick of his wrist. 'You let me know when you might like to walk out with me. I promise to behave myself like a proper gent.'

Annie let herself move a little with the rhythm of the horse and found it almost made her quite giddy, what with the trotting and the thoughts of sitting with Ed in the back row of the Crown.

They passed a tram with a huge advert for Eastman's plastered all over the side of it. The company seemed to be going from strength to strength, which the Missus wasn't too happy about, because Eastman's had a booming laundry business as well as dyeing clothes, and its vans were always coming and going around town. Esther really had landed on her feet with a job there, Annie was sure of that.

Heading down the Vale, Annie couldn't help noticing there were a lot of men in their late forties, like Bill, just hanging around outside pubs or loitering on street corners. She'd heard Mum and Bill talking about unemployment in hushed tones. There were lots of fellas down their street who were taking on odd jobs to make ends meet because they couldn't get work; they were washing windows, minding carts for people, just for pennies. Their neighbour was paid by the hour painting lorries down in Brentford and when the work dried up, he was laid off, just like that. And some of the families in Fletcher Road were going to the Poor Law to get help too because they couldn't get by on their fifteen shillings a week dole money – but no one liked to talk about that, because of the shame of it.

Uncle Arthur had a War Pension, but even he had started doing some odd jobs, in the hope that he would be able to find full-time work when he felt well enough. Annie wasn't so scared of him any more; she understood he had been a nervous wreck when he came home from the war and it wasn't his fault that he'd acted so strangely. It had taken him about a year to want to go outside the house, but once he did, he smartened himself up. He couldn't be described as exactly sociable, though.

He liked mending things, sitting for hours working on a chair or varnishing a cabinet. He rarely spoke, but he had smiled at Annie once, when she came round with a fruitcake for her aunt. She could see then that he had once been handsome because his eyes lit up. He'd joined them in the scullery for a cup of tea and a slice of cake, but when the chatter got too much, he simply got up and left, without saying goodbye. Aunt Clara shrugged her shoulders and said, 'Think we were a bit loud, Annie.' And that was that. At least he wasn't shouty and mean like Vera's dad.

As the horse made its way towards Shepherd's Bush, Ed nodded towards a crowd of men playing cards outside a pub, using an upturned crate as a table. 'Makes me glad to be in a regular job,' he said. 'People are always going to need their washing done, aren't they?'

Annie agreed. Some of the big employers in the Vale, Wilkinson's Sword, Napier's the engine factory, Du Cros cars and the battery makers Charles A. Vandervell, were laying people off and thousands had lost their jobs in the munitions factories since the end of the war.

'My dad works on the railways,' said Ed. 'He's always on at me to go and join him, but it's all union politics and I can't be doing with it.'

Annie didn't really understand politics but Bill liked to have a paper in the evening and she'd read a few of the headlines about unemployment on her way back from the shop to get it for him. The other laundry hands had seemed happy when Ramsay MacDonald and the Labour Party came to power last year but Bill wasn't into any of that union stuff. The miners were agitating about wage cuts, for a start. 'The next thing we know, it will be Communists everywhere,' he'd say, banging his fist on the table. 'Fair's fair for working men but let's not end up like bloody Russia with a revolution.'

'I don't know too much about it all, really,' said Annie. 'I think people just want food on the table and shoes on their feet, don't they? And if they get a living wage then that is fair.' But she knew lots of people around Soapsud Island were working all hours and still couldn't make ends meet, so something probably needed to change. She wasn't sure what that was or how it could happen, and she didn't feel confident talking about it with Ed because Bill had told her that opinions on politics were for the men and not for women to worry their heads about.

'Well, I would rather be out here taking the air with you, Annie, than stuck on a train or in some back room at Paddington Station discussing wages,' said Ed.

He pulled the reins and Moses came to a halt. They were parked up before the most enormous house that Annie had ever seen. It was four storeys tall and white, with fancy brickwork and a wrought-iron and glass canopy over the front path, which had black and white tiles. There was a flight of steps leading up to the front door, which was painted black and was as shiny as Moses' coat, with a polished brass door knocker. 'Wait here,' said Ed, disappearing through a side gate.

Annie clambered down and went around to the back of the cart and opened the little wooden double doors at the back, just to give herself something to do. She felt a hand on her shoulder and spun around to find herself face to face with a policeman. 'What are you up to, miss?'

'I'm just waiting for my carman,' she stammered. 'He's in there.' She pointed to the big house.

'I see,' said the policeman. 'It's just we've had a few thefts lately, so we're keeping an eye out. And Mr Felstone doesn't generally like people loitering outside his property . . .'

'Mr Felstone?'

'The gentleman who owns the house,' said the policeman, just as Ed reappeared, lugging a heavy hamper full of dirty linen.

'Well,' said the policeman. 'Mind how you go, then.' And he walked off, whistling to himself.

'That's the first lot, Annie,' said Ed, shutting the cab doors. 'One down, only about another dozen to go. I see you've met the local constabulary. They're always looking after the rich folks, and the Felstones are the richest of the lot, from what I can see.'

'Really?' said Annie, who remembered the name from the laundry. She'd washed Verity Felstone's dresses often enough.

'House-builders, I think,' said Ed. 'Made a fortune from it. Chance would be a fine thing, wouldn't it?'

They stopped at other big houses all the way along

Holland Park before turning down Campden Hill Road and wending their way around the streets there. Sometimes a servant would be ready and waiting with the laundry hamper but, more often than not, Ed would go round to a side entrance to collect it. One nice butler brought them a glass of water each to drink, on a silver tray. But by lunchtime, Annie's feet were frozen solid and she was beginning to wish she was wearing more than just a cardigan around her shoulders. Her stomach started to rumble but she didn't say anything about stopping for lunch because she'd forgotten to bring her purse.

Eventually, Ed stopped the cart at a little coffee stall. 'Come on,' he said, jumping down and offering her his hand. 'Let me treat you to something. Your stomach's growling like a blooming bear. But you have to promise not to tell the Missus, or she'll swing me, for skiving.'

He bought her a steaming mug of milky coffee and the most enormous slice of cheesecake, which was warm and had lashings of grated coconut on the top. She bit into it and it squidged over the sides of the paper it was wrapped in. She'd never tasted anything like it in her life. 'Nice to see a girl with a healthy appetite,' he said, giving her waist a little squeeze. 'I always thought you were a bit on the skinny side, Annie, but I reckon I could feed you up nicely, a bit like you feeding Moses.'

Annie giggled. 'So now you are comparing me to your horse?' She'd found her sense of humour again and it was fun to laugh with him.

'Nah,' he said. 'I think the horse is better looking.'

'Well, that is charming! No wonder I don't want to go

courting with you!' And she poked him in the ribs, so that he almost spat his coffee out.

Later that evening, as she was on her hands and knees scrubbing the wash house floor, she didn't mind that it was freezing cold and her hands were stinging as the soap found its way into the little keens on her fingers. Annie kept reliving the day she'd spent with Ed and each time she felt lighter inside, as if a weight of loneliness was lifting. She started humming to herself as she scrubbed.

The Missus appeared at the wash house door.

'Someone's cheerful,' she said.

'Yes,' said Annie, looking up. 'I am.'

And for once, she really meant it.

9

December 1925

The laundry was buzzing with excitement about the works' Christmas outing to the Chiswick Empire.

The variety shows there were legendary, with music-hall stars from the big theatres up in town doing a turn sometimes, as well as fun acts like performing dogs and acrobats and escapologists. It was the highlight of Annie's year, but the Missus was threatening to keep people back if the laundrymaids didn't stop gossiping about who was going to walk out together after work this evening.

Annie was hoping that Ed would ask her to go along with him, but she'd barely seen him all week because she'd been upstairs in the ironing room. It had been over a fortnight since their trip up to Kensington and he hadn't asked her to go out to the cinema, even though she'd been expecting him to. Now she felt foolish for thinking he would, and she was glad she hadn't told a soul, especially Vera, who probably would have blabbed about it to the other girls behind her back. She'd been a bit funny about the trip out with Ed, to be honest. Anyone would think she was jealous.

The light outside was fading and Annie could think of

nothing else but seeing him tonight, when she heard the familiar clip-clop of Moses' hooves in the street outside and her heart skipped a beat. She put her hot iron down on the board and picked up the tub of beeswax from the window ledge and gave it a cursory rub over; Mum was always on at them to wax the irons to prevent them from rusting. Then she peered out of the window to see Ed jumping down from the cart and doing up his top button before coming in to bring the day's takings to the Missus.

Mum had her back turned or she would surely have told Annie off for idling; she was teaching one of the younger laundrymaids how to iron pillowcases properly. Annie couldn't help but marvel at how patient her mother was: the poor girl had already been told how to do it yesterday, but it still hadn't sunk in.

'Now, Ada,' Mum said. 'You must iron the pillowcases very smooth, especially on the hems. You fold into thirds, so you only get two creases. That's right.'

Just then, two little faces appeared at the ironing room door. Ivy and Elsie were back from school, happily munching on a crust of bread that the Missus had given them. They were as bright as buttons, and Ivy, at seven, was the leader with all the gumption, while Elsie, just a year younger, was quieter but still had a bit of a cheeky side to her. The Missus doted on those girls almost as much as Bill did, and they were allowed to come into the laundry after lessons because Nanny Chick couldn't do with them getting under her feet at home. Poor old Nanny spent much of the day in her rocking chair because she was getting frail now. Annie and Aunt Clara took it in turns to make sure she ate something at lunch, usually just a bit of bread and cheese, but she found that difficult to manage at times, so Annie had started making soup for her, which meant that there was no time for her to eat anything herself.

The ribbons from Ivy's bunches had come loose, so Annie tied them up neatly before shooing the two girls downstairs to play in the back yard for a while. 'Will you show me how to do it?' said Elsie, pointing to the heavy irons on the pagoda stove. 'I'm nearly big enough, aren't I?'

'Soon,' said Annie, patting her on the head. Mum didn't like the girls near the heat of those irons. She'd seen too many of the younger laundrymaids scarred for life in a moment's clumsiness to risk her children getting scorched.

Annie peered out of the window again, watching Ed as he walked Moses back to the stables around the corner. He had a loping sort of walk and a broad back under his black uniform jacket. Annie remembered the way he'd smelt faintly of sweat too when she'd sat next to him on the laundry rounds. It was all the effort of lifting those hampers into the back of the cart. He'd managed it easily, of course. He was really strong and when he rolled up his shirtsleeves you could see the muscles on his forearms.

Suddenly, there was a shriek and both she and Mum made a dash for the stairs. When they got down to the wash house, Ivy was sobbing and Elsie was half naked and soaking wet, with Bessie and Vera dunking her in one of the sinks as she tried to wriggle herself free.

'She fell in the bleeding bleach tub!' cried Vera, wiping Elsie's face with a wet tea towel. 'My back was only turned for a minute.' She held up Elsie's gingham pinafore. All the colour had disappeared where she had toppled in, so it had a huge white patch on it, instead of navy and white checks.

'I just wanted to help with the washing,' Elsie blubbed.

Bill appeared at the back door and scowled at Annie: 'You were supposed to be looking after them!' He picked Elsie up and gave her a little hug. 'You'll be right as rain, don't worry, doll,' he said, shooting Annie another filthy glance. He always made it her fault, even though he was probably chatting to Chas and the other laundry hands in the boiler room out the back instead of doing any work. It was amazing how much tinkering went on in there, with spanners and so on. Vera reckoned they were busy having a whist drive and just used to clank on the boiler with a hammer every now and then to trick the Missus that they were mending it.

'I'm sorry,' said Annie, who knew her mind really had been elsewhere. 'I'll take them back and look after them.' It was silly to think of going out to the varieties anyway. She was needed at home.

'No, love,' said Mum, touching her on the arm. 'I'll take them home. You go off and enjoy yourself tonight.'

The Missus made a great show of making everyone work until six o'clock on the dot but then let the girls out a full fifteen minutes early, so that they could get to Chiswick High Road before the crowds.

As her girls stampeded out of the front door, she shooed after them, with a smile: 'Get out of here, the lot of you!' It was their one early night in the whole year and she loved playing up to being grumpy with them, just for the fun of seeing their worried faces, thinking they might have to stay behind and scrub the floors.

Ed let the other men go on ahead and fell into step with Annie and Vera. He brushed his fingers through his hair, so that it was a bit more swept back from his face. 'Hello, ladies,' he said. 'Mind if I tag along?'

'Don't mind if you do,' said Vera, giving him a smile. She had curled her hair last night and – Annie noticed – had somehow managed to get some red lipstick and slap that on, when no one was looking. Annie smoothed her hands over her hair, which was cut into a bob. She'd hoped it would make her look fashionable, like Vera, but unfortunately it just brought the kink out in the back of it. She'd stuck a clip in the side to keep it in place but the unruly waves at the back just stuck out in all the wrong places. Next to Vera, she was a total frump. She thrust her hands deeper into the pockets of her cardigan as they wandered along, their breath puffing out in front of them in the damp night air.

Ed moved a bit closer to Annie. 'Shall we sit next to each other, then?'

'She's already promised to sit with me, haven't you, Annie?' Vera cut in.

'Well, I'm sure there'll be room for me to squeeze in next to you both in that case,' said Ed, before Annie could answer. He was quite undeterred by Vera's glacial stare. Her eyes were clear blue, like icy water.

'Suit yourself,' said Vera, tossing her curls. 'I'll be watching the show in any case, not you.'

Ed raised an eyebrow and stopped to light a cigarette. He drew in a breath and then blew smoke rings in the air as they walked along. Annie watched him, quite fascinated. He looked so sophisticated. He was only a year older than her, but he seemed so worldly. It was probably because he drove all over town in the horse and cart – he got to see a bit more of life than she did at the washtub.

A queue was already forming when they got to the theatre, which stood like a palace on the Chiswick High Road. The imposing facade with its grand entrance was like a gateway to another world for Annie and the laundresses from Soapsud Island. It was a place where they could forget their daily drudgery and have a proper giggle. But they had to get in, first, and some of those sneaky girls from the Cambrian had managed to knock off ten minutes before them, so they were first in line for the cheapest seats up in the gods. There was a fair bit of jostling between some of them and the Hope Cottage laundrymaids, but the Cambrian lot were stuck to the pavement like glue.

The management had put up a notice saying they'd been 'obliged' to put the price up – just as they did every year, when they got wind of the laundry Christmas outing. Plus, the whole show was a sell-out because of one of the so-called 'trouser acts', the male impersonator Ella Shields, who was a sensation. Annie couldn't wait to see her; she'd heard Aunt Clara and Dora talking about her after they'd been to see her up in the West End. The posh folks from

Chiswick had already paid for their tickets in the circle and the stalls and were walking into the theatre, done up to the nines in their expensive coats with fur collars. That meant they missed out on the free entertainment in the street outside, of course, which was all part of the fun.

A busker with a penny whistle and a budgie in his top pocket was playing 'All the Nice Girls Love a Sailor', while a young girl tapped in time on a wooden board by his side. Further down the line, some kids were entertaining for ha'pennies, doing cartwheels and leapfrogging each other. As they got nearer, Annie nearly died of shame when she realized that one of them was her little brother George, being egged on by Vera's brother, Alf.

'Get yourself home!' she hissed at him. If Bill found out, he'd take his belt to him, but she was more bothered about being shown up in front of Ed, who would think they were common as muck to have a kid begging like that.

As George slunk away around the corner, the manager opened the door for the seats at the top of the house and the queue turned into a gaggle of excited people, surging forwards. Annie had her ninepence ready and found herself pressed up against Ed as they shuffled in. He gave her waist a little squeeze and she turned around and smiled at him. It was like a secret sign that they were here together. Annie's heart soared almost as high as the ceiling, like some bird flitting about near the ornate plasterwork.

There were so many stairs to climb, but once they were up there in the balcony, the atmosphere was thrilling, with the whole place packed to the rafters and the chatter from the plush bottle-green seats down below rising to the top of the auditorium. The walls were lit by glowing gas lights, and the light bounced off the brass fittings and made them look like burnished gold.

Aunt Clara and her friend Dora sat on the end of the row behind them and, true to his word, Ed squeezed himself in between Vera and Annie, just as the curtain went up and the orchestra struck up a tune. The first act was a woman billed as Bunty St Clair the staircase dancer, and as the music got faster, so did her prancing up and down a little set of steps. She was showing a lot of leg, and Ed wolf-whistled as she jumped down into the splits for her grand finale.

A magician was next, pulling a whole washing line full of coloured handkerchiefs out of his pockets. 'Oh, I wouldn't fancy having to wash that lot,' said Vera, with a giggle. Then came the main attraction, the male impersonator Ella Shields, who came on to a massive drum roll, dressed in a top hat, white tie and tails and spats. She was greeted by cheers as the orchestra struck up the opening bars of 'Burlington Bertie from Bow'.

Annie could hear Aunt Clara and Dora singing along in the row behind her: 'I'm Burlington Bertie, I rise at ten thirty and saunter along like a toff.'

Ella tapped her way across the stage, her voice carrying across the vast auditorium and when she took her top hat off, her cropped, slicked hair glinted in the limelight: 'I walk down the Strand, with my gloves on my hand, then I walk down again, with them off.' There were guffaws from the stalls.

When she got to the chorus, 'I'm Bert, Bert, I haven't a shirt,' all the laundry girls in the balcony were singing along. Bessie had tears of laughter rolling down her face; Annie had never seen her looking so happy.

Just as the curtain came down for the interval, Annie's mother appeared out of nowhere, at the end of their row of seats. She was flushed from running and had beads of sweat in her fringe.

'You've got to come home now,' she gasped, clutching her chest. 'It's Nanny. She's had a funny turn.'

Annie leaped to her feet and spun around, to catch Aunt Clara letting go of Dora's hand.

'So, you're off, then?' said Ed, moving his legs sideways to let her pass. She nodded. He was almost perfunctory about his goodbye, but she didn't mind too much because he obviously didn't want to get teased about being soppy with her, that was all.

'See you tomorrow,' said Vera, airily.

But as Annie was leaving, she spotted Ed's arm snaking its way around Vera's back.

10

December 1925

'Kiziah, Kizzy? Is that you?'

Nanny Chick lay in a darkened room, with the bed-sheets pulled almost up to her chin, clutching her big red medicine book to her chest.

'It's me, Nan,' said Annie. 'Don't worry yourself, everything is going to be just fine.'

The wind rattled on the windowpanes and the rain was hammering down outside as Annie went over to the bedside and held her grandmother's hand. She looked so thin and small lying there and her cheeks were all sunken.

Nanny's fingers tightened their grip: 'Don't leave me, Kizzy, please don't leave me.' She opened her eyes but didn't seem to recognize Annie standing before her.

In the hallway, the doctor was talking in hushed tones to Mum: 'It's a stroke. I have done what I can to make her comfortable, but only time will tell how well she is going to recover,' he murmured. 'I will pop round again in the morning to see how she is getting along.'

Mum stifled a sob. Annie stepped into the hallway to comfort her and found the kindly doctor standing there, clasping his black bag.

Annie handed him his coat and his hat, as Mum sank down onto the stairs, her head in her hands, her shoulders shaking as she wept. Aunt Clara rushed out from the scullery, carrying a teacup.

She offered it to Mum: 'It's a tot of brandy, Em, I think you need it.'

Annie had never seen her mum drink anything more than the occasional sherry but she knocked it back in one go and dried her eyes on her apron. It seemed to fortify her. 'Forgive me, doctor, you must think me very rude,' she said, getting up.

'No, no, not at all,' he said.

'We can settle up with you when you come tomorrow, if that is all right – it's just I haven't . . .' her voice trailed off. It went without saying that payday was Friday and she didn't have the money now to meet his bill.

'Please don't trouble yourself, Mrs Pett,' he said, in his most avuncular tone. 'You have all had a huge shock and I know this is a respectable family. There's no need to be worrying about my bill now.'

Annie opened the door for him and he smiled at her: 'And how's that little brother of yours getting along these days?'

'Fine, I think,' said Annie. She had no idea whether George had even come home yet, but the last thing Mum needed now was to be troubled with the fact that her son had been dancing for pennies outside the Chiswick Empire.

The door had barely shut on its hinges when Bill appeared from the scullery. 'Well,' he said, thrusting his hands into his pockets. 'I was hoping to give the girls a real treat this year for Christmas but I suppose that will be the money from my paying-out club going to that bleeding doctor again.' Like most of the men around Soapsud Island, Bill had been squirrelling away a few pennies a week to help pay for the turkey, trimmings and presents. Mum shot him a look of deep hurt. Aunt Clara weighed in: 'Oh, stop it Bill, you'll have your twenty shillings for Christmas! I will help out.'

Annie feared she'd say something she'd live to regret, so she retreated into the darkness of Nanny Chick's bedroom instead, with Aunt Clara hot on her heels, as Mum stormed off upstairs.

'Kiziah, Kizzy, come here, love, let me see you,' said Nanny.

Even in the half-light Annie could see that the colour had drained from Aunt Clara's face.

'She keeps asking for her,' said Annie. 'Who is Kizzy?'

'Just someone from the old days, back in Notting Hill, I should think,' she said. 'Why don't you go and get some rest? I'll sit with her for a while.'

As Annie was closing the door, she saw her aunt free the book from Nanny's grasp, smoothing the bedclothes and tenderly stroking Nanny Chick's forehead. 'There,' she whispered. 'No more talk of Kiziah, now, you'll only upset yourself. It's Clara, I'm here. I won't leave you, ever.'

Later that night, Annie fell into an uneasy sleep.

Mum and Aunt Clara were taking it in turns to sit with Nanny, and every time Annie heard footsteps pattering on the stairs, she woke with a start. Her brother was snoring softly next to her and Ivy and Elsie were tucked up fast asleep in a little single bed against the opposite wall, so Annie didn't dare get out of bed in case she disturbed them. Instead, she lay there, quietly, staring at the ceiling, thinking about the old woman who had been such a big part of her life but who now seemed so frail, as if she was fading away into dust.

It was still dark when the tap-tap came on the bedroom window from the knocker-up, who was paid to wake everyone in the street in time for their jobs at the laundry. Annie crept out of bed, her feet freezing on the cold square of linoleum which covered the boards, and made her way downstairs. Mum was already up in the scullery, pouring some tea for Aunt Clara.

'She's still sleeping and doesn't seem any worse,' said Mum. 'The Missus won't do without me, but if you can stay here for the morning, Aunt Clara will cover the afternoon and you can take over her job on packing.'

'Of course,' said Annie. 'I'll do whatever you need me to.'

Mum smiled at her and gave her a hug. 'I don't tell you enough, Annie, but you are such a good girl, my best girl, I don't know where I'd be without you.'

Once she'd cleared up the breakfast things and tidied the house, Annie opened the curtains a little way in Nanny's room, to allow some of the thin light of the winter's morning to enter. Nanny stirred and her eyelids fluttered open. Annie brought a glass of water and, cradling Nanny's head, pressed it to her lips, to help her drink.

'Annie,' she croaked.

'How are you feeling?' said Annie.

Nanny pointed to her sewing workbox, on top of the chest of drawers in the corner.

'Do you want me to bring it to you?'

Nanny nodded.

'It's all yours now. It's time,' she whispered, as Annie carried it to over to the bedside.

Nanny Chick closed her eyes with a sigh and went back to sleep.

Annie sat down in the rocking chair and opened the box. She'd spent so many hours watching Nanny sew and knit. Nanny had taught her too: how to mend and make a strong seam, how to make a nightdress pretty by buying a scrap of lace from the market for the collar and the cuffs and stitching it on. Then there were all Nanny's best buttons, the ones she'd collected over the years from the laundry floors back in Notting Hill when she first went to work there back in the eighties. The pearly ones were Annie's favourites. There were wooden buttons from babies' jumpers, big brass buttons from a gent's overcoat, delicate white mother-of-pearl ones and some fabric-covered ones, faded now, from grand ladies' ball gowns. Nanny liked to tell stories about each one of those buttons and the life it had led before it fell off in the wash. She could make up some funny things about going out dancing and the like, whirling around ballrooms and riding in carriages with the fancy horses up in Piccadilly and down Rotten Row. Annie knew it in her heart, but she didn't want to say it – Nanny's storytelling days were over now.

Annie opened the sewing box and peeked inside, her fingers finding their way over balls of wool, a button hook, a thimble – Nanny's best one. She put it on and rummaged some more – a scrap of linen, an old tobacco tin. She pulled the lid open and rifled through the needles, being careful not to prick her finger, scarcely believing that Nanny was giving all this to her. It wasn't that she didn't want it; she wasn't ready for what it meant – that Nanny wouldn't be needing it any more.

She reached the bottom of the sewing box. Nanny had never let her go through the box before. She hesitated. It wasn't right, really. Nanny was sleeping there in front of her and she was going through her things. But her fingers carried on, as if they had developed a life of their own, as if they were searching for something. Annie felt a ridge at the bottom of the box. She tapped it. It was hollow.

Carefully, she jammed her nails under the ridge and pulled upwards, gently, and a piece of wood lifted to reveal a secret compartment. There was a piece of paper in there, carefully folded. She knew she shouldn't, but she picked it up and stuck it in the pocket of her cardigan. There was something else, bigger, thicker, like a piece of card, wrapped in brown paper. The corner was stuck at the bottom of the box, so she had to twist it a bit to get it out. She closed the box, put the brown paper parcel on the top and unwrapped it, as quietly as she could. The paper rustled, but Nanny didn't stir.

It was a photograph, an old one, of a gentleman with a

jaunty moustache and his hair neatly parted. He was wearing a nice suit, by the looks of it, with a proper starched collar and a tie. He was smiling a slightly forced smile. It was the kind you made when someone told you to 'watch the birdie!' but the bottom half of the photo was missing and the card was burned, as if it had been caught in a flame.

She turned it over. There, in the faintest pencil, was written, 'To my darling Emma, love always, your Henry.'

She would have recognized him anywhere; looking into his eyes was like looking into her own.

'Daddy,' said Annie.

Time seemed to stand still. Hours passed with Annie just sitting in the rocking chair, poring over every detail of the picture of her father, Henry Austin. He had a carnation in his buttonhole and a handkerchief in his top pocket; there were wisps of hair along his hairline, just like hers, and his nose was rounded too. She wanted to reach into the photograph and touch him. She closed her eyes and imagined his voice. It would be kind and gentle, she was sure of that.

Annie almost jumped out of her skin when she heard the front door creak open. There was no time to put the picture back in its hiding place, so she tucked it down the front of her liberty bodice and sat there, with the work-box on her knee.

'Are you all right?' said Aunt Clara, brushing some raindrops out of her hair. 'You look like you've seen a ghost!'

'I'm fine,' said Annie, who hated lying – she'd been brought up to be truthful. 'I was just watching Nanny and I forgot the time.'

'How is she?'

'She woke up for a bit and said my name and told me she wanted me to have her sewing box . . .' Aunt Clara's eyes narrowed a little.

'Annie, love, she's already promised the sewing box to me, as her daughter,' she said, brusquely. Aunt Clara walked over and took the workbox from Annie's lap. 'You mustn't set too much store by what she says. She's confused, that's all.' She put the workbox back in its rightful place. Annie was crestfallen and Aunt Clara's face softened. She gave her a hug. 'Come on, chin up, I wasn't trying to upset you. You'd better get yourself off to work or the Missus'll be after you.'

Annie nodded. She darted upstairs and took the picture out from her liberty bodice, looking for a safe place to hide it. She took the folded paper from her cardigan pocket and shoved it between a couple of handkerchiefs in her drawer – the top one in the chest that she shared with George and the girls. She felt her heart thumping, nineteen to the dozen. She'd never had any secrets before, not like this, and the guilt of it was burning her up from the inside. Perhaps Nanny had promised the workbox to Aunt Clara and got confused, but she was certain that Nanny had been trying to give her the gift she'd longed for, something to remember her father by. With trembling hands, she tucked the picture inside her pillowslip and carefully placed Raggedy Annie, her doll, on the top, to guard it.

In the sorting room at Hope Cottage, Vera was humming to herself as she folded some shirts and placed them in blue tissue paper, ready to go in the next hamper.

She ran over to Annie as she came in and gave her a big hug.

'How are you doing, chicken? Your mum told me all about it, I'm so sorry, I didn't realize it was serious last night or I would have left the show and come with you,' she gushed.

'It's all right, Vera, there's nothing more to be done about it,' said Annie, staring at the floor. 'The doctor says it was a stroke and only time will tell.' To her shame, she felt annoyed with Vera. It wasn't fair to be angry with her, but she couldn't quite get the memory of Ed putting his arm around her friend out of her mind.

She picked up some freshly pressed sheets and put them in the bottom of the Felstones' hamper. There was a real sense of achievement in seeing so many things ironed and smelling lovely and clean. Of all the places to be in the laundry, the packing room was the calmest – she needed that, today of all days.

Vera sidled up to her: 'The thing is, Annie, I wanted to ask you if you'd mind terribly about something and I know the timing ain't great, with things being the way they are. It's just, we're mates, aren't we? And I wanted to be straight with you . . .'

The Missus stuck her head around the packing room

door. 'Vera, for the love of God, girl, will you stop chattering? Annie, you are wanted down in the wash house. Bessie needs help running some blankets through the mangle.'

Vera opened her mouth to protest.

'Don't stand there catching flies, girl!' shouted the Missus. 'Get on with it. You'll work more quickly on your own, in any case. This is not a gossip shop.'

Annie had to wait until teatime to find out what was on Vera's mind. Vera had to pick up some free powdered milk for her family from the Poor Law on the way home and so Annie agreed to go with her. They walked up Bollo Lane and along to the nursery on Bollo Bridge Road to collect it.

'The thing is, Annie,' said Vera, linking arms with her, 'Ed has asked me out.'

'Oh,' was all Annie could manage.

'I didn't want to tread on your toes because I thought you two might be courting?'

'No,' said Annie, noticing how the cartwheels had worn ruts in the mud at the edge of the road. Her throat had gone terribly dry. 'He hadn't asked me properly or anything.' She wanted to scream, 'but he was going to, Vera, before you butted in'. Then she saw something in Vera's eyes, a look she hadn't ever seen in all the years they'd known each other at the laundry. Her friend's face was glowing. It was happiness.

'I haven't said yes to going out because I was worried about hurting your feelings,' said Vera. 'He kissed me, Annie, after the varieties. I think he's serious about me.'

Annie squeezed her friend's arm: 'Oh, Vera! You mustn't even think about me. Don't be silly. I just like talking to him about the horse, that's all. Me and Ed are just friends and you'd be daft not to go out with him. It sounds like he is mad keen.' Inside, a new feeling was gnawing away at her. It was jealousy, she knew that, but she was determined not to stand in Vera's way and spoil her big moment.

Vera threw her arms around Annie. 'He's asked me to go to the Crown with him, you know, the one with the double seats on the back row.'

Annie sighed inwardly but forced a smile: 'Yes, it sounds wonderful, Vera, you must go of course, and it will be lovely.'

'Are you sure?' said Vera.

'Yes,' said Annie, ignoring the stab of disappointment that Vera would be walking out with Ed, in her place. 'But there is something I need to ask you.'

'Anything,' said Vera, breezily. 'Ask away!'

'Well, you know when soldiers went off to the war, like your dad, did they always get a picture done, in their uniform?'

'I think so,' said Vera. 'I mean, I know we've got one of Dad. Mum chucks it at him when they are arguing, mostly.'

'It's just I haven't got one of my dad in his uniform, at least I don't think there is one,' said Annie. She didn't want to give away too much about having found the picture of her father, but the more she thought about it, the fact that he wasn't in his uniform was a bit strange.

'Maybe it's because your dad died and so your mum is

too sad to put it up,' said Vera. 'But all the widows got one of those memorial medals – you know, the Dead Man's Penny.'

Annie looked puzzled.

'They used to be made at a factory up the road, but it was bad luck to work there, at least that is what my mum told me. Doesn't your mum have one of those?' asked Vera.

'No,' said Annie, 'but then again, even if she did, I don't suppose Bill would want it on the mantelpiece, would he?'

'He's probably traded it in for a side of bacon,' said Vera, making piggy noises, which set them both off laughing.

They parted company at the end of Stirling Road and Annie wandered home to find her mum waiting for her on the doorstep. Annie knew by the look on her face that it was bad news.

Her mother walked towards her, with arms outstretched, and Annie felt tears starting to spill down her cheeks.

'Nanny just slipped away peacefully,' said Mum. 'She didn't suffer. The doctor said it was better this way. The last words she spoke were to you this morning, Annie.'

Annie's heart leaped into her mouth.

Her mother's eyes searched her face. 'What did she say to you?'

'Nothing really,' said Annie, regaining her composure and drying her eyes. 'She just called out my name and wanted to see her sewing box for one last time, so I brought it to her.'

Mum nodded to herself, satisfied with her daughter's answer.

But Annie knew then that the photograph of her father that she had discovered in that sewing box and the lie she had just told her mother would change things between them forever.

11

May 1926

'One Out, All Out!'

The newspaper billboards up on Acton High Street were full of union workers' slogans on the eve of the General Strike.

As dawn broke on the morning of Tuesday 4 May, the railway line at the back of Annie's house was eerily quiet.

The women of Fletcher Road stood gossiping on their doorsteps, fuelling the air of anticipation, as Annie dashed up to the shops to buy some bread, before it all sold out. People were panic buying and there was even talk of food shortages.

Hundreds of transport workers from Acton and Ealing were due to gather at Ealing Common later that day but, as her mother grumbled over the breakfast table this morning, life in the laundry would still have to go on.

'It's all very well for the factory workers and the dockers and the railwaymen to walk out, but someone's got to do the washing,' she huffed, as she browned a slice of bread on the toasting fork over the fire for Annie.

'It all comes down to the miners – they're controlling it,' said Bill, grabbing the toast before Annie could get to it. 'It's all very well saying they don't want a penny off their pay or a minute on their day, but they live up north. It isn't like that down here. Who is speaking up for us?'

'I think it's just all the workers trying to stick up for each other,' said Annie. 'To speak with one voice.'

'And who asked for your opinion?' said Bill, scowling at her. 'You're beginning to sound like one of them Communists.'

'I just overheard Ed and Jack talking about it at the laundry,' she mumbled, wishing she hadn't bothered speaking. Ed's dad was among the union organizers and Jack's dad was a copper, so they each saw the argument from a different side and it had been interesting to listen in to them discussing it. Months of rumblings about strikes because of the miners' pay had come to a head and the whole country risked being crippled by it. There were fears of extremists stirring up trouble on one side and of the rich folk taking liberties with the poorest workers on the other.

'Well, that's men's talk, Annie, and no point in you repeating it, now, is there?' said Bill, with a laugh. 'As if you'd understand it, anyway!'

She stood there, as if she'd been slapped, feeling foolish for opening her mouth in the first place. Mum sighed to herself; she didn't like any unpleasantness, and she didn't want to get involved. It was all too much when she was worn down by life at the laundry.

Ivy and Elsie skipped in and kissed Bill on the cheek. He offered them a bit of bread each: 'Ah, a lovely kiss for your old dad! How are my princesses? Are you looking forward to school?'

'Yes, Dad,' they chorused.

'And who is going to be the cleverest today?' he said, pinching Ivy's plump cheek. 'Will you be top of the class in arithmetic?'

She nodded.

He turned to Elsie: 'And what about you? Still top in spelling?'

'Yes,' she giggled.

Both of her half-sisters were bright as buttons, it was true, and Miss Frobel, the headteacher, expected great things of them. She'd already had a word about them staying on at school until they were fifteen, to get the best chance of a clerical job afterwards. Annie felt proud of them both, they were so clever.

Annie knew that her brother George was no dunce either, but Bill had refused to let him try for a scholarship for the grammar school last year. Bill had moaned that if he passed, they'd have to find extra for the school uniform. 'He wouldn't fit in with those privileged kids,' Bill had said. 'Fancy your son being the "scholarship boy", with a load of toffs for mates, Em?' So the idea was quietly dropped.

Poor George just needed someone to take a bit more of an interest in him, to keep him out of trouble and away from the likes of Alf, Vera's brother, who was a wild one. Mum doted on him but she was always so busy, she didn't have time to keep an eye on what he was up to.

Lately, Annie had tried to get him to come into the laundry after school, so she could watch him. The other day he'd spent ages helping the laundry hands get the boiler going, which was something. He seemed to like taking things apart and putting them back together again. Mum would always tell him, 'Keep your greasy hands off my whites!' but if he was pulling a bicycle to bits, at least he wasn't getting up to no good with Alf.

It was too late for Annie to have any breakfast now, so she set off. She passed some tram drivers on the way down Fletcher Road, with placards slung over their shoulders, heading up to Ealing Common for their rally. Women were busy donkey-stoning their front steps to make them gleam, strike or no strike.

Annie laughed to herself at the thought of the laundry girls daring to walk out of Hope Cottage when they were forced to stay back an hour and scrub the floors, or clean the house for the Missus on a Saturday morning, or fetch her a pig's head from the butchers. There were no unions to represent *them* – the Missus wouldn't stand for it, for a start.

By Wednesday, people were starting to get jumpy about the strike and Mum and the Missus went off to a special meeting of the Acton Ladies' Laundry Association at lunchtime to listen to a BBC broadcast. Miss Toomey, who owned the power laundry in Packington Road, had a radiogram set. Men were not invited, much to Bill's annoyance. 'It's just a women's talking shop,' he grumbled. 'Load of tittle-tattle.' But he knew that the association was more than that: it was a sign that women in Soapsud Island had a voice of their own because they had financial clout, and that rankled.

Bill and the laundrymen were left to sip warm beer and pore over the only news they could get their hands on. There were two news-sheets printed but they were like gold dust. Jack, the delivery boy, managed to get one of each, the *British Worker* – that was by the trade unionists – and the *British Gazette*, the voice of the government. He appeared in the laundry yard, flushed with the effort of running from the High Street. Bill and Chas had set up their headquarters on an upturned washtub in the yard and Bessie made sure that the back door was open, so they could all hear the gossip.

'There's a tram been pushed over,' gasped Jack. 'It was driven by a blackleg, some posh boy from Cambridge University, and he ran into a load of striking drivers from Ealing who gave him what for. I wanted to stop them but I was worried I'd get beaten to a pulp.'

Bill reached out to take the news-sheets, but Jack clutched them tighter: 'I had to hand over a thruppenny bit for each of 'em, instead of a penny. So, that's sixpence you owe me.'

'Pull the other one! That's profiteering, Jack, plain and simple,' said Chas, slapping him on the back. 'No wonder the country is on strike if that is what the world is coming to.'

Bill pulled out a sixpence and ruffled Jack's hair. 'It says here they need special constables, Jack. Your old man's a cozzer – why don't you volunteer and then you can go about cracking some heads with your truncheon?'

'You're right,' said Jack. 'I'm going to do just that.' And he turned tail and left the laundry.

Ed sauntered in, to add his tuppenceworth: 'You wouldn't catch me backing either side. It's the reds on one side and a bunch of toffs on the other. Look after number one, that is my motto. My dad said there's blokes in Eton ties acting as porters down at Paddington Station and the funniest thing is watching them trying to drive the trains. There's no need for anyone to set about them. They can't bleeding well get them going in the first place.'

Bill and Chas guffawed.

The Missus and Mum walked into the yard.

'Oh, evening ladies,' said Bill, tapping his watch and making a little tutting noise.

'Mind your language, William Pett,' said the Missus. 'We have just been fully informed by Her Majesty's Government that all the trains are running as normal and there is no need to worry about your tea because they've got plenty of supplies of that, so you'll be all right. I have to say I didn't believe a word of it. Now, get back to work.'

She turned to Ed: 'Don't stand there idling, you'd better go and get the dirty linen in from Notting Hill. Where's that good-for-nothing Jack?'

Bill and Chas exchanged glances.

'He's gone to volunteer as a special constable,' said Bill, matter-of-factly. 'Felt it was his patriotic duty.'

The Missus threw her hands up. 'That is all we need!'

'Annie!' she yelled, in the direction of the wash house.

Annie walked out into the yard. She'd been lurking with Vera and Bessie just behind the sorting room door. 'You're riding out with Ed into town. Keep your wits about you. There's strikers about and I am not having them making off with any of my customers' dirty linen!'

Ed and Annie had barely exchanged a word since the trip to the Chiswick Empire. She'd stopped feeding Moses and kept herself to herself, out of embarrassment really, that she'd obviously got the wrong end of the stick, thinking that he'd fancied her. Well, either that or he'd been hedging his bets between her and Vera.

On the rare occasions they'd seen each other – mainly when he was hanging around to take Vera out somewhere after work – he avoided her gaze too. Now she was going to have to share a ride in the cart with him all the way into town and back. It was mortifying.

'Annie,' he said softly, as he picked up the reins, 'I wanted to . . .'

She decided to take the bull by the horns. It wasn't as if she'd done anything wrong. 'You don't have to explain anything,' she said, clambering up beside him. 'It isn't as if you had actually asked me out properly before you started courting Vera, is it?'

'You're a great sort, Annie,' he said, giving her shoulder a squeeze, making her heart flutter in a way which she was powerless to prevent. 'I knew you'd understand. Vera's a lovely girl, definitely the type of girl to be a girlfriend, but you are different, you know.'

'What do you mean?' said Annie, who knew she wasn't nearly as pretty as Vera, so why couldn't he just come out and say it?

'I mean you are a nice girl, someone who wouldn't . . .'

'Who wouldn't go and sit on the back row of the fleapit with you, in the double seats, you mean?' said Annie, with more than a note of irritation in her voice.

'Well, if you put it like that, yes,' said Ed, a muscle twitching in his cheek. 'The sort of girl I can talk to and be friends with is what I mean. I miss our chats. And you can come and feed Moses like you used to, if you want.'

'If I have time,' said Annie, realizing she'd missed seeing Moses and talking to Ed more than she'd care to admit. 'But I'm busy these days. Mum's asking me to help her train up some of the younger girls, and they're a giddy lot.'

She wasn't saying it to make herself feel better, either. Mum did rely on her a lot to help and she was getting older. She was twenty-one now – and that meant she was a qualified laundress, not just a laundrymaid. She wasn't going to mess that up by hanging around in Antrobus Road, whiling away the time with Ed, whose eyes still had a way of making her stomach feel all floaty. Besides, he was Vera's boyfriend.

The journey into Notting Hill was much slower than usual because of the sheer number of motor cars on the roads. There were a few buses running, but they were packed to the rafters and it seemed every bicycle from as far west as Hounslow was wobbling its way along the crammed route. Ed took a few side roads around the back of Notting Hill and then turned along the Bayswater Road to do some more collections.

Annie was shocked to see policemen sitting alongside volunteer bus drivers, and once they got near Hyde Park the grass was filled with razor wire and some temporary buildings had been hastily put up. They were guarded by armed motor vehicles filled with soldiers. Annie clasped Ed's arm in fear: 'Do you think there is going to be trouble?'

'No.' He laughed. 'I think it's all a show of strength against the strikers.'

Just then, there was the sound of horses' hooves down the Bayswater Road, followed by a convoy of lorries. A column of cavalry soldiers came riding by, making such a racket that Annie had to cover her ears and Ed had to hold the reins tightly to steady Moses, who threatened to break into a fast trot. Behind them were more than a dozen lorries and after that came armoured cars, packed with soldiers, bringing up the rear. A policeman held up the traffic as the cavalry led the convoy on its way into Hyde Park.

'My dad said that a load of food had landed at the docks yesterday,' said Ed. 'I suppose this is where they are storing it, to let everyone know that they have supplies.'

Annie didn't like any of it – things not being how they normally were. It didn't seem right to have soldiers with guns on the streets of London. It made her think of the sacrifice her dad had made for his country. Did he do all that, just so the managers could mistreat the workers and the workers could walk out and have a pitched battle in the middle of London? Why couldn't people be paid enough to live on? Life was already such a struggle, and this wasn't going to make it any easier for the poorest, she felt it in her bones.

*

It was late by the time they got back to Soapsud Island and Vera was waiting for Annie in the wash house, looking agitated.

'You took your time getting back with my boyfriend,' she said, plonking a load of dirty whites in the sink to be treated for stains.

'Don't be like that, V,' said Annie. 'There's nothing going on, I promise. It was just work. The strike made it difficult for us to get here.'

'I bet you couldn't wait to get your hands on him, once my back was turned,' she said, her eyes flashing with anger.

'No,' said Annie. 'Vera, that is not true. I told him I am happy that you two are walking out together. I would never do anything to spoil your relationship with Ed.'

Vera leaned against the wash house sink, her fingers gripping the sides. Her knuckles were almost white. She looked down at the floor. 'I'm sorry,' she whispered, 'I don't mean to be a cow to you. It's just . . .'

'What is it, Vera?' said Annie, moving closer to her friend, to try to comfort her in some way.

'I've ruined everything with Ed anyway. I think I've gone and got myself pregnant.'

12

May 1926

Annie felt the wash house floor moving from under her as news of her friend's pregnancy sank in.

'How far gone do you think you are?' she asked Vera, whispering in case any of the nosy laundrymaids were still lurking nearby.

'I'm not sure: two, maybe three months,' said Vera. 'I've never been that regular, so my mum hasn't clocked yet that I haven't thrown anything on the fire for a while. But she will do soon and then I'll be out on the street.'

'Are you sure you're pregnant?'

Vera patted her rounded belly under her apron. 'I'm surprised you didn't notice me going off to throw up in the mornings,' she said. 'I've been right off me food but I'm putting on weight like nobody's business.'

Annie was open-mouthed. She'd never expected this and she didn't know what to do or say to help.

'Can't you talk to Ed, tell him, make him do the decent thing . . . ?'

'No, I can't tell anyone,' Vera cried, with a wild look in her eyes. 'I'm done for when me dad finds out. He will kill me and then he will come and slit Ed's throat.'

'Don't talk like that,' said Annie, helplessly.

'You don't understand,' said Vera. 'He told me not to let anyone touch me, that I'm his and if I did and I wasn't married he would kill them because he killed people in the war and he knows how to do it. And now he will know that me and Ed . . .'

'When you say you are his, do you mean . . . ?' The thought was too terrible for Annie to say it out loud.

'He is just possessive of me, says I'm the prettiest of all of his girls and he wants to protect me,' said Vera, shifting uncomfortably. 'It started after the war. I think he had seen so much death he wanted to look after me, that's all. He made me promise to wait until I was married.' Vera started to snivel a bit.

Annie knew that all parents wanted to make sure their girls didn't get themselves into trouble, but there was something wrong about what Vera's dad had been up to. It was just not right for a father to say those things to his daughter, she felt sure of that. She remembered the finger marks around Vera's neck all those years ago at the Empire Day parade as well. What else had he been doing to her?

Vera went on: 'I had to hide the fact that me and Ed were going out together. I told him I was going out with you . . .'

'Oh,' said Annie.

'I'm sorry,' said Vera. 'I know it was a terrible liberty, Annie, but I didn't think you'd mind.'

That was the least of their problems now, for sure. They

hugged each other for a moment, like two frightened schoolgirls.

'We have got to find a way to put this right,' said Annie.

There was only one person experienced enough in the ways of the world they could share this with.

The penny dropped for both of them: 'Bessie.'

Bessie lived at the opposite end of Stirling Road to Vera's parents and it wouldn't be out of place for two laundry girls to pop in and see her after work, so Annie was confident that the first part of their plan would be all right.

But Bessie was rather surprised to see them – she'd left work only an hour before. She opened the door with her face wrapped in a bandage and a poultice against her cheek, which had swollen up.

'Well, you're not seeing me at my best!' She laughed. 'Me tooth is killing me, girls, but I'm not going up to the High Street to get any more oil of cloves until this blessed strike is over. Can't be doing with all the argy-bargy in the shops, for one thing. Now, what brings you round here? Not planning a walk-out over pay, I hope, because the Missus will sack you both, I can tell you that for nothing.'

'No, it's nothing like that,' said Annie. 'We've got something we need to ask, that's all.'

'I see,' said Bessie. 'You'd better come in.'

They followed her inside.

She lived in two rooms in the upstairs of one of the scruffy terraced houses, which had a rickety wooden staircase out of the back, leading down into a garden, with scrawny chickens scratching around in it. A zinc bath hung on a peg just outside the back door at the top of the stairs. Annie suddenly felt very grateful for her family's home; it seemed like a mansion compared to Bessie's.

'Well,' said Bessie, sitting down on a creaky old chair which was so tiny that her haunches spilled over the sides of it. 'What's going on?'

Annie and Vera exchanged glances. All those years together scrubbing at the washboard had brought the three of them close and Bessie sensed it was something serious. She lowered her voice; noise carried and the people downstairs were a right nosy lot. 'Is one of you in some kind of trouble?'

Vera nodded. 'I think I'm about three months gone,' she said. 'Give or take.'

'Oh, Lord,' said Bessie. 'Well, there's no point asking how it happened. I suppose it's that good-for-nothing carman that's knocked you up?' She got up and put the kettle on the stove.

Vera blushed and nodded.

'I'm not your ma, Vera, so it's not my place to tell you off. And it's too late for modesty, so you can spare your blushes in my house. The question is, what are you going to do about it?'

'We were rather hoping you might be able to help with that,' said Annie, struggling to keep her hands still in her lap. She felt guilty, just being here talking about this.

'I don't suppose you can tell him about it and ask him to marry you?' asked Bessie.

'He's not the marrying kind,' said Vera, 'I'm quite sure

of that. But I'm more afraid of what my dad will do to me. And him.'

Bessie got some teacups from a wooden shelf over the sink. Annie noticed there was a picture of a young lad in uniform which took pride of place up there. It was Bessie's son who was lost in the Great War. There was a bronze medallion next to it, in a display case. That must be one of the Dead Man's Pennies that Vera had told her about. It was still a mystery to her why she didn't have one to commemorate her father's bravery; other girls had lost their dads in the war and then their mothers had remarried and they still had pictures of them and medals and so on.

'All right,' said Bessie, eyeing them both as she plonked the cups down in front of them on the table. 'This is grown-up talk now and you must both swear you will not repeat to anyone what I'm about to tell you – not least because your mothers would skin me alive. There is a woman locally who can help girls in this sort of trouble.'

'Is there?' said Vera, brightening.

'Yes,' said Bessie, pouring some water from the kettle into an enormous brown teapot. 'But it's dangerous. It's the wrong side of the law, for a start, and it doesn't always work, so you might still have the baby anyway. But, whatever happens, you cannot go telling anyone about it or how you heard about it. And I will need to make the introduction for you.'

'Who is it?'

'Ask no questions, Annie, and I will tell you no lies,' said Bessie, sploshing milk into their cups. 'She's just a woman who helps babies come into the world, but she can also help them disappear when they are not wanted. For a price.'

'I haven't any money!' said Vera.

'Well, you should have thought of that before you went and got yourself in the family way,' said Bessie, chucking a lump of sugar in her tea and stirring it. 'You've got a wage packet. You'll have to use that or go to a money-lender – but I wouldn't advise that, because they will have you in their grasp then and it is hard to get out.' She raised her eyes heavenwards: 'God knows, I learned that the hard way.'

Annie thought for a moment and then said, 'I can help. I've been putting money by to get myself a coat for winter. Why don't we use some of that?'

'Oh, Annie,' said Vera, 'I couldn't ask you to do that.'

'I'm offering to help,' said Annie.

'Well, if you lend me a bit from your savings, I could use some of my pay because my mum doesn't always ask for it straight away,' added Vera. 'And my dad is always too drunk to notice what's going in the pot anyway.'

'I'll leave you two to work out who is paying for what,' said Bessie. 'Last I heard, she asks for a week's wages up front, so whatever you do, make sure you go with the money ready, or she won't take kindly to it. I will put the word out to her and see what she says. I ain't promising, but it is the best chance you've got, Vera.'

'It's the only chance,' said Annie, staring into the murky depths of her tea.

*

On Friday morning during their tea break, Bessie handed Vera a piece of paper with an address on it.

'It's all arranged,' she whispered, as they sipped their cuppas in the yard. 'Go straight there after work and knock twice. It's going to cost you twenty shillings. But don't tell me no more about it. I don't want to know. Is that clear?'

Annie and Vera nodded. 'I have probably done more than I should have already,' muttered Bessie, chucking the dregs of her drink on the ground. 'I don't want your mums knocking on my door about this, so let this be the end of it.'

Annie had her ten shillings of savings in a brown envelope, which felt as if it was burning a hole in the pocket of her cardigan. It seemed the older she got, the more secretive she had become, and she wasn't sure she liked that. More than anything, she felt guilty to be sneaking off behind her mum's back to do this; she'd told her that she was off out to the cinema with her friend after work.

The hours seemed to drag by through the afternoon. The Missus seemed to take ages totting up everyone's wages. She sat in the hallway with the ledger on her knee, and a tin box full of cash by her side. The ironers were paid first, with every piece they'd worked on carefully recorded, so that those who had worked extra were fairly paid. Annie feared that Vera would give the game away because when she picked up her pay packet, her hands were shaking.

'Whatever's the matter with you, girl?' asked the Missus. 'Not planning to elope with that boyfriend of yours on my wages, are you?'

'No,' said Vera, forcing a smile, ''course not! Just the pictures for me and Annie tonight, Mrs Blythe.' Annie knew she looked as guilty as sin as she collected her own pay. They were in this together now and there was no going back. They waited until the other laundrymaids were busy scrubbing the floors before hurrying out of Hope Cottage and towards The Steyne – an area even poorer than Soapsud Island, just off the High Street – and the address that Bessie had given them.

'I promise I will pay you back, a shilling a week, Annie,' Vera told her, as they scurried along. 'You are such a good friend to come with me.'

'I couldn't let you go through it alone,' said Annie. Besides, Bessie had said it was best if they went together, that way Annie could help Vera get home safely after-wards.

They stopped outside the house. The door was brown, with peeling paint, but the windows sparkled, the net cur-tains were starched and ironed nicely and there were some pot plants on the window ledge, making it look cheery. Vera stepped forwards and knocked twice. A round little woman answered, wearing a housecoat and slippers. 'You must be Vera,' she said, looking her up and down, before turning to Annie: 'I'm only doing one of you – who are you?'

'I'm her friend, Annie, Annie Austin,' she stammered. Were they even supposed to give her their names?

'Well, don't stand around on the doorstep,' she said, bustling them both inside.

She showed them through to her scullery, where a

Singer sewing machine stood against one wall, and there was a wicker basket of seamstress's work neatly folded beside it. Some crocheting was resting on the arm of a rocking chair, and there were embroidered pictures of flowers on a shelf in the corner. Annie peered at the needle-work, seeing that this woman was a very skilled seamstress indeed.

The kitchen table had been pulled into the centre of the room and covered with an old white sheet. A cushion had been placed at one end and a fat, stripy tomcat had made himself comfortable on it. 'Shoo!' said the woman, brushing him off. The cat stalked out of the back door with his tail in the air.

'Right,' she said. 'Have you got the money?'

Annie carefully unfolded the envelope with her savings and pulled out a ten-bob note while Vera counted out ten shillings from her pay packet. The woman took the money and tucked it into the pocket of her housecoat, before going over to the sink and washing her hands with a big block of carbolic soap.

The kettle was heating on the stove and it started to whistle. Annie watched as she selected a crochet hook from the work on the rocking chair and tipped boiling water over it before resting it on the side of a tin plate.

'Take your underclothes off, dearie, and climb up on the table,' the woman said to Vera, who obediently took off her shoes and put them neatly together by the sewing machine. She wriggled herself out of her cotton knickers and folded them over the arm of the rocking chair. Annie found herself blushing and looked away for a moment. It was all so personal.

The woman took a blue and white striped teacup from the draining board by the sink and picked up a bottle of colourless liquid, yanking the cork out with her teeth. She sloshed a good deal of it into the cup. 'This will hurt, I won't lie, but the gin will take the edge off it,' she said, handing the teacup to Vera. 'Down the hatch, that's right.' Vera glugged the gin down in one go and then coughed so much that Annie had to slap her on the back.

The seamstress turned and looked at Annie.

'You're Emma's girl, aren't you?'

'Yes,' said Annie.

'You're the image of her,' she said. 'Although I haven't seen her since I delivered your little brother – oh, it will be more than ten years ago now.'

Before she knew what she was saying, Annie blurted: 'So, did you know my father?'

The woman laughed. 'No, I can't say I did. Your mum was still back in Notting Hill when she had you.'

'Oh,' said Annie. She'd always thought she was born here, in Acton, not in Notting Hill. And surely her father had been here in Acton when they moved, hadn't he? This woman was a link to her past, the past she wanted to know more about. 'So, when did my mum come over here to Acton, then?'

'I've answered enough of your questions. If she hasn't told you, I'm not going to. We haven't got all day,' said the seamstress, tutting. 'We'd better get on.'

Annie couldn't argue with her; the reason they were

here was to get Vera out of her predicament, but she couldn't help being curious. It was as if her fingers were scrabbling away at the bottom of the sewing box again, looking for a buried secret.

'Help me up, Annie,' said Vera, climbing onto the table. Annie noticed that her friend's legs were shaking. 'Please hold my hand,' Vera implored, as she lay back, resting her head on the pillow, suddenly looking much younger, and more afraid than Annie had ever seen her.

The woman came over to the kitchen table, carrying the crochet hook. 'Draw your knees up and just let them flop out to the side,' she said. 'Or I shan't be able to see what I'm doing. It's important that you just relax.' She handed Vera a folded tea towel. 'And I don't want the police here, so, for the love of God, bite down on that and do not scream.'

Annie knelt down next to her friend and stroked some hair back from her forehead as the woman's hands disappeared between Vera's shaking legs. Vera's pale blue eyes were filled with panic but there was no going back. 'That's right, I'm in the right place now,' said the woman, as Vera winced. 'It will be very quickly over.' She wriggled the hook between Vera's thighs and Vera screamed into the tea towel, sobbing with the agony of it.

'There we are,' said the woman, matter-of-factly. 'Now, just get yourself into the rocking chair and we will see if that has done the trick.' She hummed to herself as she took the crochet hook, stained with blood, over to the sink, where she doused it with the remaining hot water from the kettle. Vera clutched her belly as she sat up and

Annie helped her off the table. The woman put a wodge of old tea towels onto the chair and motioned for Vera to sit down.

Vera started to moan, clutching her stomach.

'Yes,' said the woman, brusquely. 'It will hurt, but it will soon be over, bear with it.'

'Oh, God,' Vera moaned. 'Annie, help me.'

Blood started to run down Vera's legs; a trickle at first and then huge clots of it appeared. The woman handed her a rag. 'Wipe yourself up, now, that's right.' But the blood didn't stop, it came in a big gush and splattered onto the floorboards.

'Jesus, Mary and Joseph, help me,' whimpered Vera, looking at her fingers, which were stained red where she had tried to stem the flow.

The seamstress's attitude seemed to change. She stiffened and became even more businesslike, mopping up the blood and wringing it out of the cloth in the sink in the scullery. She passed Annie a heap of rags. 'You can help too, just get it off my floor,' she ordered.

After ten minutes of mopping, Vera was still moaning and groaning, doubled over on the rocking chair, with a wad of blood-soaked towels underneath her.

'Right,' said the woman, 'it's time to leave now. I have done what you paid me to do but you can't stay here any longer. Put your clothes back on, love.' She folded some muslin cloths and handed them to Vera, who dutifully shoved them into her knickers and inched the undergarment up her white thighs, which were still trembling.

She handed Vera's coat to Annie, who was dumbstruck.

'But what are we supposed to do? Where can we go? She's still bleeding.'

'That is not my problem, dearie,' said the seamstress. 'But don't you dare breathe a word to anyone about coming here.'

Out of nowhere, a fella who was about the same age as Ed the carman but twice as wide appeared in the doorway. He'd been in the front room, all along, it seemed. He stepped back to allow them to pass. Vera was doubled over but Annie looked at the floor in shame. How much had he heard?

'If you tell anyone about tonight, he won't be a gentleman about it. Remember that,' said the seamstress, with a tight little smile. 'We know where to find you.' She herded them down the dark hallway, opened the front door and pushed them through it. As they stepped into the cool of the night air, Vera almost collapsed in Annie's arms. 'Please, Vera, please, don't,' Annie begged her friend.

They staggered down the street together in the dark. Annie had made up her mind. She couldn't go home to her house and there was no question of taking Vera back to her parents' place.

'Where are we going?' moaned Vera. 'My legs feel like jelly. I don't think I can go much further.'

Annie half dragged her friend up Acton Lane, across the High Street and into Churchfield Road, ignoring a wolf whistle from some blokes outside a pub: 'Looks like you're making a night of it, girls!'

'There's only one person who can help us now,' said Annie.

*

Annie hammered on Esther's front door, praying that her friend wasn't out at night school.

The door swung open and Esther stood there, her hair in rollers. She looked older, more glamorous, somehow.

'Annie!' she said. 'And Vera . . . whatever's the matter?' Vera was swaying from side to side, her head lolling back, and blood was running down her legs. 'Oh my God!' cried Esther. 'Come inside.'

Esther took hold of Vera's arm and with Annie on the other side, they dragged her down the hallway and up the narrow staircase, leaving a trail of blood as they went.

'I didn't know where else to turn,' said Annie, with tears in her eyes. 'I didn't know what to do. We've got to help her!'

As they burst through the front door, Esther's grandfather leaped up from the sofa where he was mending shoes. He motioned for them to lay Vera down. She was murmuring softly: 'I'm sorry, I'm sorry . . .'

It was a split-second decision: tell the truth and risk getting everyone in trouble with the police, as well as that big lump of a bloke at the seamstress's house who might hurt their families – or stick to the story. 'We were in the cinema,' said Annie. 'And she started bleeding like this. I think she might have been . . .'

'Pregnant?' said Esther. 'Oh my God. We need to get a doctor.'

Esther's grandad took his family's special quilt, the one with all the woodland animals and birds on it, and laid it over Vera, who was shaking. Then he went over to the sideboard and produced a dark brown bottle. 'It's apple brandy,' said Esther, watching him pour it into a tiny glass with flowers painted on the sides. 'From his home.' He took it to Vera and tilted her head up, to help her sip it.

Annie stood there, frozen, watching the scene before her. Esther's lips were moving but it was as if the words didn't make any sense any more.

'I'm going to get the doctor,' she was saying. 'She could bleed to death. How far along was she?'

'Probably three months,' Annie murmured. 'Three months, that's about right.'

'What about her parents?'

'No!' cried Annie, grasping Esther's arm so that her nails dug into her friend's skin. 'You cannot tell her parents. Her dad will kill her.'

'All right,' said Esther. 'Let's get the doctor here and he can decide what to do, but if I don't get help now, she's in real danger.'

It was if the doctor knew, without Annie needing to say a word, exactly what had happened.

He looked straight into Annie's eyes as he said: 'I will write it up as a miscarriage. We need to get her straight to hospital. Where are her parents? They need to be informed.'

Annie gave him Vera's address, wanting the ground to swallow her up. The doctor had known her family since she was a girl and now was looking at her in a different way, a way that said he had seen this once too often and Annie was *that* kind of girl. Of course, she wasn't, but it didn't matter, because the doctor thought she was.

'But I don't think they have any medical insurances,' she said, pulling out her pay packet. 'Please, take this. I will pay for your call-out tonight.'

'Wait,' said Esther, realizing that Annie was about to hand over all her money for the week. 'Let me do it.' She offered him a crisp ten-bob note.

'Esther, you can't,' said Annie, trying to stop her friend, but Esther insisted.

'Very well,' said the doctor. 'The Poor Law will make provision for her hospital care, I can send for the ambulance now. We need to examine her properly and she'll be watched carefully over the next day or so, and then there is the risk of infection.'

He muttered under his breath as he turned to go: 'The trouble is, no one thinks about that, until it's too late.'

There was quite a bit of gossip among the laundrymaids about what had happened to Vera and why she was off work, until Bessie shut them up by giving them a clip round the ear. The ironers were a different matter. There were looks and glances in Annie's direction until her mother let it be known that the next person who mentioned Vera would be dealing with *her*. Mum pulled Annie to one side in the ironing room: 'People are talking, Annie, saying things about her trying to get rid of a baby. I need to know: were you involved in any way?'

'No,' Annie lied. 'She started bleeding and she ended up in hospital. It happened after we left the cinema, just like I said, which is why we went to Esther's house.' She couldn't tell her mum the truth, it would betray Vera and, in any case, it was too risky. That seamstress and her son, who was built like the door of the brick lavvy in the yard, would be out looking for her if she so much as breathed a word about what had happened in their kitchen. She hoped that would be the end of her mother's questions. But she was dreading the arrival of the autumn, when she'd have some explaining to do about where her coat money had gone. Her main concern, though, was what was going to happen to her friend.

Vera lay, pale as a ghost, in the Union infirmary in Isleworth, keeping up the pretence that she'd suffered a miscarriage. Her mother came to see her but her father sent word that she wasn't welcome at home any more. Annie went to visit and Vera told her, through tears, that she'd suffered a perforation to her womb from the crochet hook and might never be able to have children. 'I should have had the baby,' she said, tears rolling down the sides of her face and onto the crisp white pillowcase. 'I-I could have managed.' They both knew that was an impossibility with Vera's dad the way he was; she'd have been on the street and the baby taken away from her.

'Shhhh,' said Annie. 'Don't talk like that. You weren't to know.' None of them had known. None of them understood, until it was too late.

The ward sister bustled past and gave them a hard stare. She didn't like any fuss and nonsense, and visitors were supposed to keep the patients calm, not upset them. Plus, she must have known the real reason Vera was in here, and the way she looked at Annie made her feel as if *she* was guilty, as if *she* had stuck that crochet hook into Vera to end that baby's life.

Vera's voice fell to a whisper: 'Tell Ed . . . that I love him.'

'Of course,' said Annie, who feared that Ed must have picked up on the gossip about his girlfriend by now. Why hadn't he come to see her?

The General Strike ended the Wednesday after Vera's botched abortion and all the laundry workers piled into the Railway Tavern for a booze-up. Annie went along too, just for a quick glass of sherry with Bessie and the others, although she didn't feel much like celebrating. She couldn't get the image of Vera's shocked face out of her mind. That and the blood running down her legs – it was so awful.

Ed was there in the pub, of course, linking arms with Ada the laundrymaid, as the pianist played some tunes. Annie tried to talk to him, to tell him about Vera, that she'd been pregnant with his child and was sick in hospital and needed to see him.

'Could have been anyone's, couldn't it?' he said, drinking deeply from his pint. 'Although it's a shame because she does have a very pretty face, does Vera, and I bet her baby would have been a good-looking sort.'

The pianist hammered out another song which made everyone roar with laughter. 'Your baby has gorn dahn the plughole,' he sang, as beer sloshed over the brims of glasses and the singing grew rowdier. 'Your baby has gorn dahn the plug. The poor little thing was so skinny and thin, it should have been bathed in a ju-ug!'

Ed joined in, hugging Ada around the waist. 'Your baby is terribly 'appy, he won't need no bathing no more, your baby has gorn dahn the plughole, not lost, just gorn before. Just gorn be-fore!'

13

March 1934

The first daffodils of spring brought a burst of colour to Gunnersbury Park.

Annie loved her Saturday afternoon walks there, as she'd often catch up with Esther taking her new baby, Leonard, for a stroll in his pram.

She couldn't wait to show Esther her new hat. Now Annie was earning more than a pound a week as a qualified laundress, Mum had insisted she put some money aside to spend on herself. She'd spent ages window-shopping up at the big department store on Ealing Broadway before choosing a bottle-green felt cloche hat with a black grosgrain ribbon around it.

Annie had never been one to follow fashions; until now, she simply couldn't afford to. But with her new hat and a coat she'd picked up second-hand at the market and put some new buttons on, she had to admit, she really did feel quite smart.

Esther was waiting for her, ready to soak up any gossip Annie had from the laundry, like a sponge. She had her hands full being a home-maker now, after her boyfriend, Paul, who worked at Wilkinson's Sword factory down the

Vale, had popped the question. Although she'd only admit it to Annie, she was wondering what on earth she'd spent all that time bettering herself with exams for.

The laundry business was one place where married women could go back to work, not like working in factories or shops, but people still frowned on it, and if you could afford to stay home, like Esther, then you did.

'I miss working, Annie,' she confided. 'I know I shouldn't say it because I love being married, but I hardly see anyone all day and now he wants another one. He thinks it'll make me happier.'

'But Leonard is beautiful,' said Annie, gazing at the cherubic baby, sleeping soundly, tucked up in the pram. 'Of course you will have another, won't you?'

'I expect so,' said Esther, with a sigh. 'But what about you? Why don't you find yourself a nice man and settle down?'

'Oh, I just haven't had the time to meet anyone yet,' said Annie, who had steered clear of any romantic involvement at work after what had happened to Vera; the last thing she wanted was to get herself into any kind of trouble or find herself forced into walking up the aisle too soon and then regretting it. 'Mum and Bill rely on me so much to look after the girls, I just don't think it would be right. My family needs me to be living with them to help out with the rent and running the house.'

Esther gave a little nod, as if she didn't quite believe her friend. 'But if the right man came along . . .'

'Well, he hasn't so far, has he?' said Annie, rather too quickly. She'd got used to catching the bouquet at other people's weddings, always being the one without a partner when they went on work outings. She felt sad about it, of course she did, but then she'd catch Ed the carman chatting up some unsuspecting laundrymaid and she'd feel sick to the pit of her stomach. He had sowed a seed of mistrust about men, a secret flower that she nurtured every night as she lay in bed, thinking about her life. It blossomed in the darkness and she fed it on her heartache.

It was a constant source of amazement to Annie how much dust could gather under the beds.

She was giving the bedroom a thorough spring clean, with her hair tied up in a headscarf and a feather duster in her hand, while her sisters Elsie and Ivy got to work cleaning the windows downstairs.

Annie sang to herself as she got into all the nooks and crannies, imagining she was one of the Hollywood movie stars she'd seen in the talkies, singing and having fun as she went about her chores. She pulled open the top drawer of the chest in the corner to give it a tidy and carefully took out her few things; some woollen stockings, a chemise and some handkerchiefs.

Of course, she knew there was a little piece of paper in there, which along with the photo of her father, was the most precious thing she owned, taken from Nanny Chick's sewing box the day she died. She looked at it in the rare moments when she was alone in the bedroom, without Elsie or Ivy. She'd carefully unfold it and trace over the words with her finger: 'I love you Emma, now and always, Henry', imagining her father saying that to her mother.

Quickly, she got up and ran to the top of the stairs to check what the girls were up to. They were nearly young women now, with Ivy turning sixteen soon and learning to type, while Elsie was leaving school this year. But they seemed younger than other girls their age in some ways, more sheltered, because they'd not been out at work and picked up the ways of the factory girls. Bill liked it that way and Annie had to admit, she was glad they hadn't had to toil in the laundries from a young age as she had. They both still had a cheeky streak to them and were as thick as thieves if they'd been up to mischief. The last thing Annie wanted was for them to catch her pulling the paper from its hiding place: they'd run and tell their mother, or worse, Bill. She could hear them singing 'On Mother Kelly's Doorstep' together in the front room; Elsie had a nice singing voice but Ivy, God bless her, was tone deaf.

There was almost a thrill in her little secret, unfolding that paper, and reading his declaration of love. It was written in pencil, on top of what looked like a payslip, for eighteen shillings, from Silchester Mews Stables in Notting Hill. If no one else was around, she'd pull the photograph of her father out from its hiding place under the mattress and look at that too, searching his face for similarities to her own, now she was a grown woman. What would he make of her? Would he be proud of her working so hard each day in the laundry and looking after her sisters and George?

A footfall on the stairs brought her back to reality and she swiftly tucked the paper into the pocket of her pinny as Elsie burst through the door. 'Come and judge who's done the best job, Annie!' she cried. 'Dad's got a sixpence for the winner and I want it to be me.'

Annie glanced at her wristwatch. It was nearly six o'clock and she had promised to pop in and see Vera this weekend. She was a fiercely loyal friend to Annie but was building a reputation as a woman not to be messed with around South Acton.

As far as work was concerned, Vera was completely unreliable; the Missus had to sack her in the end for her poor time-keeping. Well, that and the fact that she lamped Ada the laundrymaid one day for making snide remarks about her 'trouble'.

After Vera left hospital and found herself homeless, Bessie had persuaded the Nosy Parkers downstairs to sublet one of their rooms. It wasn't completely without self-interest, mind you, because having Vera around gave Bessie more clout when she wanted to use the shared copper in the scullery to do her smalls. Vera, meanwhile, found herself a new job as a helper in the council nursery on Bollo Bridge Road, which meant she was able to see her mum's new baby, Evangeline, and lavish her with so much love, as if she were her own child. Annie knew that Vera was seizing the chance to be with the baby, for fear that she would never be able to have one of her own.

And there were signs that she was trying to bury the sadness of everything that had happened in her life. Once her pay packet arrived on a Friday afternoon, Vera would start drinking more than it was thought polite for a young woman – or any woman, for that matter. Her father would be propping up one end of the bar, sinking pints, and she'd sit at the other end, knocking back port and lemon or sherry, glowering at him. As the night wore on, he'd sling an insult and she'd sling one back. The landlord of the Railway Tavern had tired of them both and turfed them out, so for the time being, they were both to be found, in their cups, at the Anchor up the road.

Saturday teatimes were Annie and Vera's regular meet-up because that was when Vera's dad went out to the eel pie and mash shop down Acton Lane for his tea, giving Vera's mum the opportunity to sneak her wayward daughter into the house to see her siblings. There were ten of them, including Vera, but the six oldest had all grown up and moved out and started families of their own, so that you only had to turn a corner in South Acton and you'd bump into one of the O'Reillys or their offspring.

Just when it seemed that Vera's mum had surpassed herself with the twins, Ernest and George – who were constantly in trouble with the Old Bill – and told everyone that these two had just about killed her off with worry, she'd fallen pregnant again, unexpectedly, with Evangeline. The child was angelic – sweet, blonde and beautiful – and was doted on by the whole family, and Vera most of all.

As Annie hurried off towards Stirling Road she was almost knocked flying by a gaggle of kids careering down the middle of the street on a crate they'd hammered some old pram wheels onto. It seemed like yesterday that George was doing the same, but now he was to be found zooming around town on a motorcycle with a gleaming sidecar. He'd landed a job as a delivery boy for the Cherry Blossom shoe polish factory down in Isleworth and was cock-a-hoop about it, not least because all the prettiest girls wanted to jump in for a lift.

There seemed to be plenty of opportunities for keen young blokes like George who were prepared to move with the times and learn new skills. It was the older fellas who still suffered the most from the worst of the unemployment and wage cuts. Even Alf, Vera's brother, had got himself a job as a delivery boy for the grocer and he brought his pay packet home to his mum every week, to make her life a bit easier.

Annie rapped on the tatty black door at Vera's mum's house and then gave it a shove and let herself in. She knew better than to stand on the doorstep and wait – she'd be there all night – for politeness did not feature highly in their world. She walked into the hallway, which had mud marks and scuffs all up one wall, as if it had been used for football practice. Ernie and George were fighting on the stairs, pulling each other's hair and screeching their heads off. The O'Reilly family lived in a continual cacophony of noise, tears and dirt, but Vera's mum did her best to love them – even through the black eyes which were the mark of Vera's dad having had a particularly busy weekend, drink-wise.

In one sense, the O'Reillys had gone up in the world, in that they now had the run of the entire house, as the old woman upstairs had given up the ghost and died, so the landlord had let them have her rooms for next to nothing. On the other hand, the house was as near to a total slum as anything Annie had ever seen, with beetles infesting the walls and mould sprouting strange mushroom-like growths from the damp and peeling extremities of each room.

Annie pushed open the door to the scullery, which was probably not more than nine feet square, and was confronted by the smell of a burning sausage in a pan on the stove, which did little to disguise a sweet, fetid stench. Vera was holding Evangeline on her lap on a worn-out old sofa and trying to spoon watery mashed potato into the child's mouth. The little mite didn't have the strength to protest or wriggle, so she merely clamped her lips tightly shut and tried to turn her head away. Meanwhile, her mother was mopping sweat from her brow and browning a single sausage to a crisp; it would then have to be carefully sliced and divided between the children for their supper, along with a dollop of mashed potato each.

'Come on, Evangeline, eat, please, for me,' Vera crooned. 'Eat for your best big sister.'

She turned and looked up at Annie.

'Oh Ann, I'm worried half to death about her,' she said. 'She's not been right all week, right off her food, and she's got the runs something terrible.' Vera kicked a porcelain jerry under the sofa, for the sake of decency, but the smell lingered.

'The poor little thing,' said Annie. 'Has she seen a doctor?'

Vera lowered her voice to a whisper: 'Ma says she can't afford it but I'm going to take her myself on Monday. It ain't right. It's coming out like water, Annie, and there's not a picking on her to start with. She's all skin and bones.'

It was true, even for a two-year-old Evangeline was tiny, and her skin was almost translucent, except for two blotches of pink on her cheeks, and the hand-me-down nightdress she was wearing seemed to swamp her scrawny frame. Annie put her hand to the toddler's forehead. It was burning hot.

Vera's mum called for the twins and there was a stampede of little feet into the kitchen. The boys wolfed their food down and then charged back out of the room, wild-eyed and with their hair sticking up on end, to knock seven bells out of each other while their mother washed up.

'I'll get you a nice drink of milk,' said Vera, patting Evangeline's dirty blonde curls. She went over to a zinc bowl by the draining board and lifted a grey-looking cloth to reveal a milk bottle. There was nowhere to keep it cool, so this was the best Vera could manage, but a couple of flies buzzed about as she did so.

Vera sniffed at the milk bottle and then poured some of the milk into a little teacup and took it to her sister.

'Are you sure that's good for her?' said Annie. She didn't want to interfere but she knew that the dairyman who delivered around Stirling Road was one to avoid; her mum had refused to buy his milk because of the filthy churns. He'd merely dropped his prices and moved his cart a few streets away, of course. The poorest in the community didn't have the luxury of paying a few pennies more for cleaner milk, but she thought Vera's family should have qualified for the free powdered milk that the council gave out.

'They stopped the powdered stuff, the Poor Law did,' said Vera. 'Caught me dad working at the tyre factory and because me mum is working they took it off us. But milk is milk, Annie, and everyone knows it's good for littl'uns.'

'I don't know,' said Annie. 'I think you should try to speak to the doctor . . . but Nanny Chick always used to say if you had a dicky tummy you should steer clear.'

Evangeline took the cup and gulped it down. 'She's thirsty,' said Vera. 'I'll get her some more.'

Vera filled the cup up again and then smiled at Annie. 'See, it's doing her good. She looks better already.'

Annie nodded, ignoring the dreadful sinking feeling inside her, as she looked into Evangeline's beautiful blue eyes.

Bessie was busy grumbling about the difficulties of washing rayon undergarments without shrinking them when Mum came in to the wash house waving a poster about a public meeting.

There in big, bold black letters were the words which made her mother see red: 'The Health RISKS of Acton's LAUNDRIES: Acton's Medical Officer will address councillors' concerns about health problems related to Soapsud Island.'

'It's outrageous,' she said. 'We can't have people saying our laundries are a health risk. I'm going to take it to the Ladies' Laundry Association, but I will expect you lot to back me up at the council meeting.'

'And so will I,' boomed the Missus, looming over her shoulder. 'It's just a lot of busybodies spreading lies, girls, and we have got to stick up for each other.'

Annie had to admit, it did seem like some of the councillors from the other side of the tracks were always complaining and blaming every cough and splutter in the district on the laundries, while making full use of their services to keep themselves looking spick and span.

She yanked some dirty sheets out of the Felstones' laundry hamper with renewed vigour. She had quite a few thoughts about things, but she tended to keep them to herself.

'There's been a lot of that upset tummy business going around,' said Bessie, as she held up the most ridiculous-looking pair of red rayon bloomers; it was cheaper than silk, so a lot of people had it nowadays, but if you got the water too hot, it would ruin it. 'People say it's dirty milk. I don't see how that is our fault!'

Bessie was right. Soapsud Island was just an easy target for people who wanted to point the finger of blame, but the truth was that it employed well over a thousand women in the district and the Ladies' Laundry Association was going from strength to strength, giving the women a voice, as well as a Christmas club and outings. With other industries laying men off left, right and centre, families were only too pleased to have mothers and daughters out at work at the washtubs, and someone needed to remind the council of that.

But the mood didn't stay serious for long in the wash house, not with Bessie around. 'Oooh, Annie,' she said, putting on a silly voice. 'Look at me in my long, red raffia drawers! I bet you'd love a pair like this, wouldn't you?'

Annie laughed: 'I thought they belonged to you!'

'Oh, you cheeky minx,' said Bessie. 'Don't think you're too old for me to give you a clout!'

Annie hadn't heard from Vera for a few days, so she decided to call round to see her at Bessie's on the way home from work, to catch up on how little Evangeline was doing. Plus, she could bring her friend along to the meeting up at the council offices, off the High Street. The Missus wanted bums on seats and that was what she was going to get.

But when she got to Bessie's house, Mrs Nosy Parker from downstairs answered the door, with her hair in rollers. 'She's out. Gone round to her mum's.'

Knowing that Vera only dared venture home on a Saturday tea time, when her dad was out, Annie hurried off down the street to the O'Reillys to see what was going on. When she got there, the curtains were already drawn downstairs and the house was unusually quiet. She knocked, tentatively, and then let herself in. Vera was sitting at the kitchen table, clutching Evangeline's favourite doll. She glanced up as Annie entered, her eyes red-rimmed from crying. 'It's the baby, she's really sick with her stomach trouble,' she sobbed. 'Mum's gone up to the hospital with her, she went so floppy that the doctor had to come out and Dad went off on one because of the cost of it.'

'Where are the other kids?' said Annie.

'They've gone to my aunt's around the corner, although God knows where she's going to put them all, but she insisted, so that my Mum could go and be with Evangeline up at the hospital.'

'Do the doctors know what's wrong?'

'Not yet,' said Vera, 'but there's a few kids gone down with some kind of fever and they're blaming the milk churns. The doctor took the milk bottle away to test it or something.' Her face darkened and she balled her hands into fists. 'That dairyman better not show his face around here if he has done something to hurt my Evangeline!'

'There's a meeting this evening,' said Annie, hesitantly. 'It's about health. Maybe you could ask some questions about it – or at least take your mind off things. It can't be good sitting here on your own.'

Alf appeared around the scullery door: 'You go, Vera. I'll get up to the hospital and keep an eye on things.'

Vera sighed. She looked so much older than her years, haggard and hunched over the table. 'You're right,' she said, standing up. 'It'll be good to get out for a bit at least. I'm just sitting here worrying myself sick about everything. I know my mum has gone up there with her, but I feel like it should be me, Annie, I'm the one she loves the most.'

Annie put her hand on her friend's shoulder, realizing how painful this was for Vera: 'Of course you are, Vera. And she loves you right back, you can see it in her eyes every time she looks at you.'

*

Annie had never seen so many washerwomen crammed into one room before, and with them taking the weight off their feet for once, too, rather than bent double over their washboards. The noise of them chattering to each other echoed around the hall, to the obvious irritation of the councillors sitting on a little stage at the front, who wanted to get on with the meeting.

The town hall was such an imposing building, with a grand clock tower in white stone looming over the High Street. Annie had always wondered what went on in there, with smartly dressed men bustling in and out of it whenever she'd walked past. Now she was inside, it made her feel quite nervous and her throat had gone terribly dry. She was warm too, even though it was only spring, and she took off her cardigan and held it in her hands, which had gone all clammy.

She recognized the doctor sitting up there, shuffling some papers about, but he was murmuring to another man, who had a silvery beard and not much hair on the top of his head. The Mayor was next to him, weighed down by his chains of office, and then along the row were other men in sombre suits and starched collars. A sturdy-looking woman sat at the end of the table, and next to her was a fine-boned slender little bird of a thing, wearing the purest white dress and silk stockings that Annie had ever seen. Annie couldn't help wondering how much those stockings had cost; she'd laundered quite a few pairs of those in her time and loved the feel of the silk, but she couldn't imagine what they'd be like to wear. The woman crossed her legs and stifled a yawn behind her gloved hand

and then turned her gaze once more to the men beside her, with a look of concentration, as if she were willing herself not to fall asleep.

Annie could just about see the top of her mother's best hat in the front row, alongside the Missus. There was no sign of Bill or the other laundry hands anywhere; they'd probably taken the opportunity to sneak out for a sly pint.

The Mayor stood up and banged a gavel on the table in front of him, calling the room to order: 'This is a very impressive turn-out indeed and it's pleasing to see so many of you prepared to take an interest in the health of our borough. Without further ado, I'd like to hand you over to Acton's Medical Officer . . .'

The man with the silvery beard stood up and began to read from a sheaf of papers in front of him, glancing around the room as he did so. 'Infant mortality in Acton has long been a problem and a topic of much discussion among the council members in this very chamber. Regrettably, we have found that deaths from diarrhoeal diseases and respiratory causes have always been high, and the reason is probably that the extra food and higher standard of living that a woman working outside the home in the laundries can provide and negated by the effect on the babies of the mothers leaving them in the care of others, in order to work.'

Vera leaned over to Annie, whispering, 'What a bunch of stuffed suits this lot look, don't they, Ann?' Meanwhile, as the Medical Officer's words began to sink in, the women in the rows in front of Annie started to shift uncomfortably in their seats. Annie spotted Bessie, twisting her handkerchief over and over in her hands.

'The employment of married women outside the home means that premature weaning is likely, and that is one of the causes of diarrhoeal diseases, of which we have seen an upsurge in recent weeks . . .'

Bessie could no longer contain herself: 'But it is bad milk that makes the babies sick, not the mother working in the laundries, everyone knows that! Wouldn't you be better off spending your time making those dairymen clean up their act?'

The sturdy woman up on the podium glared at Bessie for interrupting. 'That's Mrs Knight, who runs the council nursery where our Evangeline goes,' said Vera. 'She's a right old dragon. I wouldn't fancy Bessie's chances if it came to blows.'

'That is a fair point, madam,' said the Medical Officer. 'But if babies were not weaned so early in order to get the mother back to work, there would be no question of them needing other milk . . .'

'And if none of us worked, who'd keep your suits looking so smart, then?' said another woman, from the row behind Annie.

The woman in white simpered slightly as she gazed up at the Medical Officer and they exchanged glances. He ran his fingers through what was left of his hair, in exasperation.

The Mayor stood up and banged his gavel on the table. 'Ladies, this will not do! The Medical Officer is trying to bring to your attention a very serious issue about the health of the children in this borough – the least you could do is listen politely.'

Vera, who was not the brightest button in the box, leaned over to Annie again: 'So, are they saying it is our fault that kids are getting sick, because women have to go out to work?'

'That's about it, yes,' said Annie, who had started to feel properly unwell herself; she was burning up from the inside and her throat felt as if she had swallowed one of Bill's rusty old razor blades.

The Medical Officer started off again, reading out a long list of ailments which affected the tiniest tots in the borough: 'Bronchitis, pneumonia, tuberculosis, malnutrition due to want of breast milk . . .'

Annie had started to feel quite giddy and she barely noticed the tugging at her sleeve at first. Vera was pointing to the door, where her brother Alf was standing, waving frantically at them. 'I've got to go, Annie,' she said. 'Come with me?' They slipped quietly from the hall and into the cool air of the atrium. Alf was standing there, waiting. The look on his face said it all; he had been crying, that much was clear, but he couldn't get the words out.

Vera seized him by the shoulders and shook him, hard: 'What's happened to her? Is there any news from the hospital? Tell me or I will box your ears right off that stupid head of yours.'

'No, Vera, don't,' said Annie, struggling to hold her friend back; Vera in a temper was like a ship in full sail. 'He's your brother, he's only trying to help.'

'I'm sorry, Vera, I'm sorry,' he said, as tears spilled

down his cheeks. 'Mum was there with her at the end. There was nothing more to be done.'

Annie had never realized how loudly a scream could echo around a hallway with a marble floor, but Vera's cries for her baby sister Evangeline brought an abrupt end to the meeting as the women of Soapsud Island abandoned any thoughts of listening to the men who were trying to tell them how to raise their kids, and burst through the doors to comfort one of their own.

On the morning of Evangeline's funeral, Annie woke to find herself bathed in sweat. It was a fever like no other, not even when she'd had German measles as a child; the sheets were wringing wet.

Elsie and Ivy took one look at her and hopped out of their bed, running to get Mum. They bobbed about over Mum's shoulder, to see what was wrong, before they were shooed away downstairs.

Annie looked down at her arms, which were covered in red blotches.

'Let me see,' said Mum, peering down the front of Annie's nightdress; it didn't matter that she was a grown-up, in her mother's eyes she would always be her little girl. The rash was spreading across her chest and her face was burning up. 'I don't like the look of it,' said Mum. 'Looks like scarlet fever.'

Annie wanted to speak, to tell her mum not to fuss, that she'd get better, but her head just felt too big and heavy to even lift off the pillow.

'You need to keep away from me,' said Annie, her voice

a whisper. 'Keep the girls away from me, don't let them catch it.' Mum nodded and Annie closed her eyes for a minute. When she opened them again, the room seemed to be moving from side to side; she'd never been on a boat but now she imagined herself being rocked on a gentle tide, and the sea surrounding her was so warm that she needed a drink, yet she could barely swallow the water that her mother offered her.

The next thing Annie knew, sunlight was streaming through a crack in the curtains. She must have slept for hours. A damp cloth had been laid across her forehead and she tried to sit, dislodging it, so it slipped down over her face.

'Don't move, I'll do it,' said a voice. Aunt Clara drew nearer and dipped the cloth in a basin of water on a stool at the bedside. 'You need to rest.'

'Don't come too close,' croaked Annie. 'It might be catching.'

Aunt Clara smiled, her broad face beaming with kindness: 'I've had scarlet fever. Don't worry, I'm safe to look after you. Your mum and Bill and the girls have gone to my house and George is sleeping at the neighbour's. The doctor says the best thing is to keep you here, to stop it from spreading.'

'I don't want to be a trouble . . .'

It didn't seem right that everyone had to move just because she'd fallen sick, but Annie didn't have the energy to say any more. She flopped back into the bed as Aunt Clara dabbed the cloth over her face. She was on the boat again, swaying gently, as her eyelids closed.

'It didn't take me, and it won't take you, Annie, I promise,' whispered Clara, laying a kiss on Annie's forehead as she drifted back off to sleep.

That night, Annie's fever worsened and the rash spread all over her body, burning her up from the inside, as the skin started to peel from her hands. Aunt Clara sat in a chair in the corner, sewing by candlelight, rising occasionally to give Annie a drink or to pile more blankets on her, in the hope of making her sweat it out.

When she closed her eyes, Annie saw Moses the horse coming out of the bedroom wall towards her, pulling a hearse with a glass coffin filled with flowers. She climbed out of the bed, her feet wading through murky waters which lapped almost to her knees. Moses sploshed forwards to greet her and she reached out her hands to him. As she drew nearer, she realized that the hearse was carrying her body, pale and lifeless, and she recoiled in horror. She looked up at the carman and he lifted his black silk top hat to her, and she came face to face with her father, just like he was in the photograph. Annie woke with a blood-curdling scream and sat bolt upright.

'Whatever's the matter?' said Aunt Clara, rushing to her side.

'I'm dying,' croaked Annie, 'I'm dying and there are things I have to tell you. Things I've taken, I shouldn't have . . .' She was boiling hot but her legs were shaking and she felt that no matter how many blankets Aunt Clara put on top of her, she'd never get warm again. Her teeth started to chatter and she resembled one of those little monkeys jumping up and down for pennies at the fair in the summer.

Aunt Clara's expression was placid in the half-light: 'Shhh, don't upset yourself. It's the fever talking, Annie, it makes people say silly things.'

'No,' Annie whispered, curling herself into a ball, to try to get warm, 'I found a picture in Nanny's sewing box before she died, of my dad, and a piece of paper.'

'What picture? What paper?' said Aunt Clara, her voice rising slightly.

Annie pointed to the chest of drawers and Aunt Clara opened a drawer and rifled through it, pulling out the note. She unfolded it and held it to the candlelight to read, making a little 'Hmph' noise as she did so. Eventually she said: 'You're a dark horse, aren't you, Annie? If there's things put away so you won't find them, it's for your own good . . .'

'Please,' croaked Annie. 'I know it was wrong of me, but I'm not a child, I need to know. I have been keeping the picture I found since Nanny died. I don't want there to be any more secrets, not now.'

'Tell me where you hid it,' said Aunt Clara, gently.

Annie pointed beneath her, under the mattress.

Aunt Clara ran her hand underneath and pulled out the old photograph, gazing at it for an instant, smiling in recognition: 'Oh, yes, that's him, that's Henry Austin.'

'Nanny kept it,' said Annie.

Aunt Clara stood up and walked over to the window. When she turned around, Annie could see that there were tears glistening in her eyes.

'It was all such a long time ago now, some things are best forgotten, Annie.'

'There's nothing wrong with me knowing he was my father, or having a picture of him, is there?'

'No, not as such – it's just it was very difficult for your mum, losing him so young, and people have to move on, get on with their lives, and memories don't help put bread on the table, do they? It's probably best not to tell her you found it, I'm not sure what Bill would say, for a start . . .'

Annie was exhausted with the effort of talking and, sensing this, Aunt Clara offered her a sip of barley water. A solitary tear started to trickle down Annie's face as she drank.

'Don't, Annie, please, you mustn't tire yourself,' said Aunt Clara. Annie had no energy left to talk now. She lay back, her body aching; it was as if she was being run through the box mangle, with its heavy stones pressing down on top of her. She coughed, a horrible, rattling cough, which shook her bones. She could almost feel Moses' breath warm on her fingers, and her father was motioning to her to climb up on the driver's seat of the hearse beside him. He looked so handsome sitting up there and it would be peaceful to ride along beside him, with Moses stepping out gently all the way. There would be no more pain, she knew that.

Aunt Clara sat down in the chair by the bed and held Annie's hand, sensing that her niece was giving up the will to fight the fever. She squeezed her hand: 'Stay with me Annie; stay with me and I will tell you what I can about Notting Hill in the old days.'

Annie's eyelids fluttered open.

'That's right, you listen to me and I will tell you a story about three sisters living in the Potteries and Piggeries of Notting Hill, working in the hand laundries. Those places make Hope Cottage look like a palace. Oh, they were tough times but they had each other. Emma, Clara and their older sister . . . Kiziah.'

14

Notting Hill, January 1900

Susan Chick pulled her shawl tightly around her shoulders and set her face against the bitter wind as she pushed her handcart full of clean laundry up Holland Park Avenue, the wealthy main street through Kensington, lined with white stucco houses.

Silently, she cursed the day she'd left her job as a lady's maid; it had been twenty long years of spit and polish, but at least she'd have been warm inside one of the mansions on a day like this, instead of splitting the worn leather on her boots walking for miles on end.

The cold made her rheumatism play up, the pain spreading through her joints with every step, and then there was him indoors to worry about.

He was always keeping money back from her, spending it down the boozer with the other workmen, instead of bringing it home. Every man kept a few shillings for himself – for tobacco and beer – but Will, well, he seemed to need a bit more than most to keep him happy, which meant she was often running short of housekeeping money. She didn't like to complain because the one time she'd given him a piece of her mind, he'd refused to get

out of bed and go to work at all and then they almost
starved. She'd had to beg his forgiveness and he found
another job soon enough, but it had frightened the life out
of her because she honestly thought he'd have seen them
all in the workhouse.

Sometimes, she could have sworn he did it out of spite,
because she hadn't given him a son, just three daughters.
They were three of the loveliest girls you could wish for,
everyone in the laundry said so, but only her eldest, Kizzy,
seemed to be good enough in his eyes – and that was
because she had a wild streak and would stand up to him
and his moods.

The worst of it most days was when he'd start on at
Susan for not cooking him a decent tea. 'A man's got to
have his relish!' he'd yell, as he picked over lumpy mash
and gravy. Once, he'd chucked a plate of kippers at the
wall in a fury because he'd wanted a nice lamb chop, but
she couldn't afford it, not after she'd fed the girls, even
though she'd gone without. It had left a greasy mark on
the wallpaper, like someone pointing a finger at her every
time she set the rickety little table for them to eat. It made
her hate him, although she tried not to because she'd
meant her vows – to love, honour and obey – and, God
knows, she'd left it late enough to find a husband. She'd
still had flaxen hair when he'd walked her up the aisle, but
by the time her third came along, she'd turned as grey as
the flagstones on the laundry floor. Sometimes she was so
tired from standing all day at the washtub that she felt as
if she had one foot in the grave, in any case.

Whenever he shouted because his wife's food displeased

him, Clara, her youngest, would start quaking in her boots and her middle one, Emma, would try to placate him, smoothing things over by offering to run to the shops to find something else, which he would only find fault with, in any case. Only Kiziah would tell him that the food tasted fine and he'd feel better for it, if only he'd just try a mouthful. He'd watch her for a minute, through eyes that were already bloodshot from boozing, and then stroke his whiskers before tucking in, the juices dribbling down his chin – until Kiziah mopped them up with his handkerchief. He was like a little kitten with her.

His other favourite habit was to start harping on to all and sundry about the first Mrs Chick, who was no longer of this earth. She was so bleeding marvellous, she should have been a cook at the Savoy Hotel, apparently. Everything she did was better than Susan, according to him; it was a wonder she hadn't got her halo caught in the mangle when she did her washing.

Susan knew she didn't have it as bad as some of the other laundresses, though, and she was grateful for it. Oh, the endless black eyes and busted lips she saw at the washboards on a Monday morning were a sight to behold. Will had never raised his fists to her, but he was such a miserable so-and-so, she breathed a sigh of relief when the front door banged shut in the morning and he took his scowl off to work, wallpapering the grand mansions in Belgravia.

Susan pushed the cart on up towards Notting Hill Gate, as a beautiful glass-topped landau carriage pulled by two glossy black high-stepping horses came clip-clopping past.

She remembered seeing them for the first time when she came to London from Suffolk as a servant, marvelling at the footmen who rode on the back, with their shining buttons on perfectly pressed uniforms. Now all she could think about was how long it would take her to get those uniforms looking so smart, just so the fella in the silk top hat, studiously ignoring her as he sat safely inside, could keep up appearances with his posh friends.

Mind you, she was only too pleased to have a bit of extra work on from the wealthy lot who paraded up and down Rotten Row. It was helping to make ends meet, taking in some extra laundry, even if it meant she was working seven days a week. Once she'd finished at Mr Ranieri's place on Latimer Road, she'd haul buckets of water from the yard into the scullery and get the copper going and get scrubbing with the washboard again until the light faded. Emma and Clara helped her run it all through the mangle, and she had a good solid sad iron for pressing things just right. She'd perfected her skills working for a rich American widow in Bayswater during her years in service. The mistress was blind, the poor old dear, but she could feel a wrinkle in a sheet or a crease out of line on a handkerchief and then there'd be trouble.

It wasn't a bad life, not as bad as some folks thought it was when you said you came from the Potteries and Piggeries. It was just a stone's throw from the posh houses up on Notting Hill, but the rows of grim little two-up, two-downs that had been hastily thrown up there to house the poorest in the parish were a world away from that. There were still a few old dears who remembered the days of cut-throats in the back alleys, cock-fighting and the tumbledown wooden shacks of the pig keepers, who were driven out of Marble Arch and settled there, in the mud and the filth, back in the 1840s. Then came the bricklayers, digging out the clay pits to build rows and rows of back-to-backs which were crammed full of people struggling to make ends meet, every family as poor as the next. By the time Susan and Will moved in, the area was a network of little streets and every square inch of dusty earth seemed to be put to use to scrape a living; whether it was basket weaving on the front step, pig fattening, or rag-and-bone men picking over the rubbish from the houses up on the hill.

Susan was glad of her friends and neighbours in Manchester Road, the row of sooty terraced houses – which all the do-gooders who came to help at the Mission Hall on Latimer Road on Sundays spoke of, in whispers, as a 'slum'. Slum it might be, but it was home. She kept it as clean as she could, scrubbing the front step on a Friday, just like all the women who worked with her in the laundries and whose husbands were all plasterers or decorators like her old man Will.

When the girls were little, back in the eighties, you could barely venture out without a clothes peg on your hooter, it was true, because of the stink of those blooming pigs running everywhere and all the old claypits filled with black, slimy water and pigs' muck. The totters' kids from Silchester Mews called the biggest one the Ocean and used to dare each other to dip their toes in, but Susan had warned her girls to stay away from it. One poor love never made it home from the pub when she slipped and fell in and drowned – what a way to go! It was a park now because they'd filled it in for health and decency's sake, but Susan didn't like to go down there, near Pottery Lane. Some said it was haunted by the ghost of that poor drowned woman – and she believed them.

They were a respectable family, the Chicks. They went to church and believed that cleanliness was next to Godliness, even if him indoors did like his drink a bit too much. All the girls had good jobs, although Kiziah was a worry because she had ploughed her own furrow. She hadn't lasted five minutes in the laundry, she was just too spirited to be bossed about by a Laundry Missus. Kiziah even told the Missus where to get off when she'd found fault with her ironing. Susan had told her daughter that was no good, it was not the way to get on in this world, but Kizzy just laughed and tossed her auburn hair and said she'd go out and find another job. And, do you know what? She blooming well did!

First of all, she'd tried the posh shops down Bond Street, but they were all snooty and didn't want a girl from the Potteries who didn't know how to address a lady. Susan could have taught her, if she'd only listen, but she was headstrong, that one, with a fire in her belly, and so she'd gone off to find work doing the thing she was good at: sewing. Being a seamstress was hard work, poorly paid, but Kizzy loved to see what the ladies about town were wearing and she had such a way with her nimble fingers, it was as if the silks just flowed like water in her hands. She'd done some samples for one of the tailors down on Westbourne Grove and just about knocked spots off his best seamstresses, so he'd taken her on, just like that. She was paid per piece, and sometimes she'd bring her work home with her to finish off in the evenings. The light of the gas jet in the scullery was dim and so Kizzy would sit with her sewing on her lap, making tiny rows of perfect stitches by candlelight, until she was happy with it, while her dad almost glowed with pride at her work.

'You'll make someone a fine wife, Kizzy,' he said, pressing some baccy into his pipe. She'd be eighteen soon enough, a good age for marrying.

'Oh, I'm in no rush,' she said, with a laugh. 'I'm waiting for a proper gentleman to sweep me off my feet.' Dad nodded to himself, as if he were pleased with her answer, and then smiled at her.

Emma looked up from the sink where she was peeling spuds, and rolled her eyes at her mother and said under her breath: 'And I bet that would be just your luck, an' all!'

Emma was bringing in a half-decent wage as a presser at Mr Ranieri's. She was learning the ropes from Eliza Blythe, who was a right stickler, but Emma didn't mind. Emma was a different kettle of fish to her older sister, Kizzy, everyone said so. It wasn't just their looks – Kiziah was tall, fiery and striking, with red hair, where Emma was small, like her mum, with thick, sheeny chestnut locks and a quiet way about her. Emma was secretly proud that she had the patience needed to become a best ironer. It would take years of hard work, she knew that, but she'd only just turned sixteen, so she had time. She hoped it might make it easier for her to make a good marriage, too, because as the old saying went, 'marry a silk ironer and marry a fortune' – that's what all the women around the Potteries said. The other part of the saying was that the painters and decorators who married laundresses were a lazy lot who lived off their wives' hard work, but she knew better than to repeat that within earshot of her father.

Her younger sister, Clara, well, she was a bit of a clumsy clot and a bag of nerves whenever she got scolded, but she was such a sweet girl. She was in packing at Mr Ranieri's because she'd not long left school and he'd been kind enough to take her on, as she was family, although no one expected too much of her. Mum worried about her, but Emma promised she'd always take care of her, and she did, too – she was always checking she was all right and making sure she didn't make any mistakes by getting things in the wrong hamper. The family needed her wage, for starters, so it would be no good if she got the sack.

Mum was only too pleased that Emma and Clara were out of the wash house because it was down a steep set of stairs right in the basement of Mr Ranieri's two-up, two-down. Gawd, it was like the Black Hole of Calcutta down there some days, with all the bugs crawling out of the dirty sheets and stinking clothing, the filth sloshing out of the washtubs onto the floor and the steam rising and no air to be had anywhere. Old Ranieri would have his two daughters and his missus and as many women from the neighbourhood who'd work for a bob a day down there in his cellar, scrubbing away and mangling for dear life. It wasn't legal, of course, to have so many women working in such squalor, and when the factory inspectors came a-calling they'd all have to hightail it out of there with their washboards and away down the back alley. He was allowed to employ his family and two others, that was all, and then he could just about get away with murder on the pay and conditions because he wasn't covered by the Factory Act, and he knew it. It wasn't that Ranieri was a bad sort, he was just running a business – like all the others in Notting Hill. He was kind-hearted enough to bring them bread and cheese and beer for their lunches every day, from the Black Bull pub round on Silchester Road.

Emma looked forward to that because sometimes one of the local workmen would carry the beer in cans suspended from a long wooden pole and deliver them to the laundry. She'd got chatting to him lately because he knew her dad from working on the houses, and his mum, Jane, worked as an ironer at Mr Ranieri's. He was called Arthur and had a cheeky grin and the greenest eyes she'd ever seen. He'd made a point of talking to her on the doorstep long enough for Mr Ranieri to get annoyed the other day too, so maybe he quite liked her, although she couldn't be certain because she'd never had much experience of talking to fellas. Her dad wouldn't stand for any nonsense with blokes, she was pretty sure of that, because he'd tell his daughters not to dress up like the costergirls, who put feathers in their hats and hung around the pubs after dark.

Hanging around the pubs was a different matter as far as he was concerned, of course, and Emma was often sent off by her mum to fish him out of his favourite watering hole. Sometimes he'd be propping up the bar at the Black Bull, talking to Cornelius, the old barman, but lately he'd taken to supping pints down at the Bridport, off Avondale Park Road, because that was where the best card-gaming went on.

Emma buttoned up her jacket against the cold and lifted the hem of her skirt as she stepped over the rubbish strewn all over the street. The tinkers made a living collecting rubbish from the big houses up Holland Park and then whatever they couldn't use, they just chucked out in the street; what with the mud in the winter, you never knew what you were going to step in. The road narrowed into a little alleyway at the top of Pottery Lane, where the last of the brick kilns stood. She hated going down there in the dark, as the gas lamps barely lit the way and the shadows they cast up the narrow walls gave her the jitters. She took a deep breath and made a run for it, her boots tapping on the cobbles as she went.

A dog barked nearby, almost making her jump out of her skin. The local pig-keepers had dogs, too, and those mangy old things ran wild sometimes, which was scary if you got a pack of them coming after you. Some of the women carried walking sticks to beat them off and Emma was regretting coming out of the house empty-handed but, as she reached the end of the lane, the barking grew more distant and she slowed to a walk.

The costermongers were already making a night of it down the pub because Emma could hear them singing 'Molly Malone' when she came around the corner:

Alive, alive, oh,
Alive, alive, oh,
Crying, 'Cockles and mussels', alive, alive, oh!

A down-and-out minding the barrows was slumped against the green-tiled walls of the pub, looking for all the world like a bundle of rags, but he held out his hand as she drew near: 'Trouble you for a penny, miss?'

Emma knew her mother would scold her for it, but she dipped her hand into her jacket pocket and tossed a coin into his tin mug; it was a cold night, and she hated to see people on the streets in this weather.

As she pushed open the doors, Emma was enveloped by a thick fug of tobacco smoke which rose above the bar; the walls were stained yellow from years of men puffing away in there. One of the locals was hammering away at the piano, while a costermonger, in his shirtsleeves and waistcoat, was playing the spoons by way of accompaniment.

A costergirl with wild raven-black curls was standing on a table, her skirt hitched up to her knees, swishing it from side to side, with a circle of admirers at her feet. She had the tiniest waist that Emma had ever seen, and all the men seemed enthralled by her; it was like watching a music-hall star, close up. A hush fell over the room as she sang:

She died of a fever, and no one could save her,
And that was the end of sweet Molly Malone.
Now her ghost wheels its barrow, through streets
*   broad and narrow,*
Singing 'Cockles and mussels, alive, alive, oh!'

And then the whole pub erupted into the chorus, with hoots of laughter, as the singer jumped down to join her friends. They linked arms with each other, swaying as they screeched the refrain at the top of their voices: 'Alive, alive, oh!'

'Well, here's a pretty face,' said the spoon player, giving Emma's waist a little squeeze as she nudged her way through the crowd to find her father. 'Come and join in, love, don't be shy. I bet you can sing like a bird.'

'No, really, I'm fine, thank you,' said Emma, staring at the floor in shame. She hated coming into places like this. 'I'm just looking for my dad, Will Chick.'

'Will's girl, are you?' he said, smiling to reveal teeth like a row of moss-covered tombstones. 'He's round the back, playing whist with Charlie D and the boys.'

Emma elbowed her way through to the back room, where her dad was sitting at a table, his brow furrowed in concentration as he thumbed through the cards in his hand.

He glanced up at Emma and slapped the cards down on the table, chucking a small pile of coins into the middle. 'I'm folding, lads,' he said to the other three players. 'Here's what I owe you – any more than that, you'll have to wait till Friday.'

'Probably best you do, before you lose your shirt,' said a bearded man, with a wry smile. Emma swallowed hard. This must be Charlie D. He didn't sound as if he was joking. They couldn't afford for Dad to gamble away his wages like this.

Emma didn't want to ask her dad directly to come

home, it made him look foolish and he might take it out on her mother, but there was another reason she didn't want to speak; one of the men gazing up at her from the card table was Arthur.

It was as if she had fallen into his eyes and was drowning in them.

'Cat got your tongue, girl?' said Dad.

'Mum sent me,' she said, staring down at the workmen's hobnail boots, which – when you looked closely – were covered in flecks of paint.

Dad stood up and plonked his tatty bowler hat on the back of his head and adjusted his cravat. 'Let's be off, then.'

They barely said a word as they made their way home, back up Pottery Lane, but Emma didn't mind. She was too busy wondering whether she might lace her corset a bit tighter tomorrow, just a little. Maybe then Arthur would look at her the way those fellas were gazing at the coster-girl; that would be something, wouldn't it?

15

May 1900

'Roll up! Roll up! All the fun of the fair, for just a penny!'

The man in the top hat, whose face almost matched the scarlet of his waistcoat, glanced down at his gold fob-watch for a moment before gesticulating to Emma, Clara and Kiziah to come closer. Behind him, the merry-go-round of painted horses bobbed up and down as a little steam engine chugged away inside it.

'I'll give you three young ladies a ride for tuppence, just because I like the look of you, how's that for a bargain?'

Clara clapped her hands with glee, but Emma hesitated.

'Oh, go on, Em,' said Kiziah, pulling some pennies from her purse and pushing her sister forwards. 'Do something daring, for once in your life! It won't kill you!'

'I'm worried it might make me feel a bit sick,' said Emma, who would have preferred to have a go on the shove ha'penny or just watch the strong man lift weights. The May Fair at Shepherd's Bush was full of exciting things to see and there were toffee apples too, which were her favourite. Shepherd's Bush was such a bustling hub of a place, it made Emma feel anything was possible; there were shops skirting the green, their awnings flapping in the breeze, and horse-drawn trams crammed with passengers. The trams were vying with each other to get down the road, past barrows filled with fruit and vegetables. The people on those trams didn't have to spend all day at the washtubs or the ironing boards, Emma was sure of that, and she almost got caught up in a daydream about what their lives were like until Kiziah shouted 'Come on!' Kiziah had already chosen her steed and had clambered astride it, in the most unladylike fashion, unpinning her straw boater and letting her hair flow free: 'I'm going to enjoy myself!'

Quite why Kizzy always had to make such a show of herself, Emma would never understand, but she sighed and followed her to the carousel, where Clara was already making herself comfortable in a gaily coloured chariot.

'I'll help you up, if you like?'

Emma spun around to see Arthur offering her his hand.

She had hoped he might be here, at the fair, with some of the other workmen, but now he was beside her, she didn't quite know what to say. It wasn't like meeting briefly on the doorstep of the laundry, where they could have a little chat about the weather or how busy they both were. This was different.

He took her by the hand and led her to a dappled grey horse with a bright red saddle and golden reins. The pony had a fixed grin which Emma feared might resemble her own, as she was almost struck dumb by Arthur's presence.

In an instant, she felt his hands around her waist, lifting her up to sit, side-saddle. She clasped the gilt-painted twisted wooden pole which rose from the horse's back, to steady herself, inwardly praying that her long wool skirt wasn't hitched up too much because that wouldn't be seemly.

'Mind if I climb up there and join you?' he said. He was clean-shaven, with a freshly pressed shirt and collar, and the way his waistcoat was buttoned up showed off his muscular frame. A smile played on his lips as she murmured her consent and he clasped the pole, his fingers almost touching hers, and swung himself onto the horse's back, his long legs dangling over the footplate at either side. Just to be this close to him, well, it probably wasn't decent, but it was as if all the golds, reds and greens and blues on the carousel were swirling around inside her and she couldn't help smiling.

Emma turned and caught a glimpse of Kiziah, sitting on the horse behind her. She could have sworn that her sister was scowling.

Just then, another bloke appeared at the carousel and waved at Arthur, before jumping on, just as a bell rang out and it started to turn.

'Thought I'd lost you for a minute,' he said, catching his breath. 'I was in the hall of mirrors – almost scared myself witless! I might have known you'd have found some fine fillies to keep you occupied, Arthur.'

He tipped his bowler hat at Emma: 'And who might this be?'

'This is Emma, from the laundry in Latimer Road,' said Arthur. He added, with a laugh: 'The girl I was telling you about, Henry.'

'I'm his younger brother,' said Henry, giving Emma a wink. 'The better looking of the two Austin lads, so they say . . .' He was shorter than Arthur, wiry too, but he was right – there was a roundness to his face which made him almost boyishly handsome, even with his neat little moustache.

The merry-go-round owner appeared at their side and motioned for Henry to find a seat and pay his penny, so he sat down in the chariot, beside Clara, whose mouth was just about hanging open. She'd better not go telling Mum and Dad about this carousel ride and all these blokes appearing, or they'd be for it.

A crowd had gathered to watch, and their faces were a blur as the carousel whirled round, faster than Emma had ever gone in her life, as the organ piped out 'Pop Goes the Weasel'. Her heart was pounding in her chest and her face was flushed, she could feel it. Some wisps of hair escaped from the plait which she had so carefully pinned into place under her hat, but she let them fly about, as she leaned a bit closer to Arthur. Some children on the horses in front of them were waving frantically to their parents, and the music and the spinning and shouts all made Emma feel rather giddy. But with Arthur beside her, she was enjoying the ride, rather more than she had expected.

'Is that your sister?' said Arthur, glancing over his shoulder, as their dappled horse bobbed up and down in time to the music. His words almost broke the spell.

'Yes,' said Emma, 'that's Kiziah, she's my older sister.' She almost had to shout above the din to make herself heard. 'She's a seamstress!'

Right on cue, Kiziah tossed her head, her flaming red

hair billowing in the wind, and smiled a dainty little smile, right at Arthur, who grinned back at her.

'Your dad must be very proud of you both,' said Arthur, holding Kizzy's gaze.

Desperate to take the attention away from Kizzy, Emma pointed to Clara, who looked as if she might catch flies in her gawping mouth at any moment.

'And that's my younger sister, Clara, who works at the laundry with me.'

Arthur nodded. He whispered in her ear: 'So, might you think about walking out with me one of these Sunday afternoons? It's nice up at Kensington Gardens.'

He was actually asking her out courting!

'I'm not sure what my dad would say . . .' she replied, her heart sinking into her boots. She wanted to go out with him, more than anything, but if her father found out she'd been messing about on fairground rides and getting asked out, he'd have her guts for garters.

'Look, I understand how things are,' he said, before she could say anything else. 'Why don't we meet next week at two o'clock at the park gates? You can bring your sisters along with you and I will bring my brother, then there won't be anything to worry about, will there?'

Sunday couldn't come around quickly enough and the whispered conversations between the sisters in their bedroom every night that week only seemed to make each day drag a little more, building the anticipation of what was to come.

With Clara sworn to secrecy, Kiziah and Emma had

agreed they would all meet up with the two Austin brothers at the gates to Hyde Park after lunch, without mentioning it to their parents. It wasn't that they were going to lie, as such; they just weren't planning on telling the whole truth.

'Sometimes it's best not to tell Mum and Dad everything,' Kizzy said, giving Clara's hand a little pat. Emma nodded in agreement. Clara was a sweet and trusting girl who'd been brought up to be truthful, but if Dad got a whiff of their plan, they'd be forbidden from setting foot outside the house. He was protective of his daughters, to the extent that he'd once slapped Kizzy after word reached him she'd been dawdling down a back alley with one of the delivery boys from the grocer's. It was nothing more than a bit of hand-holding and sweet talk, but the way Dad had walloped her had taken the wind right out of her sails. Kizzy had steered clear of boys after that, just to keep the peace.

And the message to Emma was clear – don't even think about dallying with the local lads. It was fine when the girls were Clara's age, but now they were young women, it just didn't seem fair. Mum wanted a quiet life, so she wasn't going to fight their corner, but they weren't children any more and it was only natural that they should want to go courting, so this was a good compromise.

'If we all stick together, he won't suspect anything, and in any case, we can all keep an eye out for each other, can't we?' said Emma, after church on Sunday morning.

'I don't want to be a gooseberry with you two getting

all pally with those Austin boys, though,' said Clara, twiddling a lock of her hair, as she sat on the bed.

'You won't be!' said Kizzy, kneeling down beside her and clasping her sister's hands. 'I will make sure you won't be left out. We can have a laugh at all the hoity-toity ladies and their ridiculously expensive dresses.' Kiziah leaped to her feet, stuck her nose in the air and pretended she was strutting along with a walking stick.

Clara looked slightly mollified.

'And if you don't like that,' said Emma, 'we can take a stale crust and feed the ducks!'

Clara nodded in agreement, and the plan was set.

Mum called them down to lunch – a cheerless affair of boiled neck of lamb with some carrots and gravy so thin it looked – and tasted – like dishwater. The girls did their best to eat with gusto but, if the truth be told, Emma's appetite had all but disappeared.

'You'd better not be sickening for something,' said her mum, reaching for the big red book on the shelf over the range. 'I can mix you up a tonic.'

'No!' said Emma, rather too vehemently, knowing her mother's foul-tasting home-made medicines only too well. 'I'm fine, just not feeling that hungry today, that's all.' Her stomach was full to bursting with butterflies at the thought of spending the afternoon with Arthur, in any case.

'I'll tell you what,' said Kizzy, putting her knife and fork down in the middle of her plate, in the hope of bringing the meal to an early conclusion. 'Why don't I take you and Clara out for a nice long stroll. Down Hyde Park way, perhaps? That might sort you out . . .'

'Oooh, yes!' chimed Clara. 'That would be lovely.'

Mum looked at all three of them. 'Well, as long as you are back in time to help me finish off the ironing, I don't suppose I mind being left here on me own.'

Dad looked up from his plate, where he was struggling with the last of the scraggy end of the lamb. 'Just remember you've all got work in the morning, so no staying out late.' He couldn't wait for opening time, when he could sink a decent pint, and then this bloody awful meal would be a distant memory.

The three girls almost skipped up Holland Park Avenue, they were so excited. At one point they considered hopping on a horse-drawn omnibus, but Kizzy told them to save their money, so they could at least afford a cup of tea while they were out.

The roads were chock-full of carriages, with people wearing their Sunday best, out for a ride. It was a warm day and Emma could feel little beads of sweat gathering on her brow as they strolled along. She only had one best skirt, of black wool, the same as Kizzy, which was quite hot in the afternoon sun, and she'd put on her finest blouse, which had some lacework around the collar. She'd done her best to tame her wavy hair, pinning it up above her ears and pulling the back into a low bun under her hat. Kizzy had pulled the sides of hers up but put the rest into a long ponytail, secured by a ribbon, and she wore her hat at a slightly jaunty angle. Emma had to admit, her sister looked really pretty in her blouse. Kizzy had made it herself, with lots of pin-tucks down the front, and lace trimmings on the cuffs. She had a sort of glow about her, whereas Emma just felt a bit flustered, to be honest.

Arthur was leaning nonchalantly against the park railings, puffing away at a smoke, while Henry looked almost anxious, pacing up and down, with his hands in his pockets. He waved at them as they walked up, while Arthur just raised his hat.

'Couldn't have picked a nicer afternoon for it, could we?' said Arthur, breaking into a grin.

'Well, Saturday afternoon might've been better for me, to be honest,' said Henry, 'because I did get a bit of earache off the boss for missing out on fares.'

'Oh,' said Emma, 'do you drive one of those omnibuses?'

'No,' said Henry, with a laugh. 'I'm a cabbie and Sunday is normally one of my busiest days out in the hansom.'

'Oh, Gawd, I'm sorry . . .' said Emma, who always felt the need to apologize for something or other, even when it wasn't her fault.

'It's fine – nothing to worry about,' said Arthur, chipping in. 'He'll make it up with a double shift, won't you?'

'Yes,' said Henry, thrusting his hands back into his pockets. 'Charlie D will see to it that I do. That fella will get his pound of flesh out of me, and that's no lie.'

'Isn't he the one who runs the card games down in the Bridport?' said Emma, remembering the big bloke with the bushy beard and the commanding manner from a few months back.

'Yeah, that's him,' said Arthur, with a laugh. 'He runs a lot of things around our way, but his main job is running the stables. He's the master, runs a lot of the horses for the hansom cabs on behalf of Mr Felstone and generally does his bidding on other things too . . .'

'Who's Mr Felstone?' asked Emma. He sounded intriguing, but Kiziah stifled a yawn: 'Oh, I don't want to spend the day talking about boring work! That's men's talk, Emma. Let's go and feed the ducks.'

They set off together, with Clara linking arms with her two sisters, so that Arthur and Henry were forced to walk at either end of the line. Arthur walked beside Emma and Henry started chatting to Kiziah as they headed down towards the duck pond. Clara had brought a hunk of stale bread with her in the pocket of her pinafore and she tore great lumps off it and started throwing them into the water, so that all the ducks came flocking towards them.

'Fancy a ride in the rowing boats down on the lake?' said Henry, looking over at Emma. 'That might be fun . . .'

'Oh, I'm not sure; I don't know how to swim,' she began.

Kiziah rolled her eyes: 'You're not sailing the seven seas, Emma! Of course we want to go on the rowing boats. It sounds wonderful, the best fun ever. Come on!'

She grabbed Clara by the hand and marched off towards the Serpentine at the other end of the park, with Arthur trailing in her wake.

Henry fell into step beside Emma. 'I can stand on the

side with you, if you like,' he said. He looked at her in such a sweet and caring way, Emma found herself blushing.

'No, I'll be fine, honestly. I was just being silly before,' she said. 'It's only a rowing boat, just like Kizzy said.' She glanced over to the water's edge, where Arthur was paying a man to take a boat out. Kiziah was standing right by him but gazing in the other direction. Then he started rolling up his sleeves and Emma noticed that Kiziah had turned and was watching him intently. She glanced away again when he caught her looking at him.

Some ladies in the most beautiful white dresses with ornate lacework were sitting on a bench nearby. They were shielded from the sun by hats with huge brims, which almost appeared to be floating above their curls. Occasionally, one of the ladies would raise a gloved hand to her face and whisper something. Emma suddenly felt ashamed of her clothes and her hat, which wasn't in the least bit fashionable, and shrank under their gaze. Kiziah turned and stared at them and seemed to grow taller, swishing her auburn ponytail and carrying her head high as Arthur held out his hand for her to get into the boat. She stepped lightly, like a ballerina, and took up her seat with barely a wobble. Emma tried to follow her with as much poise as she could muster and Clara, well, she fairly clattered into that boat like a baby elephant; at least it didn't capsize. When Emma looked over, the women were tittering. 'Just ignore them,' Kiziah said. 'Snooty lot, they're no better than us!' And she gave them a little wave, which left the two women open-mouthed.

Arthur and Henry took up their places opposite the girls and began to row slowly out into the middle of the lake to join at least a dozen others who were paddling gently up and down, as the sunlight dappled the water. Emma forgot to be scared; she was too busy marvelling at how strong Arthur was, his muscles flexing with every stroke of the oars. Kiziah closed her eyes and let her hand trail languidly over the side as Clara started to hum 'Row, row, row your boat' – she'd learned that in the bath-tub in front of the fire, as a baby.

'So, how long have you been a seamstress, Kizzy?' said Arthur.

'Almost too long.' She laughed. 'But it's better than working in the laundry like Emma and Clara.' Emma bristled at that comment. She wanted to say something back, but she couldn't. It was as if Kiziah had stolen her thunder.

'You must be very skilled,' Arthur went on. 'I can't imagine what's it's like making all those tiny stitches.'

'Well, I suppose it's the only thing I have ever been good at,' said Kiziah, with uncharacteristic shyness, batting her eyelids at him. 'To tell the truth, Arthur, I got the sack from the laundry and I didn't want to go out charring and my family needed me to have a wage. But what about you?'

'Oh, I'm a jack-of-all-trades in the decorating business, plastering, painting, always plenty of work to be had,' he said blithely. 'Not like Henry, here, who seems to be in love with his blooming horse when the whole world is getting on the omnibus or that new tuppenny tube.' Everyone in

the neighbourhood had been talking about the new railway line which ran in a deep tunnel under Notting Hill
Gate and had recently opened a station at Shepherd's Bush.

'People will always need cabs, Arthur,' said Henry,
stiffly. 'That's just the way of things in London, especially
in Theatreland or when it's raining, which seems to be half
the time, don't it?'

They all laughed at that, although Emma had seen the
cabbies and their horses standing waiting for fares in the
pouring rain, soaked through. And she knew it was no
laughing matter to be stuck out there in all weathers, not
to mention the pea-souper fogs, which made you feel you
were choking.

'I'd like to see you in your cab, Henry,' said Emma,
before she knew what she was saying. She wanted to make
him feel a bit better after Arthur's comment to him, which
had seemed rather mean.

'Well, you can come and visit me at the stables any
time,' said Henry, his nose crinkling a bit as he gave her a
little smile.

Just then, Arthur caught a crab with his oar and
splashed some water over her blouse, making her gasp in
surprise. 'Oh, I'm sorry, Emma, forgive me, that was
clumsy,' said Arthur. He pulled a pristine handkerchief
from his pocket and she took it and dabbed at the wet
patch on her front. He did his best to be gallant about it
but Kiziah was smirking, as if she found it terribly amus-
ing to see her sister soaked like that.

'Oh, don't fuss, Emma,' she said. 'It's only a splash of
water, you're not drowning!'

'Don't worry,' said Henry. 'It will soon dry.' He beamed at her: 'You're still wearing the prettiest blouse in the park this afternoon.'

Arthur gave his younger brother a sideways glance and they rowed back to the edge of the lake in silence.

16

May 1900

The sound of the horses clattering up and down the cobbles and the wheels of the carts rolling down the road was just a part of everyday life for Emma: the milkman and the tallyman and their wagons, the beer dray coming to and from the pub around the corner and the deliveries from the coal lorry, with blinkered carthorses hauling prime Wallsend by the hundredweight.

But since the park outing with Arthur and his brother Henry, the clip-clop of horses' hooves had brought Emma to the bedroom window, peeking out expectantly from behind the curtains in case she caught a glimpse of his hansom cab trotting by.

At first, she'd told herself that she was just being foolish; she wasn't really looking out and hoping to see Henry. Besides, she was still sweet on Arthur, she was certain of that, but he hadn't been around to the laundry since the weekend because he was working on a house up in Hampstead with her father. Kiziah had feigned disinterest when Dad told Mum he'd be late back because he was doing some extra work for Mr Felstone, the housebuilder, along with a team of lads including Arthur Austin. But Emma knew her sister well enough to notice little blotches of colour rising above the collar of her blouse when Arthur's name was mentioned. She was blushing.

When Dad had left and Mum was tidying up in the scullery, Emma followed her sister up the stairs.

'You fancy Arthur, don't you?' she whispered to Kiziah, as they entered their bedroom.

Kizzy spun around and said indignantly, 'I do not!'

'Because I saw him first, Kizzy, and he asked me out to the park, not you,' hissed Emma, giving her a sister a little prod. 'Never mind all your hair tossing and little smiles at him.'

'Don't you shove me!' cried Kizzy, pushing Emma hard, so that she sat down on the rickety bed, next to Clara, who was putting her hair in plaits, ready to go to work.

'Do that again and I'll give you what for!' shouted Emma, springing to her feet.

'You girls better not be fighting up there!' came a voice from the foot of the stairs. The walls and floors in their house were as thin as newspaper, and a cross word would be heard streets away, so their mother wouldn't stand for any argy-bargy. 'Or I'll bang both of your heads together. Get to work, the pair of you!'

'See!' whispered Kizzy, triumphantly. 'You and your big mouth. If you start causing trouble, we'll all be for it. Just keep your trap shut, Emma, and stop imagining things.' She flounced out of the room and down the stairs, banging the front door shut, for good measure.

*

Emma brooded on how much she disliked her sister all day. Kizzy had been trying to get Arthur to notice her, she was sure of it, and the thing was, she wouldn't admit it, which made it even worse. Emma knew that Kizzy was the more striking, with her beautiful mane of hair and her sparkling blue eyes and her dainty little neck. She made Emma feel leaden and dull and quite plain by comparison.

She found herself kicking along the cobbles on the way home, lost in her thoughts, just as a gleaming black two-wheeler rounded the corner, pulled by a silver-grey horse. The carriage stopped beside her and she glanced up to find herself gazing into Henry's eyes. He lifted his bowler hat as he smiled at her: 'Fancy meeting you here! Can I give you a lift somewhere?'

'I was just on my way home,' she began, ignoring the floaty sensation inside her; she felt as if she were on the boat on the Serpentine again.

'I'm just on my way back to the stables. Why not hop up for a ride? I can show you around, like I promised the other day . . .'

He reached out his hand to her and before she knew what she was doing she was climbing up to sit next to him, on the driver's seat of his hansom cab. She'd never ridden in a carriage before; it was quite high up, and some of the local kids came chasing around, shouting for her to chuck them a penny. She felt a bit like a princess, sitting up there. 'Don't be daft, you lot!' she said, 'I'm not made of money.'

Henry flicked his long whip and said, 'Get on,' and the horse trundled on, down Manchester Road, before turning through a narrow archway into the stables in Silchester Mews. It was a hive of activity, with half a dozen horses being led into their stalls for the night, while others were being hitched into waiting cabs. 'It's a shift change,' said Henry. 'I'm bringing her in but I'm taking another one out, to make up for Sunday.'

'Sorry,' said Emma. 'I hope it was worth taking the day off.'

He turned to her: 'Wouldn't have missed it for the world!' He did have a look of Arthur about him when he smiled, so of course she thought he was handsome.

He jumped down and started to undo the buckles of the harness holding the horse in the shafts of the carriage, as a stable boy brought a bucket of water for the animal to drink. Arthur patted his horse and said, 'I'd better intro-duce you to Old Nell, here, or she'll get upset with me.'

The cobbles were black and greasy with bits of straw all over the place, and the smell of the dung heap was quite overpowering, but Emma loved seeing so many ani-mals in one place. She peered into the stable block to see a row of stalls, filled with horses munching on their hay; others stood patiently in the yard, as the grooms brushed them down, making their coats gleam.

'You come up to her from the side, so she can see you, and then she won't get scared,' said Henry. Emma followed close behind him, reaching out her hand to feel the animal's muzzle – it was soft and warm. Henry grabbed a handful of hay from a heap in the corner and showed Emma how to feed the horse, with her hand flat.

She giggled as Nell took it from her, her big teeth grazing against the flesh of her palm: 'It tickles a bit, don't it?'

'And who's this you're bringing into my yard?' a voice boomed across the cobbles.

Henry and Emma spun around to see Charlie D – the big fella from the pub – standing full square, his thumbs tucked into the pockets of his waistcoat. He pulled out his fob-watch and added, with a beady eye on Henry: 'You'd better be getting out again or I'll dock you a shilling, boy.'

'Sorry, Charlie,' said Henry. 'I'm just showing one of Will Chick's girls around. I'll be back off out in just a tick.'

Charlie D came over, slapped Henry on the back and started laughing. 'Of course, it's all right, I'm only teasing, she's welcome here any time.'

He turned to Emma: 'How's that father of yours?'

'Fine,' said Emma. 'Working in Hampstead at the moment.'

'Ah,' said Charlie D, stroking his bushy beard. 'Not seen him in the Bridport lately and he owes me a couple of bob. You tell him old Charlie D is waiting to see him back at the card tables now, won't you?'

'Of course,' she said, realizing, to her horror, that if she passed the message on, she'd have to explain to her dad how she'd come to be chatting to Charlie D in the stables at Silchester Mews in the first place.

Emma didn't mention her little ride in the hansom cab to her sisters – it was none of their business and, in any case, Kiziah would probably only use it to stir up trouble after their spat. Besides, the person she really wanted to hear from, Arthur, hadn't been in touch at all, which bothered her. Henry was nice and all that, but Arthur was the one she was really interested in.

Imagine her delight then, the very next day, when a little note arrived at the laundry with one of the workmen delivering the lunch from the pub around the corner. He tapped the side of his nose and slipped it, silently, into the pocket of her apron as he handed over the bread, cheese and beer for the women. Emma waited until everyone was busy tucking in at their ironing boards before turning her back and unfolding it: 'Meet me at seven tonight in the park, Arthur.' And he'd even added a little kiss. It was a secret meeting, just the two of them! So, he was keen on her, after all. There was just one problem: how was she going to slip out of the house unnoticed?

After mulling it over, she decided to rope Clara in on the plan. 'I'll give you a penny for covering for me and another for coming along and just hanging around some- where close by – that way, if anyone sees us, you can say we were out for a walk together and just bumped into Arthur.'

Clara wasn't too certain: 'But what if Dad finds out? He'll belt the both of us, that's for sure.'

'He won't ever find out,' said Emma. 'And we won't tell Kizzy either because she's bound to let it slip out of spite that Arthur hasn't asked *her* to meet up.' She was barely able to disguise the note of triumph in her voice as she spoke. Yes, Kizzy, her beautiful older sister, was not the one that Arthur wanted, despite all her showing off.

That evening, Kizzy sat darning some socks by the range and Mum was doing extra washing, as usual, when Emma stood up and announced she needed some air: 'I don't know, I'm feeling like I could be getting one of those stuffy headaches. Do you fancy coming for a quick stroll out with me, Clara?'

Clara leaped to her feet. 'Yes, that would be nice, it's a warm evening.'

Mum glanced up from her washboard. 'Well, you could do worse than seeing if you can dig your father out of the pub while you're out, too, if you go down that way.'

'Well, we'll be off then,' Emma said, grabbing Clara by the hand, marching down the hallway and out through the front door, before Kizzy could open her mouth to say she wanted to join them.

Outside in the street, some of the old fellas were sitting out on chairs, talking to each other, while boys played kick the can and the girls swung a huge skipping rope across the width of the street and called on Clara to jump in. Emma remembered how much she'd loved playing those games when she was a girl, but she was too old for that now, she was about to be someone's girlfriend – her skipping days were over. Clara made to join the game, just for a minute, but Emma touched her arm: 'Remember, we've got important business tonight' – and they hurried off towards the park.

Arthur was leaning against the park gate post, drawing on a ciggie, when they arrived: 'I thought you'd be alone,' he said, looking over at Clara, his eyes narrowing a little.

'Oh, we will be. Clara is just making sure I don't get

into trouble with my parents, that's all,' said Emma. 'She can sit on a bench while we take a stroll . . .' Clara looked at the floor and shuffled her feet about, embarrassed.

'That's good,' said Arthur, beaming at Emma, 'because I'd hoped to have you all to myself.'

Clara walked over to a bench and sat down and started fidgeting with her hands in her lap.

'We won't be long,' said Emma. 'You stay here – and we'll be back in a while.'

Arthur offered her his arm and she took it as they wandered off, towards the bandstand. The light was fading and the scent of the first blossom on the trees filled the air.

'I wanted to ask you about walking out with me, more often,' said Arthur, turning to face her. 'I want to spend more time with you, time when we can be alone together. Maybe I could take you up to the varieties at the Shepherd's Bush Empire?'

Faced with the reality of having to tell her father, Emma was completely flummoxed. 'I'm not sure, it might cause me so much trouble indoors,' she said. 'Can't we just meet up like this from time to time?'

They had reached the bandstand now, and Arthur took her by the hand and walked her around to the back of it, near some bushes, before turning and pulling her to him. Suddenly, his mouth was covering hers and his tongue, probing and insistent, was pushing its way in between her lips. She'd never been kissed before and she found that she wasn't enjoying it, not in the way she'd expected to, at least.

She put her hands up to his chest and began to try to

push him away, but he was too strong. He enveloped her in his embrace and kissed her harder, so that she had no choice but to let his tongue explore the softness of her mouth. 'I want you, Emma,' he breathed, his hands running their way up her ribcage and brushing across her bosom. It was like being on a carousel with him, but she had no control over getting off when she'd had enough, she could see that now.

'I'm not ready for that,' she said, using all her strength to pull away. 'I don't know what you think of me, Arthur, but I'm not that kind of girl.'

He looked crestfallen. 'I'm sorry. It's just I thought you liked me,' he said.

'I do,' said Emma, straightening her blouse. 'I think of you all the time, Arthur. But we need to take things slowly. Perhaps you could come and meet my parents properly? We could get their permission for us to go out for walks together – that would be a start, wouldn't it?'

He didn't have a chance to reply because Clara came running towards them, screaming and crying, her hair and clothes all dishevelled. Emma ran to her sister: 'Whatever's the matter?'

Clara's lip was cut and she was crying too much to speak at first, she just took great gulping sobs of air, as Emma threw her arms around her to try to comfort her.

Arthur ran to her. 'Who did this to you?'

'I shouldn't have, but I left the park, just so I wasn't spying on you two,' she cried. 'I only made it as far as Pottery Lane when two of them jumped on me and started pawing at me like a pair of dogs.'

Arthur's green eyes blazed with anger: 'Did you get a look at them?'

'Just ruffians,' said Clara, wiping her eyes. 'Not from round here, I'd say. They wanted money and when I didn't have any, they . . .' She couldn't finish the sentence and dissolved into a heap of tears.

'I'm going to get some of the lads from the Bridport and we'll find them and beat them black and blue!' said Arthur, drawing himself up to his full height. 'No one comes around here and messes with our girls.'

He made to leave but Emma grabbed him by the arm: 'No! Wait! If you go and tell anyone about this my dad will find out we were here meeting you and then we'll all be for it.'

Her heart was racing as she turned to Clara: 'You can't tell anyone about this, do you understand?'

Her sister looked up at her, the livid cut on her lip was swelling up now but she was such a good girl, she always did what she was told: 'Yes, Emma, I won't tell a soul, I promise.'

Emma's mind was whirring. 'We'll just say you tripped and fell and busted your lip, you clumsy clot, and I will not let you out of my sight again, I swear. I will never make you come out like this again, I promise you, Clara. It's all my fault. I'm so sorry.'

Arthur thrust his hands deep into his pockets and kicked at a stone as they walked out of the park and muttered to himself, 'Well, I'm still going to have a look up and down the lane to see who I can see. It ain't right to have girls being bothered like that.'

Emma turned her back on him and put her arm protectively around her little sister as they walked away, back to Manchester Road, back home, where they belonged. None of this would have happened if it hadn't been for her silly ideas of having a boyfriend: 'No one will hurt you ever again, Clara, I promise you that. I will always be there to protect you.'

'There's a visitor for you, Kiziah!'

Mum stood with her arms folded, eyeing Arthur Austin when he came calling the following Saturday afternoon, cap in hand. She knew his mum, Jane, from the laundry, and what's more, she knew that she'd never married. Jane had raised her kids properly, of course, but the Chicks were a very respectable family.

'I was hoping I might have a word with Mr Chick first,' he said, stepping over the threshold, as Emma stood, open-mouthed, at the top of the stairs. Kizzy was there in the hallway, looking as pretty as a picture, her hair flowing over her shoulders, some needlework in her hand.

Dad ambled out of the scullery, stroking his whiskers. 'What brings you here, Arthur?'

Arthur straightened his collar and came straight to the point: 'I wanted to ask your permission, sir, to take your Kiziah out from time to time . . .'

17

August 1901

It was a lovely summer wedding.

Emma would always remember that, and how her sister scrimped and saved to buy the offcut of claret silk from the draper's to make a beautiful bodice for her big day; how she sewed it in the scullery every evening, until it was finished.

Emma never told Kizzy that Arthur had kissed her first and she had turned him down. After what had happened at the bandstand that evening, she knew she wasn't ready for boyfriends just yet and he had made his choice – her beautiful, funny, spirited older sister. And although Kizzy could have been triumphant about Arthur, when it came to it, she wasn't. Instead, she held Emma's hand and asked her: 'Are you sure you don't mind me walking out with him? I know you saw him first.'

Dad had taken some persuading to let Kizzy go out with Arthur. In fact, he'd almost said 'No', but Kizzy was his favourite and she'd wheedled round him to be allowed to go to the park on Sunday afternoons and then, once in a while, to the new varieties at the Shepherd's Bush Empire, as long as she didn't come home late.

After a few months, Dad was singing Arthur's praises at every turn: 'He's a clever lad, that Arthur Austin. He's got plans for the future, that one, and a good career too. He's a hard worker, never misses a day and always happy to buy a man a pint or lend him a bob when he's running short.'

And that, thought Emma ruefully, was probably what lay behind Arthur's newfound popularity with her father. Dad was spending more and more time at the card tables, but with Arthur by his side his debts never quite caught up with him.

Six months later, Arthur called round again, to seek permission to marry Kiziah, and the next thing anyone knew, they were walking up the aisle, with Emma and Clara behind them, as their bridesmaids. Arthur acted as if nothing had ever happened between them – that was the thing which hurt the most, to be honest. He had just moved on and only had eyes for Kizzy; he planned to whisk her off to a new life in Acton, where lots of new houses were being built.

'The air's better down there, so they say,' said Arthur, as everyone in the Black Bull raised a toast to the happy couple. 'But we won't be strangers, will we Kizzy?'

She looked up at him and said: ''Course not.' She was Mrs Austin now, leaving the Potteries and Piggeries for a new life and she glowed with delight on her big day.

'You know, you will meet the right man soon, Emma,' said Kizzy, handing her the bridal bouquet, a spray of lily of the valley. Kizzy looked around her and glanced over to where Henry was drinking with his mates, giving Emma a little nudge.

'One day, but there's no rush,' said Emma, who still felt a stab of jealousy whenever she saw Arthur gazing adoringly at her sister. At least with them moving she wouldn't have to see him so often, even if he was family now. There was so much guilt about what had happened to Clara that dreadful evening down Pottery Lane. It was all mixed up in Emma's head – Clara getting hurt by those boys, Arthur kissing her in the way that he did. Her sweet, innocent sister was like a shadow, barely speaking much any more, and most nights, she'd wake up screaming in the bed next to Emma.

'I don't know,' said Mum. 'It must be her age, these night terrors. I ought to have a word with the tallyman and see if he can recommend a good tonic.'

He was a wily sod, that tallyman, and he could sell coals to Newcastle given half the chance. Emma was convinced that half of the little glass phials he touted were filled with nothing more than cochineal and tap water, but Mum was convinced he was genuinely helpful, and she was always checking up in her big red book, *Consult Me for All You Want to Know*, for advice on any kind of ailment. She'd had to buy that on tick as well; it had taken her the best part of a year to pay for it.

'No, Mum,' said Emma, with a sigh. 'I don't think that will help; it's just nerves, I think, that's all.' Poor Clara. Emma had tried to talk to her about what had happened but she just clammed up or got angry with her:

'It don't matter now, in any case,' Clara would say,

turning on her side to face the bedroom wall. 'What's done is done.' But the nightmares would return, with Clara waking up shouting 'No!', and Emma did her best to comfort her then, holding her close and stroking her hair until she went back to sleep.

There was no one she could confide in and, as the nights started to draw in, Emma found herself wandering the streets as dusk fell, alone with her thoughts. On one rainy evening, she was walking down Latimer Road, when a familiar voice called out from a passing hansom cab: 'Need a lift, Miss Chick?'

She turned and saw Henry, smiling down at her through the rain, which had soaked right through his jacket and was dripping from the rim of his bowler hat.

'It's no kind of evening to be out on your own, Emma,' he said, offering her his hand.

She climbed up next to him and he threw a blanket over her legs, to keep her warm.

'How have you been lately?' he said, his eyes searching her face, as Nell walked on.

'Down in the dumps,' she murmured. What was the point of pretending to be happy?

'Me too, Emma,' he said. 'I've had a terrible week. People don't want to take a cab with a grey horse, you know. They think it's unlucky, that's why Charlie D lets me have her on the cheap. But sometimes I struggle to cover my costs.'

'Oh, I'm sorry,' said Emma, who realized she was being terribly selfish, wallowing in her own misery. 'Can't you change her for another horse?'

'Wouldn't be fair to the old girl,' said Henry. 'We're a team, me and Nellie. Things will get better, but the weather gets us down a bit, don't it?' Emma nodded. It was as if he understood how she was feeling.

They sat for a while in silence, just letting the carriage rock them gently from side to side as the horse found her way back to the stables. Just before they arrived, Henry turned to Emma and blurted: 'I know I wasn't your first choice, Emma, but might you consider walking out with me? I think I could make you smile again, if you'd let me try. And you have such a pretty smile.'

There was a warmth to his voice and his face was open and honest, his brown eyes eagerly awaiting her answer.

'Yes,' she said. 'I'd like that.'

He may have been Arthur's brother, but Henry Austin didn't find much favour with Dad.

To his credit, he put up with all the grumbling about what a waste of time being a cabbie was every time he showed his face in Manchester Road.

'I don't know about you taking my daughter out,' Dad would start complaining. 'It's not as if you could afford to keep her. A shilling a mile, is it? And how much of that goes to Charlie D?'

'He takes eighteen shillings a week at the height of the season and half that in the winter,' said Arthur, with a resolute grin. 'I don't do so badly, you know.'

'Most people are getting on the omnibus these days, they can't afford cabs. And what's with that grey horse of yours? The best mares are all brown, everyone knows that!' Dad mumbled into his tea, determined to press home his point.

'Oh, do stop it, Will!' said Mum, flicking her dishcloth in his direction, in irritation. She'd grown fond of Henry, who had a kind way about him. 'Henry is doing the laundry deliveries and collections on Mondays and Fridays now too, which must be bringing in a pretty penny or two.'

'Indeed, I am,' said Henry, giving Emma a wink. It meant they got to see each other during the week, more often than not, which had only made Emma realize how fond she was of Henry these days. The strain of working so hard had started to show in his face, which was looking drawn, and so she'd taken to bringing him a bite to eat in the stables if he was doing a double shift.

Henry wasn't like some of the other cabbies with their hirelings; they'd just bring them in and walk off down the pub, leaving the grooms and the stable boys to get them out of their heavy harnesses, brush them down and give them their feed. Not Henry. Even if he was working a double, he'd make time to unhitch Nell, walk her into the stable and give her a drink, even before a drop of water passed his own lips.

The flies troubled the horses something rotten that summer, no matter how hard the stable boys worked to keep the stalls clean, digging over the straw with their pitchforks. The dung heap lurked in the corner of the mews and stank to high heaven, which can't have helped, either.

Emma watched Henry running his hands down the

horse's fetlocks and lifting her hooves to check for any stones Nell might have picked up on the roads, which could lead to lameness and infection. Then he rolled up his sleeves, took up a brush and started to groom the horse, from her head all the way down her flanks, as she munched away at clumps of hay from her hay net. Some of the horses had to be tied to each side of the stall to keep them still, but not Nell. And Henry had a look of such concentration on his face, it was as if everything else was lost to him, except making sure Nell was well cared for.

'Show me how you do that,' said Emma, who'd always been rather afraid of horses; they were such huge animals and she'd seen carts overturn when they took fright. But now, with Henry beside her, she felt brave enough to get closer. He gave her the brush and she put her fingers through the leather hand strap, allowing him to guide it down onto the horse's coat.

'You stroke downwards, quite firmly, and you can talk to her at the same time if she looks like she's getting jumpy,' he said.

Nell whinnied a bit, making Emma laugh. 'I think she likes it.'

''Course she does,' said Henry. 'How could she not like you paying her attention?'

A lock of hair had fallen down over his forehead and his face was flushed in the heat of the afternoon. Emma turned to him; their lips were just inches away from one another.

She moved closer still.

'I wish every day was like this in the stables,' he murmured. 'I don't think I'd earn a penny, though, because I wouldn't want to leave.'

Then, she kissed him.

18

January 1904

The banging on the front door was loud enough to wake the dead, never mind the whole street.

Emma and Henry were toasting muffins in front of the fire in the front room with Clara, while Mum and Dad drank their cuppas in peace in the scullery, when there was such a loud knock, the door practically flew off its hinges.

'What in the name of God Almighty?' yelled her father, storming into the hallway to answer it.

Emma and Henry rushed out to follow him, to be greeted by three burly shapes looming across the front doorstep, with their hats pulled low and their collars up, to cover their faces. One of them was carrying a shillelagh and he waved it towards Dad's face.

A thick yellow fog hung in the air, muffling the shouts of 'Who's that?' and 'Keep the noise down!' as their neighbours complained about the disturbance on a quiet Sunday teatime.

'Mr Felstone says he's been patient enough with you and he wants his money,' said one fella, whose front teeth appeared to be missing. 'You've got until the end of the week or we'll be back.'

Mum marched out of the scullery, her hands on her hips, as Dad shrank back into the house.

'Don't you come around here threatening us!' she shouted, waving a knitting needle near their faces. 'Or I'll have the law on you!'

'Tell your wife to keep her trap shut, or we'll do it for her,' said a smaller, ratty-looking bloke with pockmarks on his cheeks. 'You know what you owe and it's time to pay up.'

Mum slammed the door shut and leaned against it, clasping her hands to her chest, as if she was struggling to breathe.

'Tell me, Will,' she said, with a look of terror. 'What money are they talking about?'

Dad sat down on the stairs and put his head in his hands. 'It's me gaming debts, Susan. Got a bit out of hand since Arthur left, that's all.'

She could barely get the words out: 'What do you mean?'

'It started off as a fiver, but with the interest on the loan it's double that by now,' said Dad, staring at his hands, as if the money might magically appear from somewhere to dig him out of this hole.

'Oh my God!' cried Mum. 'We'll be out on the streets! Where are we going to get that kind of money? How could you? You bloody fool!' She turned her face to the wall and started to cry, as Emma and Clara went to comfort her.

Henry stepped forwards and put his hand on her shoulder: 'Mrs Chick, I work with Charlie D, maybe I can talk to him about it, see if there's a way to sort this out . . .'

'It's no use!' said Dad, leaping to his feet. 'D'you think I haven't tried calling in all the favours under the sun with Charlie? He's a good bloke an' all but he works for Felstone and when his boss calls in the loan, the loan has to be paid, as sure as eggs is eggs.'

'In that case,' said Henry, puffing out his chest a bit. 'I'll help pay it off. But we need to talk first, man to man.'

'What do you mean "man to man"? You're little more than a boy yourself!' Dad scoffed.

'I'm young, yes, but I have a good job and I'm earning a decent wage,' said Henry. 'I'm offering to help you pay off your debt but now seems like a good time to ask you something which has been on my mind lately . . .' He cleared his throat. 'I would like to ask your permission to marry Emma.'

Emma gasped; she couldn't believe her ears. They spent as much time as they could together, and Dad accepted him in the house now – albeit with a bit of a grumble from time to time – but marriage wasn't something they had ever discussed. Even though she was nearly twenty she still needed her father's permission, and she knew he'd never give it.

'Marry my daughter?' Dad's face had twisted into a sneer. 'Marry her? What kind of a future can you give her?'

'A better one than you,' said Henry, staring him down. 'At this rate, all you can offer is the workhouse or the soup kitchen at the Mission Hall. I'm offering to help pay off the debt and I will be a good husband. We can get married later in the year . . .' He hesitated and glanced over to the doorway, where Emma was helping to support her mum, who looked as if she was about to faint with this latest turn of events – 'If Emma will have me.'

Dad turned to Emma: 'Well, he's got some brass neck.' He stroked his whiskers, weighing up the offer. 'Do you want to get married to him?

'Yes,' Emma whispered, knowing that this was what she wanted, more than anything in the world, 'I do.'

Henry was as good as his word and, with Charlie D acting as his broker, handed over his savings of a pound that Friday, with a promise that he'd pay back Mr Felstone at a rate of five shillings a week; it was just enough to keep the bully boys away from their door. Meanwhile, Dad promised to stay away from the card tables and also chucked a couple of bob a week into the pot, which was the least he could do. Mum still wasn't speaking to him.

No one was exactly sure how long it would take to pay off the debt because the loan continued with exorbitant interest, at whatever rate Mr Felstone saw fit to impose. They were caught, like flies in amber.

Henry worked double shifts every day in the week and on Sundays too, and Emma couldn't help but notice how much thinner he was looking. He never lost his spark, though, and all that spring, they'd snatch what moments they could in the stables together.

One Saturday afternoon, she arrived from the laundry

with some bread and cheese for him and he was waiting for her, with Nell in her stall. As Emma drew near, he swept his hair from his forehead, dropped down on one knee and pulled a little silver ring out of his waistcoat pocket.

'It's just a token, until I can afford to buy you a proper ring, Emma,' he said. 'But I wanted to ask you properly all the same, so will you marry me?'

'It's beautiful,' said Emma, slipping the silver band onto the third finger of her left hand as her heart skipped a beat. 'Yes, I will marry you, Henry, because I love you with all my heart.'

He pulled her to him and they kissed until Nell started nudging them.

'Oh, I think she's jealous,' said Henry, patting the horse on the cheek. 'Or perhaps she's reminding me, there's something else too . . .'

He fished inside the other pocket of his waistcoat and pulled out a little brass charm of a horse on a gilt chain.

'This is from Nell, to show she approves of us getting together,' said Henry, fastening it around Emma's neck. 'She can be a bit jealous, so I thought I'd better include her.'

'Oh, it's lovely!' said Emma. 'Thank you, Nell, old girl!' She grabbed a handful of hay and fed it to her, as a treat.

Charlie D appeared in the doorway to the stable block. 'Well, ain't that a pretty picture, you two lovebirds!'

'Oh, get out of it, Charlie!' said Henry, making as if to shoo his boss away.

'Look, call me soft if you like,' said Charlie, grinning

from ear to ear. 'How about you borrow one of my cabs to take you to the church on time, Emma? Better than that – I'll drive you there meself!'

As the sun rose on a bright May morning, Emma rubbed sleep out of her eyes and jumped out of bed with excitement at what her wedding day would bring.

Clara slept on, her fingers clutching the pillow, as they always did. She seemed much more like her old self these days. At least, she'd found a friend to talk to – Dora, from packing at Mr Ranieri's – and they seemed to spend so much time together, giggling upstairs or putting their heads together wandering off down the street, arm in arm. It was a relief, after what had happened down Pottery Lane, to see her smiling and laughing again.

Emma's wedding outfit lay across the back of the wooden chair in the corner of the room. Kiziah had made the trip up from Acton last weekend specially to bring it for her, and check that it fitted right. She'd unpicked the seams of her best claret silk bodice – the one she had worn to walk up the aisle with Arthur – and took it in, to fit Emma, who was smaller and slighter than she was. She'd wear her best black woollen skirt as well and, with her boots polished up, she'd look her best.

'You will look proper beautiful in it,' Kiziah told her sister. 'I promise.' She didn't get up their way much these days because she was working at a tailor's shop in Chiswick and the hours were terrible. Arthur had been away in Hertfordshire, building some houses and, much to everyone's disappointment, there had been no patter of tiny feet yet.

Emma tried to imagine what married life would be like with Henry and got butterflies just thinking about it. They couldn't afford to move out into a place of their own but Mum and Dad had said they were welcome to have the front room downstairs as their bedroom; it was the least they could do, given that Henry was still working his fingers to the bone trying to pay off Dad's gambling debt.

Mum came in to help her get ready, looking brighter than Emma had ever seen her: 'You enjoy today, my girl. It's the happiest day of a woman's life.' It was as if the wedding lifted all the misery of the debt and the past few months, for all of them.

Emma started to cry, thinking that she could have made a mistake and gone with Arthur all those years ago, when Henry was there all along, and he was the right one for her.

'Now, no tears, you'll spoil that pretty face,' said Mum, helping her into her corset.

'Wait,' said Emma, as Mum was buttoning her into her bodice. She reached down under her pillow and pulled out the little brass horse charm that Henry had given her. 'I need to put this on, for luck!'

Mum had bought white roses from the market and tied them into a little posy with some string, and Clara was to carry a single white rose of her own. Emma had never had flowers before – it was a luxury they couldn't afford – so these were really special.

Charlie D kept his promise; he turned up at her door

in Manchester Road with a gleaming hansom cab, pulled by Nell, with white roses tied on to the lanterns. Emma gasped when she saw the cab. She could scarcely believe she was going to ride inside it, looking like a real princess. All the kids in the street started running around it excitedly and just about every front door was flung open so that the neighbours could get a look at the blushing bride.

Dad was flabbergasted: 'Charlie, my son, I think you're losing your touch, ain't you? Going all sentimental.'

'Nonsense,' said Charlie D, fixing his collar. 'I'm just doing what's right for the young couple, that's all.' He opened the cab door to Emma, and she climbed inside.

Charlie D took Emma around the streets of Notting Dale a few times to show her off, as everyone stopped and waved at the bridal carriage. Anyone would think he was relishing the prospect of making Henry a bit nervous, as she was a full ten minutes late getting to St Clement's Church on Treadgold Street.

Henry was waiting for her at the altar, in his best bib and tucker, looking the most handsome he had ever done, with Arthur as his best man. Both of them were smiling at her as she made her way up the aisle on Dad's arm, but she only had eyes for Henry. Kiziah beamed at her little sister from the congregation, which seemed to include a few of the local urchins, who had run behind the cab all the way from Manchester Road and sneaked into the back of the church.

Emma had practised her vows and had promised herself she wouldn't weep, not on such a happy occasion. But as she gazed into Henry's eyes and swore to be with him forever, she was overcome with emotion and there wasn't a dry eye in the house.

It didn't matter, because as Henry slipped a simple gold band on her finger, she knew the tears she was crying were tears of joy.

19

Acton, May 1934

The road to recovery from scarlet fever was a long one – the illness had sapped so much of Annie's strength, the doctor said she'd been lucky to survive.

Aunt Clara moved back home once Annie had been given the all-clear, but before she did, she sat beside her on the edge of the bed and held her in her steady gaze: 'Do you remember the stories I told you when you were so sick?'

'Some of it, yes,' said Annie, propping herself up on a pillow. She wasn't even sure if she'd dreamed parts of it, because when she closed her eyes at night, she could see her mum and her dad, riding together on a hansom cab pulled by a beautiful grey horse, around the grimy streets of Notting Hill. She loved thinking about them together, so young and so in love until the war came along and took him away.

But she wanted the story to go on and, especially, to know more about what happened to Kiziah and Arthur, her uncle. She only knew him as a haunted shell of a man, a victim of the horrors of war, but finding out about his past made her see him differently now. And her Aunt

Kiziah sounded so spirited and determined. Where was she?

'I've got some questions for you about Kizzy – things that don't make sense to me, or maybe I was asleep when you explained them,' Annie began.

'Oh, Lord, I've probably said too much already,' said Clara, twisting a handkerchief over and over in her hands. 'I can't answer any more questions, Annie. I just wanted you to know how much your dad loved your mum, that's all, because it's only right that you know that.

'It's not that I've done anything wrong . . .' She glanced away for a second. 'It's just I don't think you should mention any of this to your mum. She won't want to rake over the past, she's got a lot on her mind, with you being so sick and everything.'

Gazing at her aunt, Annie realized that unearthing one family secret had only led to another layer of hushed-up truths, too painful to talk about. Arthur had suffered so much in the war, and with Kizzy no longer there to help him, it was no wonder his nerves were shot to pieces.

'I understand,' said Annie. Mum's hair seemed to have turned grey with worry, it was true, and she knew that something was up, because Bill seemed to be around the house a lot. He kept himself to himself and had started a little project; building some shelves to keep food away from the mice in the scullery. And they weren't having a roast on a Sunday any more, but to save face with the neighbours, he still went out into the back yard every Sunday and sharpened the carving knife, with great flourish.

He'd even taken it upon himself to advise George about

getting a really good career, rather than just being a driver. With that in mind, George had got himself a job as an apprentice – albeit on a lower wage but with better prospects – to be a cabinetmaker, and he was only too pleased to show Bill what he had learned at work. The pair of them would stand about in that back yard for hours, sawing at bits of wood, hammering nails in. Annie was pleased that Bill had started to show an interest in his stepson; it was as if they had, after all these years, found some common ground.

Deep down, Annie felt better, knowing at least something about her mum and dad's past, and that made her look on her stepdad more kindly. Mum's first love had been Henry Austin, her father, she was sure of that now. But the trouble was, in her heart of hearts, despite Aunt Clara's warnings not to rock the boat, she wanted to know more.

It was weeks before Mum would let her set foot outside the house, and when she did, people in the street greeted her as if she had just returned from a long and perilous journey: 'Nice to have you back with us, Annie!' and 'Good to see you again, love!' She got used to them giving her a cheery wave as she took a tentative stroll up the road, on her mum's arm, and it was comforting to know that the whole community had been willing her to get better.

'I'm well enough to go back to work now, aren't I?' said Annie, after Mum decided to take her for a walk before their tea one evening. They rounded the corner, onto Acton Lane.

'There's a few things I need to tell you, Annie,' said Mum, scarcely pausing for breath, as if she just needed to get the words out. 'Hope Cottage has had to close.'

'What?' said Annie, pulling away in shock.

'Now, you are not to upset yourself,' said Mum, calmly, taking hold of her arm again. 'I haven't told you until now because I didn't want to knock you back when you'd been so ill, but the council Medical Officer came into the laundry when you got scarlet fever to do some investigating and, the thing is, they reckon that the cause of it was some infected sheets that had come from one of the big houses . . .'

'What do you mean?' asked Annie, who felt as if the rug had been pulled from under her feet; she'd been so focused on her own illness, she hadn't given a thought to anyone else these past weeks.

'It was the Felstone hamper, the one you were sorting – at least that is what they think, because their daughter had been sick with the scarlet fever and she'd been lying in the sheets you took out of their basket. They were supposed to have been treated with carbolic by the nurses looking after her, but they weren't . . .'

'You mean Verity Felstone?' Annie flinched visibly at the mention of the Felstone name. 'I think I remember seeing her name in the clothes I washed in the laundry.'

She had seen Verity's name, day after day, of course, on so many lovely clothes in the years she'd worked at Hope Cottage. It was as if she knew her because she'd watched her clothes change from the pinafores of a girl to the beautiful dresses of a wealthy young woman. Some days,

Annie had even imagined Verity Felstone going off to glamorous parties or drinking tea in the afternoon with her friends in their mansions around Holland Park.

'I don't know her name, love, but it was the Felstone girl who had the fever.'

'And she got better, like me, didn't she?' said Annie.

'Well, I don't want to dwell on it, Annie, but as it happens . . . no, she didn't get well again . . .' Mum's voice trailed off. She gave Annie a hug. 'We are just thanking our lucky stars you are still here, love. We can only look forward now, not back.'

Annie took in the enormity of what her mum was saying. She wanted to cry but found she couldn't; there were no tears for someone she had never met. She'd never look on that family the same way now, knowing what she did about how Mr Felstone's bully boys threatened poor people who owed him money. But none of that was Verity Felstone's fault, of course, and Annie felt guilty somehow, that she had survived and Verity hadn't.

'But what about the laundry? It can't just be closed down! It wasn't the laundry's fault I got sick,' she said eventually.

'It couldn't be helped,' said Mum, with a sigh. 'The thing is, there were stories in the paper about the scarlet fever spreading because of the laundry, and once word got around that the doctors thought it had come from the sheets, people didn't want to send their linen in, in case they caught it too. The Missus had the authorities round and they advised shutting up shop for a while, but in truth, the takings were already down and the Missus was going to have to lay people off. She sold off what she could to raise enough money for her to retire: the box mangle and the cart . . .'

'But what about Moses?'

Mum stopped and held Annie's hand.

'There's not much call for laundry carts these days, Annie. Everyone's switching to motor vans, but she got in touch with a rag-and-bone man in Notting Hill and he took him. He's using him to haul his wagon.'

'It's all my fault,' said Annie, as tears began to spill down her cheeks. Her whole world had changed overnight. 'If I hadn't got the stupid fever in the first place, none of this would have happened.'

'Now, crying will not solve anything, my girl,' said Mum, brushing the tears away with a clean handkerchief.

'What's everyone doing for work?' said Annie, sniffling a bit.

'Well, the other laundries have taken on as many of us as they can,' said Mum. 'I'm around at Miss Toomey's Power Laundry with Aunt Clara and Dora and most of the ironers.' Mum forced a smile. 'It's taken a while to get used to the steam irons, I can tell you, but perhaps it's for the best. The old ways of doing things have got to move on at some point, you know.'

'What about Bessie and the washerwomen?'

'Bessie and the others are down at the Cambrian and the Sweet Lavender, but they aren't getting as much pay per day now,' said Mum. 'It ain't fair but there's nothing to be done about it. At least they have got work. It's the men who've been the hardest hit.'

So that's what Bill had been doing, kicking his heels around the yard at home.

'The laundries don't need any more fellas, there's so many going for one job, with unemployment being what it is.' It had always been difficult to get work since the days of the General Strike, and more families than ever in Soapsud Island seemed to be relying on the women's wages, it was true. There was money to employ apprentices, because they earned next to nothing, but a man of Bill's age could find himself out of work and signing on the dole before he knew it.

'I've got to get back to work and start earning,' said Annie. She almost asked whether Elsie and Ivy might be sent out to earn something, but then she stopped herself. Her sisters were clever as anything and Mum and Bill were rightly proud of them. They were on to secretarial college and a better life. Annie didn't begrudge them that; in fact, if anything, she was prepared to work harder to ensure they stayed out of the factories and the laundries.

'There's barely a job to be had round here, love,' said Mum, staring straight ahead. 'You can try, Annie, you're a good worker, but I've got my ear to the ground and I know the laundries in Soapsud Island aren't hiring.'

'Well, I'll go further afield, then,' said Annie. 'I'll get the tram up towards Shepherd's Bush tomorrow and see what I can find.'

'Don't push yourself before you're ready,' said Mum. 'But the truth is, Annie, anything you can bring in will be a godsend because we're down to our last brass farthing at the end of every week and I'm going have to start putting things on tick, or we won't be able to pay the rent next month.'

As Annie pulled on her coat and her green felt cloche hat to set off looking for work the next day, she realized that her hands were shaking with nerves.

Mum eyed her warily. 'Do you need another cuppa before you go?'

'No, I'm fine,' she replied, jamming her hands into the depths of her coat pockets. Her fingers traced the outline of some folded paper: the note from her father, Henry. 'I'd best be off. The early bird catches the worm!'

By the time she'd reached the tram up on Acton High Street, her plan was set in her mind. She handed over her penny and the tram conductor issued her ticket, with a little 'ting' on the bell punch as he stamped it for her to get off at Shepherd's Bush; it was just a short walk from the tram depot up to Notting Hill, she knew the route well enough from her trips with Moses on the laundry cart.

She put the ticket in her pocket and carefully unfolded the note from her father, written on a payslip from the stables, the paper now yellow with age. She examined it, memorizing the address – Silchester Mews. It wasn't as if she was doing anything wrong, she just wanted to see where her dad had worked and maybe walk down her family's old street. There'd be plenty of time after that for her to go and have a look around the laundries in Latimer Road and the shops up Holland Park, to see if anyone was hiring.

The tram was a rickety old thing and the clattering of

the metal wheels on the rails in the road was almost deafening, so it came as a relief to get off. The tram didn't run up past the big houses at Holland Park, and she suspected that the noise might have had something to do with that: who'd want that kind of racket outside the front door, morning, noon and night? She turned off Holland Park and into a side street, trying to remember the landmarks that Aunt Clara had spoken about. The road ahead narrowed into a mews with a kiln at the end of it and she found herself on Pottery Lane.

It was a like a gateway to another world; one with tumbledown houses with peeling paint and net curtains grey with dirt. The streets were alive with kids, hordes of them, with suspicious little faces and filthy knees. They were skinnier even than the Stirling Road mob and meaner-looking too. She wanted to stop to ask directions to the stables in Silchester Mews but, faced with women in grubby housecoats staring at her from their front steps, Annie was lost for words. In the end, she plucked up courage to ask a couple of navvies who were hauling open a manhole cover in the dusty road. They wolf-whistled at her as she turned her back and a boy shouted a rude comment about her hat, so she took that off and held it close to her, quickening her pace, wondering whether this had been such a good idea after all.

She smelt the mews before she saw it. As she rounded the corner into Silchester Road, she was hit by an overpowering stench of horse dung and rubbish. A large heap of the stuff was piled at the far end of the mews and some kids were chucking stones at one of the stable doors, which was hanging off its hinges.

A broken cart was jammed hard up against another of the stables. Annie dreaded to think what might be lurking underneath the tarpaulin covering it, because it stank of rotting flesh. A pile of old pram wheels and metal poles stuck out at crazy angles in a tangle of metal next to that. She inched her way across the greasy black cobbles, trying not to slip or step in anything which might ruin her only pair of smart shoes. They had a slight heel to them and she felt very foolish for having worn them, in case she needed to make a run for it.

She glanced around her. This wasn't how she'd imagined her father's work to be; in her mind's eye she'd seen a bustling stable filled with beautiful horses and ruddy-cheeked stable lads fetching and carrying buckets of water and bales of hay. Instead, she was confronted with decaying horse manure and piles of junk concealing God knows what.

'Get out of it!' a voice boomed from a cracked window-pane above one of the stable doors. 'Sling yer hook or I'll give you a thick ear!'

Annie glanced nervously around her as the boys scarpered back down the road. A heavy door was pushed open and a bulky figure appeared, with sacking tied around his legs up to his knees. He wore an ancient bowler hat and his grey beard was flecked with the remnants of his dinner, by the look of it.

'Clear off, you too!' he said, tucking his thumbs into his belt and glaring in her direction.

'I'm sorry,' she began. 'I'm just looking for someone who used to work at the stables here . . .'

He laughed. 'The horse has had his day, or are you blind?' There was the sound of whinnying from one of the stalls. 'Except for that old thing: he pulls the rag-and-bone wagon for me.' He spat on the ground in front of him.

'I don't want to be a trouble, I was just hoping that someone might have heard of Henry Austin, that's all.'

He looked at her closely. 'And who's asking?'

'My name's Annie Austin. He was my dad and I think he was a cabbie here.'

'Well, I'm not saying I did know him and I'm not saying I didn't, but I'd better take a closer look at you,' he said, ambling down the flagstone stairs towards her. He wasn't too steady on his feet and he held onto the wall with an outstretched hand as he did so. Annie stood rooted to the spot, afraid to move, as he drew nearer. He was a big fella, standing nearly six feet tall, but he walked with a stoop which made him look lopsided. And he smelt almost as bad as the manure heap. His jacket was covered in greasy stains and his neckerchief had once been red but was now almost black with filth. With the sacking tied around his legs with twine, he cut a very strange figure indeed.

'Keeps the rats away,' he said, spitting on the floor again, as he caught Annie staring at his legs.

She tried her best not to shrink under his gaze.

'Well, you do look quite like him, I'll give you that much,' he said. 'But you have your mother's face more than his, I'd say.'

'So, you knew them both?' said Annie, with barely disguised excitement.

'Yes, I suppose I did,' he said. 'A long time ago. It was a different world then. Your dad worked for me here, at the stables.' He paused, as if he was thinking: 'Horses ruled the roads, not like the motor cars they have now.'

The penny dropped for Annie then: 'You must be Charlie D?'

'Most folks know me as Charles Doncaster these days,' he said, with a laugh. 'Makes me sound more respectable, for a totter, at least. I'd like to talk to you, but I have got a terrible thirst coming on . . .' He touched his throat with blackened fingernails.

'I can buy you a drink if you'd like?' she offered, catching his drift.

'Well, if you insist.' He smirked. 'Let's go round to the Black Bull and see if a pint or two can jog my memory.'

The fact that Charlie D, the scruffy totter from Silchester Mews, was walking out with a well-dressed young woman was enough to turn a few heads on the way round to the pub.

A shopkeeper unloading some boxes from a wagon gave them a cheery wave and shouted, 'Whose your new bird, Charlie?' which made Annie wish the ground would swallow her up.

She studied him closely, thinking that all those years ago, her dad had spent every day working for him. It was hard to say how old he was. She guessed he was about ten years older than her mum and Bill, perhaps, but he looked ancient because of the years spent working outside in all weathers, which had given his skin the appearance of worn leather.

He pushed open the doors to the pub; it stank of stale smoke, and was darker than a coal hole inside, with drab walls. The floor was old, with broken floorboards, and Annie couldn't help noticing the pile of sawdust at the foot of the brown-painted bar, filled with abandoned matchsticks and fag ends. A tatty chalkboard with 'No Tick' stood on a shelf lined with grimy glasses and half-empty bottles of dubious-looking spirits.

She'd never bought a drink herself before and certainly not in the middle of the day, so she fished her purse from her coat pocket and handed some coins to Charlie D, while she settled herself on a stool near the fireplace because her legs were shaking so much with nerves, she wasn't sure she could stand much longer.

'Now then,' said Charlie D, returning with a port and lemon for her and a pint for himself, 'it's all starting to come back to me. What is it you want to know?'

She took a teeny sip of her drink, just to be polite. 'I wanted to know what my dad did up until he went away to the war, I suppose . . .' she ventured.

He looked at her, puzzled: 'Oh, he was long gone before that.'

'What do you mean?' said Annie, completely flummoxed. 'Where did he go?'

Charlie D hesitated for a moment before taking a large swig of his ale. 'They never told you the truth, did they?'

20

May 1934

'You were still a babe in arms the first time your mother brought you along to visit my stables.'

The bar stool screeched on the stone floor as Annie shuffled closer to Charlie D so she could hear him better; he was muttering into his beard as he spoke.

'What about my dad?' she asked.

'Oh, he was a good worker, reliable, but he never got as many fares as some of the other lads because of that old grey mare he liked so much,' said Charlie with a laugh.

'You mean Old Nell,' said Annie. She touched the brass horse charm which she was wearing under her blouse. It had seemed right to put it on this morning, and now she was glad that she had.

The pub had started to fill up with lunchtime drinkers, workmen mostly, who nodded a 'hello' to Charlie. One fella with a pronounced limp hobbled in and was handed a pint by the barman without having to ask for it. He sank it in about three seconds flat, handed over his money and then limped out again.

She lowered her voice: 'I know about the gambling debt and my dad working to pay it off.'

He raised an eyebrow. 'Well, there's a thing. All right, so I'll speak plainly. Not many months after you came into the world, the old man Will died.'

'Oh,' said Annie, 'that must have made things even more tough for my family.'

'I can't say that it did,' said Charlie, shaking his head. 'Liked two things in life, he did. Drink and gaming.'

'But I thought he'd promised my nan he'd give all that up after he got in money trouble!' said Annie, her voice rising an octave in disbelief.

'Well, there's one thing I've learned in this life, and that's that a leopard don't change his spots. Will drank so much he fairly pickled his liver,' said Charlie. 'And he was still owing people money left, right and centre. So, I can't say he was mourned too badly when he went, though I always had time for him.'

'I bet you did,' muttered Annie, under her breath.

'What's that you say?' said Charlie D, a flicker of malice in his eyes.

'Well, you were working for Felstone all along and encouraging him to gamble!' she said. 'You were partly to blame.'

People at the bar turned and started to talk to each other, pointing over at them. Charlie grabbed her by the arm and gripped it tightly. 'Now, see here,' he hissed. 'A man makes his own choices. And you don't come onto my manor and start hollering Mr Felstone's name too loudly, not if you know what's good for you.'

'Let go of me!' she said, trying to pull her arm away, but he held her fast.

'You think you can come into this parish, take a trip down memory lane and then just waltz off and leave the past behind?' he said. 'Well, it ain't that easy; the past ain't finished with you yet.'

Annie wanted to scream, but she didn't think for one minute that any of the men at the bar would help her. She was a stranger here, out of her depth. 'I'm sorry,' she stammered. 'It's just that my Aunt Clara told me . . .'

He relaxed his grip and patted her arm. 'Your Aunt Clara was little more than a girl back then and she didn't know the half of it,' said Charlie. 'No more hollering, either. I don't want any of Felstone's men breathing down my neck, wondering what a pretty little thing like you might want, talking to the likes of me. Clear?'

He pushed the glass of port and lemon towards her and steered her to a table in the corner. 'Take a drink of that, you'll need it.'

'I was boss of these streets back around the turn of the century, had a nice little earner going with my stables and the hansom cabs and a bit of looking after the pubs round here on behalf of Mr Felstone,' said Charlie. His face lit up as he remembered his glory days. 'He owned the houses and the horses, but I was his eyes and ears – at least, that was how it was at first, but business got bigger and he got more respectable and needed more people keeping an eye on his interests. That was when the real trouble started.

'I didn't like 'em, fellas from Kensal Town. They'd hit you first and ask questions later, which wasn't my way of doing things. I knew people round here would pay eventually, you just had to give them time. It was like a family business, the debt collecting, so when Will got himself in deep, I told Mr Felstone he'd pay in time and made it clear I didn't want that lot bothering him, not on my manor.

'Henry was head over heels with your mum, he'd have done anything for her, so he was working all hours to try to clear the debt and, to be fair, he was meeting his payments at first, but then the work started to dry up.'

'Why was that?' said Annie, sipping her drink and feeling the port warming her from the inside.

'People just stopped using hansom cabs as much,' said Charlie D, tracing a finger around the rim of his beer glass. 'They were on the omnibuses or the tuppenny tube, or the trams. Things started changing so much that, by the time you were born, it was like a different world and London went from being a city of horses to a city of motor cars. We were all feeling the pinch at the stables and with a new mouth to feed and Will gone, Henry missed a couple of payments.

'I told him I'd talk to Mr Felstone about it, but I never got the chance.' Charlie stopped and took a large glug of his pint and wiped his mouth on the back of his sleeve.

'Why?' said Annie, 'I thought Mr Felstone listened to you.'

'The Kensal Town mob waited until I'd gone out on some business one morning and they came into the stables to find Henry,' he said. 'He was in the stall, tacking Nell up, when they caught up with him . . .'

'What did they do to him?' said Annie, her voice a whisper. She could hardly bear to listen to what Charlie was saying, but she'd come this far . . .

'One of my stable lads heard the shouting and came to see what was going on. He was given a thick ear for his trouble, but he saw it all. They were roughing Henry up and he was fighting back. He had the whip in his hand and whacked one of them round the face with it, good and proper, but there was three of them to one of him and they got him in the corner and knocked him down. It weren't a fair fight.

'He stood up, fists at the ready, but that was when Nell panicked and bucked. She didn't mean to, I know she didn't, but she kicked him right in the chest and he went down hard on that stable floor . . .'

Tears started to roll silently down Annie's face.

'I came running as soon as I heard about the commotion,' said Charlie. 'We picked him up and got him in a cab and I rode like the clappers down to Paddington to the hospital, with him moaning and groaning in the back. But by the time I got there, it was too late.'

'Too late?' said Annie.

'Doctors said his heart had given out. He'd gone.'

There was a moment's silence as Annie took in what Charlie had just told her.

'What about my mum?' she asked. 'Did she see what happened?'

'No, love, thank God she didn't, but we sent word to

the laundry and she came to the hospital as quick as she could. Of course, he was dead as a doornail by then. She practically screamed the place down, calling for him. She wouldn't believe it until the nurses let her see the body and then she didn't want to be parted from him.'

All the colour had drained from Annie's face. It was such a waste of her father's life, dying in a fight like that, and everything she had been told since she was a baby, her whole life, had been founded on a complete and utter lie. Her heart was racing and so many thoughts were flitting around her mind that she couldn't quite get close enough to grasp them. She needed to know more: 'But why didn't Nan or my mum tell me what had happened? I thought he was working here in London all the years I was away in Suffolk.'

'There's plenty of things children don't need to know,' said Charlie. 'Perhaps they told you a little story to make you feel better. And in any case, with Henry gone, your family still owed money to Mr Felstone, see?'

'So how did they pay it off?'

Charlie sucked in his paunch and sat up tall.

'The truth is, they didn't.'

'What? The money is still owing?' said Annie.

Charlie D shifted uncomfortably and lowered his voice. 'Yes, it is. Folks round here are dirt poor, but we look after our own, Annie, and when it came to it, Henry was one of ours and I didn't like the way things had got out of hand on my turf. Without Henry, there was no way the debt could be paid – your mum and your nan both knew that.'

'Didn't someone tell the police? To get them on to Felstone?'

'The cozzers?' said Charlie. 'Oh, you have got a lot to learn, my girl. Mr Felstone was untouchable then and he still is now. All the top brass are his mates. Besides, no one round here breathed a word about what had happened in the stables that day. If anyone official had come around here we'd all have said it was just an accident with the horse getting spooked and poor old Henry being in the wrong place. A tragedy, if you like.

'But once he was buried, it wouldn't take long for the Kensal Town boys to come back and start asking for the cash, would it? They knew where your mum lived, for starters.'

'So, how did they get out of it?' said Annie, who was desperate to know more.

'Well, I may have had a hand in it . . .' said Charlie. 'Although, God knows, Felstone couldn't prove it and if he thought I had, even now, he'd make my life difficult.'

'I won't tell a soul,' said Annie. 'I promise.'

'I'm counting on that, Annie, because I have a long memory and I bear grudges,' said Charlie, looming over the table towards her, so that she caught a whiff of his foul breath.

He smiled and went on: 'It was your Aunt Kiziah's idea, really, to get away to Soapsud Island. She was always a clever one. Your mum weren't thinking straight, she was barely eating enough to feed a fly, and your nan was holding everything together, making sure you were looked after. Girls at the laundry took it in turns to mind you, but your nan knew it made sense to get away somewhere else, somewhere safe.

'It can't have been more than a few days after the funeral and I remember it was winter because it was still freezing cold and the horse didn't want to come out of her stable,' he said, chuckling to himself. 'Oh, I had to whisper sweet nothings in Old Nell's earhole that night to get her out of that stall. She weren't right after Henry went, it was like she'd lost the will to work, the old nag, but once I got the harness on her and into the shafts of one of my wagons, it was as if she knew what she had to do. She was as sprightly as a foal by the time we got to Manchester Road.

'Your nan had packed up everything they owned – lock, stock and barrel – and we piled it onto my carts. The neighbours helped. It was pitch black and a pea-souper to boot. You were tucked up safely next to your mum in a blanket. Oh, and then she ran back into the house because she almost forgot some dolly or other your dad had bought you as a baby. Then off we went, in a moonlight flit, as they call it.'

'What about Felstone's men?'

'Oh, they came calling, 'course they did, but you were all long gone by then. And if anyone did know where you were, they weren't going to tell the Kensal Town boys. There was a lot of bad feeling about the way Henry died.'

Annie swilled the last of her port around her glass, trying to take in everything that Charlie D had told her.

His face softened. 'I always knew your nan was a strong woman, Annie, putting up with her old man Will the way she did all those years, but I only really saw the mettle in her that night. She got hold of your mum and told her: "This is the hand that life has dealt us, so for God's sake, stop crying now, for the sake of the baby. There's only one way out of this mess, Emma, and that is sheer bloody hard work.'"

21

May 1934

'Well, you look like you've seen a ghost!'

Vera stood, stick thin, with bony arms outstretched, on the doorstep at Stirling Road.

Annie had cried all the way home on the tram back from Notting Hill – so much so, she'd almost missed her stop, so she probably did look a complete sight.

'I'm sorry I haven't been around earlier, Vee,' said Annie, almost falling into her friend's arms. 'I wanted to be sure I was clear of the fever and then Mum needed me to go out and look for work.'

'It looks like it's knocked the stuffing right out of you, there's barely a picking on you these days!' Vera cried, swaying slightly. 'You could do with a drink, I bet?' She started to pull her friend up the staircase before she could refuse her offer.

A woman in a flowery housecoat appeared in the hall-way below them. 'All right, Mrs Smith, I'm not sneaking a fella in,' said Vera, poking her tongue out at her land-lady's back as it disappeared into the scullery. 'Honestly, the old bag, she's like a rat up a bleeding drainpipe every time the front door goes.'

She muttered under her breath: 'Thinks it's a knocking shop up here, probably 'cos she ain't getting any!' She'd moved out of Bessie's when life with the Nosy Parkers downstairs became unbearable, but her new place didn't seem any better.

Vera pushed open the door to her room, which had a bed against one wall, a wooden chair with a bottle of sherry open on it and a small rag rug on the bare floorboards.

Vera grabbed a chipped teacup, poured some sherry into it and handed it to Annie. She then raised the bottle to her lips and threw her head back: 'Down the hatch!'

Annie hesitated. She hadn't eaten all day, and drink was the last thing on her mind after her time in the Black Bull pub with Charlie D.

'Come on, Annie,' said Vera. 'It will do you good and we've got a lot to catch up on, ain't we?'

Annie sat down on the bed and drank a little as Vera plonked herself down next to her. She'd missed her friend.

'I'm just sorry I wasn't there for you when you buried Evangeline . . .'

'Don't worry yourself about that now,' said Vera. 'You were really sick. Everyone was worried we were going to lose you, but I knew you'd fight.'

'But did you get to say goodbye to her?' Annie knew how difficult things were for Vera indoors.

'Well, my dad tried to say I couldn't go but my mum wasn't having any of it, so he had to let me come. And anyway, he was dead drunk, he could have done us all a favour by falling into the grave himself, and then at least we'd be rid of him, the miserable old git.' She clutched her sides, as if she'd told the funniest joke ever, but Annie couldn't muster a laugh.

'How's your mum coping?'

Vera stopped for a second and then took another swig of sherry. 'She's got her hands full, hasn't she, with the twins, so I don't think it's hit her so hard as me. I've got time on my hands.'

'Aren't you still working up at the nursery?'

'Let me go, didn't they?' said Vera, staring at the wall. 'Said I wasn't right to be around the kids no more because someone had seen me round the back of the Railway Tavern with a fella. Well, so what if I did? None of their bleeding business, is it?'

'No,' said Annie, who had a horrible, sinking feeling about how Vera was scraping a living these days.

'Means we are in the same boat, both looking for work,' said Vera, tipping a drop more sherry into Annie's cup. 'So, how far did you go on the tram today? Bessie said they're not hiring even up round Shepherd's Bush now. Three girls for every one job in the wash houses round there! Can you imagine?'

'I went up Notting Hill way,' said Annie, who was not sure why she was even telling Vera this – her friend was probably too plastered to make sense of it all. 'I went to where my mum and dad used to live, where I was born.'

'Gawd, it's rough as houses round there, Annie,' said Vera. 'No wonder you came back looking like the wreck of the *Hesperus*.'

'Well, I found out something while I was there too.'

'Come on, spill the beans,' said Vera.

'You know I was always wondering why my mum didn't have my dad's war medals or a picture of him in his uniform when he'd died in the Great War, like Bessie's boy?'

Vera nodded.

'Well, she never had them because he never went to the war. He died ten years before that, when I was still a baby, after a fight in Notting Hill, and they kept it secret from me, all these years.' A spark of something had ignited inside her as she spoke. 'My mum and my nan and my Aunt Clara told me a pack of lies from the moment I could crawl, letting me believe in him as a war hero when he was nothing of the sort,' she spat.

'That's awful, Annie,' said Vera, holding her friend's hand. 'But there must be a reason for it, mustn't there?'

'I think they were trying to protect me from the upset of it, of him dying so young,' said Annie, who didn't want to mention the gambling debt nor the fact that her family still owed money to the Felstones. She'd promised Charlie D not to talk about it to anyone; in any case, it was shameful to have to admit to it. 'But it makes me feel that my whole life has been a lie. I used to dream about him fighting in the trenches – it made it better somehow, especially with Mum marrying Bill.'

'But, hang on a minute,' said Vera, scratching her head, as if the fug of alcohol was clearing. 'If your dad died when you were a baby, what about your brother George?'

She really had opened a can of worms by seeking the truth about her father.

Annie didn't take much convincing to have another stiff drink, and then another, while she and Vera picked over the bones of her mother's deceit.

'Who'd have thought it?' said Vera, shaking her head. 'She must have done it to cover the fact that she'd got knocked up when your dad had gone all them years before. But George don't look anything like old Bill, does he? Far too good-looking, if you ask me!' Vera cackled to herself.

'I just can't believe it,' said Annie, over and over. 'She lied through her teeth. Took me for a fool, good and proper. Why didn't she just tell me the truth?'

Her head was reeling by the time she left Vera's, and not just from the drink; and as she rounded the corner to home, she went hot and cold and then felt vomit rising in her throat. She held on to the lamppost, and – to her shame – threw up in the gutter. Glancing around to check that the neighbours hadn't spotted her, she wiped the flecks of vomit away from her mouth with her handkerchief, straightened herself up and tried to sneak into the house without Mum or Bill noticing. That plan went awry when she bumped into one of the wooden chairs in the scullery and knocked it flying; it was as if the world was spinning.

Mum appeared in the doorway: 'Where on earth have you been, Annie? I've been worried sick!' She took one look at her daughter and, leaning in closer, said, 'Have you been drinking?'

'I just popped in to see Vera and she got some sherry out to celebrate me getting better, that's all,' said Annie, with a note of defiance in her voice. All the while she looked at her mother, she was thinking, 'Liar!'

'And meanwhile we were sitting here thinking you'd fallen ill again and were lying in the gutter somewhere! You could at least have let us know you were safely back from Notting Hill, Annie.'

Something snapped; all the years she'd done what she was told, been good, put up with Bill, slaved away in the laundry for pennies without question and waited and waited to see a father who was never coming home. 'I'm not a child!' she shouted. 'You can't expect me to tell you everything any more!' And she stormed off upstairs.

'I don't know what got into you last night, but I don't expect to see a repeat of it!' Mum scolded, as Annie sat, with a thumping headache, at the breakfast table.

She served Annie a piece of bread and marg and a steaming mug of strong tea: 'You'd better drink that.' And as she turned her back and bustled off to the sink, Mum muttered, 'Sherry, indeed!'

'I'm sorry,' said Annie, to keep the peace. She was sorry but only up to a point. Mum had made her question everything in her world. The one certainty in her life had been taken away from her. She'd always taken such comfort in the fact that she and George had both lost their dad in the war, and George had been there before Bill came into their lives.

Yes, she adored her sisters, but she'd always imagined that her dad would have been so proud of George and now it turned out that her dad couldn't possibly have fathered her brother because he was six feet under at the time. It was as if life had given her back her father, with what Charlie D had told her, but snatched her brother away from her somehow.

There was a heavy footfall on the staircase and then Elsie appeared at the table, with Ivy following close behind. Ivy was smiling cheekily and holding her hands behind her back.

'What you got there, Ivy?' said Mum, pouring them both a cuppa before they headed off to school.

'I'm not sure,' said Ivy, 'but it was under Annie's mattress. I think she might have a fancy man and she's keeping a picture of him under her bed!' She gave a little snort of laughter as she waved the old photograph of Henry Austin under Annie's nose. 'Maybe that's what she was doing last night!'

Annie made to snatch it back from her, but Mum was too quick. All the colour drained from her face as she grabbed the old picture from Ivy and held it between her shaking fingers: 'Ye gods and little fishes, Annie! Where did you get this?'

Annie opened her mouth to reply but her mother had coloured up now, like a kettle coming to the boil, and steam was almost coming out of her ears: 'You have no right to have this! You have no right, my girl!'

Right on cue, Bill ambled into the scullery, with his little mug of hot water and a shaving brush from his daily ablutions. 'What's all this, then?'

'Nanny Chick gave it to me, years ago,' said Annie, who was shaking almost as much as her mother's fingers. 'It's just a picture of . . .'

'It was never hers to give, Annie!' Mum cried. Realizing

this was no laughing matter, Ivy and Elsie retreated to the safety of the hallway.

Bill peered at the photograph, made a little 'hmm' to himself and then turned his back, walking slowly over to the sink and sloshing his dirty shaving water down the plughole. He wasn't going to get involved.

Annie clasped her hands in front of her, like a cat's cradle, the game she used to like to play with Nanny with a ball of wool when she was little. 'Nanny wanted me to have it, Mum. She wasn't trying to cause any trouble, I know it. She just wanted me to have a picture of him, of my dad.'

'How long have you had it?' said Mum, holding the picture to her chest.

'Years, since just before Nanny died,' said Annie.

'And you never once thought to tell me about it?' Mum shouted. 'Never once! You went skulking about behind my back and hiding it under your bed, for the love of God. Lying to me. What's got into you!'

'No!' said Annie, standing up. 'You lied to me! You made me into a liar because you let me believe he was alive all those years I was in Suffolk, and now I know he wasn't.'

It was as if someone had taken the wind right out of Mum's sails then, because she sat down, deflated, at the table. Bill came over to her and put his hands on her shoulders. He glared at Annie: 'Don't you dare talk to your mother like that, you cheeky little blighter.'

He raised his hand to her, as if he were going to strike her. But Annie moved away from him and stared him down. 'I'm not a little girl any more, Bill. Do you think you are just going to belt me one and get away with it?'

'Oh, don't you work your ticket with me!' he shouted. 'Or you'll find out.'

'Please, both of you, stop it!' Mum sobbed, burying her face in her hands.

'I know the truth about what happened to my dad in Notting Hill when I was just a baby,' Annie began, 'despite all your best efforts to hide it.'

Mum glanced up at her, as if she were looking at a total stranger who had just walked into her kitchen, dragging the past in with her, uninvited.

Annie could feel the triumph of what she was saying surging through her body, as if the years of secrecy, of creeping around and hiding things were finally being thrown off: 'Yes, I found out! I know you loved him, I know you did, Mum, so why didn't you just tell me he'd died like that?'

'You've no right to be meddling about in my business . . .'

'It's my past!' cried Annie. 'It's not wrong to want to know about my own father, is it?'

But Mum had heard enough. She stood up, opened her hand and delivered a resounding slap right around Annie's face, sending her reeling backwards, into the kitchen door.

'That's right!' Mum yelled, as Annie fled the room, clutching her face. 'Get out of my sight!'

22

May 1934

You can see a lot of London from the top deck of a bus.

Annie had never had the time to travel about up in town, but now, with her few belongings stuffed into Nanny Chick's old carpet bag, she had all the time in the world and nowhere in particular to go.

The noise of Oxford Circus thrummed in her head as the policeman standing in the middle of the road directed the traffic with his white-gloved hands. Lorries were parked up haphazardly as motor cars chugged through and a sad-looking dray horse waited his turn, surrounded by choking fumes. Paperboys yelled the headlines, while women in fancy coats and mink stoles stepped lightly along the pavement on the arms of men wearing trilby hats and wide-legged trousers with turn-ups. Everyone was so smart, it made Annie feel rather small and shabby, watching it all from her vantage point but not really being part of it.

She hopped off the bus and made her way down the warren of backstreets, past some dodgy-looking blokes at a betting shop joshing around with some girls leaning out of a window above them, wearing a lot of make-up, by the look of it. Annie hurried on, her fingers working over the coins in her pocket, wondering whether she should stop for a cup of tea now or keep going a bit longer.

In truth, she hadn't a clue where she was heading. She'd never been this far into town before but had no intention of going home. She'd waited until the front door banged shut, signalling that her mum was off out to work and Elsie and Ivy had gone to secretarial college, before grabbing her things – including her precious rag doll – shoving them into Nanny Chick's old carpet bag and scarpering down the stairs and out of the front door, before Bill could say another word to her.

Her mum didn't want her there, she was sure of it, and she didn't want to spend another moment living with the lies under that roof. She'd been a fool to believe everything she'd been told, she could see that now. She just wanted a fresh start. But where would she go?

Her feet were aching by the time she reached Covent Garden, with its burgundy-tiled station. Outside, the barrow boys were shouting to each other as they loaded wicker baskets and crates onto the backs of carts. There was barely room to move, with so many wagons vying for space, and there was such a cacophony of noise that Annie almost had to cover her ears. Flower-sellers, old girls in long skirts, stood on the street corners with their shawls drawn around their shoulders as the afternoon drew to a close, shouting, 'A penny a bunch!' to anyone who'd listen.

Annie stopped outside a cake shop, her stomach rumbling. She couldn't really afford to waste money on such luxuries, but she was starving hungry, so she went inside and bought herself a nice iced bun. She sat down on a bench and ate it, watching the world go by, feeling a bit better for having some food inside her.

A plan began to form in her mind. She needed a job, and although she'd only ever worked in a laundry, she knew how to be polite to people. So, perhaps she could try some shop work? Licking her fingers, she went back into the baker's shop and asked whether he might need any help. But he just shook his head apologetically.

'You could try some of the pubs, love,' he said. 'They're often happy to take on a nice-looking girl to help behind the bar: the punters like it, if you know what I mean.'

He was trying to be helpful, she realized that, but as she skirted around the pubs near the market, she couldn't quite get up the courage to go inside and ask; mainly because of the drunken oafs falling out of them into the gutter.

She'd almost lost hope and dusk was starting to fall when she spotted the sign in the window of a little pub with a bow window, down a side street next to the Theatre Royal. A solitary figure stood outside in the semi-darkness, the light of his cigarette burning brightly.

Annie drew nearer so she could read the notice. It said: 'Help wanted.'

The man opened the door for her, and she stepped inside.

Ralph and Mavis Hartwood were an East End couple, born and bred, who had been in the pub trade for generations, but since Mavis had had their daughter,

Daphne, four years ago she'd been getting cold feet about being up West and was hankering after a return to their home turf.

'She could use an extra pair of hands around the place to keep her happy,' said Ralph, almost conspiratorially. 'I need someone to take the weight off her feet and a load off her mind. She's not been herself lately and she worries about our little girl hanging around the pub all day with nothing to do. We've got a spare room at the back, nothing fancy, but you'll be comfortable enough and I won't charge you rent. Are you any good with kids?'

'I helped raise my two stepsisters,' said Annie, brightly. 'So, yes, I suppose so.'

'Well, if you can take Daphne out during the day and help out behind the bar in the evenings, that would be just what we are after,' said Ralph. 'I'll get you to meet the wife.'

He disappeared around the back of the bar and yelled up the staircase: 'Mavis! I think I've found the right girl for us.'

A ruddy-cheeked woman appeared at the foot of the stairs, carrying a beautiful dark-haired little girl in her arms. The little one smiled shyly at Annie.

'Annie here is looking for work and is good with children. She's from a laundry family in Acton,' said Ralph.

'What brings you this far up into town, then?' asked Mavis, with a note of suspicion in her voice.

'Didn't get on with my stepdad, really, so I fell out with my mum,' said Annie. It was more complicated than that, of course, but she didn't want to go into the ins and outs of her family secrets with complete strangers.

Mavis smiled and her whole face lit up: 'Oh, you poor thing. Sounds terrible. Chuck you out on your ear, did she? You can tell me all about it over a cup of tea. Not that I would tell a soul, you understand, I'm as silent as the grave, not one to gossip.'

Ralph raised his eyebrows but said nothing and Mavis popped the child down at Annie's feet.

'Say hello to Annie, then.'

Annie knelt down and looked into Daphne's big brown eyes and eager little face. She was so sweet, Annie almost cried.

'Will we go out and have fun together?' said Daphne.

'Yes,' said Annie, climbing the stairs behind Mavis, with Daphne in her arms. 'I promise we will.'

Later that evening, as she was settling herself into her new room, the pain of the row with her mum had diminished a bit, so that she felt numb, she gazed out across the back yard of the pub and the rooftops of Covent Garden, their tiles all glossy in the rain.

She'd grown used to Elsie and Ivy clattering up and down the stairs, Bill shouting for something or other and her mum asking her to help get the plates washed up. But now there was a completely different set of noises: the creak of the old pub staircase, the shouts of the market traders, the drunks in high spirits, people bustling about, motor cars in the street, right outside.

There were times she'd dreamed of having a room of her own, and now she had one, with dark wooden

furniture, a dressing table and even a mirror, just for her.
It was like being cast adrift in a little boat on a vast sea
and not quite knowing where she was heading.

There was a gentle knock on the door and Mavis
appeared.

'Mind if I come in?' she said.

Annie wasn't used to anyone knocking on the door and
asking her permission to enter, so she nodded and Mavis
came in and sat beside her on the single bed.

'I thought this might help you sleep,' she said, handing
her a mug of Ovaltine.

Annie sipped. It was delicious.

By the time her head hit the pillow, the shock of the
row with her mum had faded into the background and she
slipped willingly into a deep sleep.

Annie relished the chance to go off visiting the museums
and parks around London with her young charge.

'I really want the best for my girl,' said Mavis. 'So I'd
like you to take her to places that I don't have time to go.
Show her a bit of history. I don't want her growing up
thinking that drinking in pubs is all that life has to offer.'

Ralph rolled his eyes but said nothing. Bringing up the
girl was Mavis's responsibility and he just didn't understand what she was so worried about. It wasn't as if
Daphne was sitting at the bar, drinking pints, was it?

Annie was only too pleased to take her off and see a
bit of culture. All the years she'd missed out on schooling
and the time she'd spent stuck scrubbing away at the

washboards meant she was probably more excited than Daphne to go and have a look at some proper history.

In the mornings, after sorting out breakfast for the family and tidying up the beds, while Mavis went for a lie down, they'd set off through Covent Garden, marvelling at the porters with stacks of wicker baskets balanced precariously on their heads bringing the fruit and veg in. The record was held by one man with a dozen baskets up there; the women were wider than the pub doors, and probably stronger than the fellas.

Ralph liked to tell a funny story about a bet that one of the costermongers' wives had years ago, that she couldn't carry her hubby down to the Borough over the water without dropping him – she did it, stopping only to consume a whole bottle of gin on the way, with him still slung over her shoulders.

Annie and Daphne rode the Underground up to the Natural History Museum, to see everything from huge dinosaur skeletons to beautiful butterfly collections in glass cases, with their wings like brightly coloured silk hankies.

Daphne's favourite day out was at London Zoo in Regent's Park, and Annie loved seeing the animals, but she was careful not to let the little girl stick her fingers through the bars of the cages. 'You can look, not touch!' was her watchword, just as it had been with Elsie and Ivy up at the baker's shop in Acton High Street.

In the evenings, she helped out behind the bar, which was Ralph's pride and joy – he was always mopping it down and cleaning it. She quickly learned how to tot up drinks bills in her head and give the right change, how to pull pints using the brass-topped china pump handles and even change a barrel of beer – although the cellar was damp and creepy, so she hated going down there. The Nell of Old Drury had been a pub for centuries; Ralph had teased her it was haunted, and she believed him.

The pub was a popular watering hole for lots of actors and music-hall stars, with the Theatre Royal being just across the way, and Annie got used to seeing some very famous faces horsing around before a show, cracking Ralph up into a booming laugh and making Mavis smile more than she had ever seen. There was something about the way the light bounced off all the gleaming glasses and reflected in the mirrors behind the bar that made the whole place glitter with life.

The first time she spotted the comedian Arthur Askey he was pretending to have trouble climbing up onto a bar stool. He was a small man, and the way he flailed his legs about had the whole pub in tears of laughter. At the end of his little routine, he took a deep bow and said, 'I thank you,' but the way he said it, sounded like 'I thang yew', which gave Annie a fit of the giggles. He said it to her every time she handed him a drink after that, just to make her laugh.

Annie was a bit shy at first, but she found a scrap of paper and he signed it for her. That was the start of her autograph collection. Ralph gave her an old notebook and she stuck the signatures in, one by one.

Max Wall was a particular favourite. She was a bit scared of him when she first saw him drinking moodily in the corner one lunchtime.

'He's a funny one, looks a bit miserable, if you ask me, but it's just because he's working on his routines, Annie, don't take it personal. He's bleeding hilarious once he's in the limelight,' Ralph explained.

When he came over to chat to Annie one lunchtime, Max was so charming, she was quite smitten with him; he was a handsome bloke. She also liked the music-hall duo Flanagan and Allen, who had a play on over the road at the Royal, and they would take it in turns to tease Annie by ordering drinks for each other and changing their minds at the last minute, until she told them to stop it. There was never a dull moment behind the bar.

Ralph was delighted because Mavis seemed more like her old self too, just having Annie around. She'd stopped going for long lie-downs in the middle of the day and was always there to provide a listening ear to her regulars from the market when they popped in for a natter, which was good for business.

One day, after closing time, when they were wiping the tabletops down, Mavis said to her: 'Do you ever think about your family, Annie? Your mum must be worried about you.'

'Oh, I haven't had any time to think about them much these days,' Annie said, scrubbing the table with renewed vigour.

'Well, perhaps you should get in touch, just to let them know you are doing well?'

'No,' said Annie, firmly. 'I don't think that would help. It was difficult, the way I left things.'

'But a mother would never forget her daughter. I'm just

thinking if I ever fell out with Daphne when she was older, it would kill me not knowing where she was or what she was doing,' said Mavis. She glanced over at her little girl, who was quietly flicking through a picture book.

'I'll think about it,' said Annie, turning away.

The truth was, most nights, when the shouts of chucking-out time had died down and the streets of Covent Garden fell silent for a few short hours before the market got going again, she lay there missing her mum, George, Ivy and Elsie, Aunt Clara and even – and she couldn't work this one out – Bill, of all people.

She wasn't sorry for saying what she had said, though, and the lies still hurt, like a kind of ache in her chest when she thought about it all. Then, before she knew it, dawn would break and she'd have so much to do with little Daphne and all the excitement in the pub, it was easy to push it all to the back of her mind.

And as the days turned into weeks, the distance between her and the folks back in Soapsud Island seemed to grow, until it was so vast that she didn't know how to cross it any more, or whether she even wanted to.

23

September 1934

'Oo's the omi of the carsa?'

A bird-like little fellow with startling blue eyes and razor-sharp cheekbones perched himself right on the edge of the bar, like some kind of acrobat.

'Evening Wilf – not seen you for a while. Pint, is it?' said Ralph, flicking a tea towel at him, to tell him to get down.

He jumped back onto a bar stool and pulled his jacket pockets inside out. 'Nunty dinari, mate, don't get paid till Friday.'

'I'll stand you a half – we can put it on tick,' said Ralph.

Annie started to pour him a drink; she could barely understand a word the man was saying but he seemed friendly enough.

'Ooo, bona polone, where d'you find 'er, then?'

'This is Annie, she just blew in on a gust of wind, Wilf, right to our front door,' said Ralph, giving Annie an avuncular smile. 'She's been great with the little one too, takes the worry out of it all for me and the missus.'

'Tell you what, Annie, I could zhoosh your riah right

up and you'd look fantabulosa!' he said, with a wave of his hands.

Was he making fun of her?

'Wilf works backstage at the Royal, Annie. He's just saying he could do your hair for you sometime, in theatre-speak. It's called Polari.'

'Oh, I see,' she said, trying not to blush. She probably did need to make a bit more of an effort with her appearance.

'I'll lend you some slap and we'll get your glad rags on, love,' said Wilf, giving her a wink. 'Paint the town red.'

Another man, taller and suave-looking, in a well-cut suit, his straw-coloured hair slicked back from his face, came over to join the conversation.

He leaned over the bar towards Annie: 'I bet you can sing, can't you?'

'Well, I can hold a tune,' said Annie, who'd got used to having a bit of a banter with the locals. 'Does that count?'

'What about dancing, I bet you move like a ballerina.'

Annie grinned at him. 'Two left feet, I'm afraid.'

'Ah, such a disappointment,' he said. 'There was I thinking I'd found the next Big Thing, working right here in Theatreland, pulling pints. Perhaps you just dropped in from the sky, because you look divine . . .'

'Oh, stop teasing her, Stanley,' said Ralph, handing him a whisky and soda. 'Stanley's always on the prowl for new talent, but you can't have her, old man – she's my best barmaid.'

'She's certainly the prettiest,' said Stanley, flashing Annie a smile. His face was so clean-shaven, he had smooth skin, like alabaster, and even his fingernails were manicured. Annie had never seen a man looking so well kept, so smart. She tried not to gawp at him.

'Where've you been lately, Stan?' said Ralph, drying some glasses on a tea towel.

'Away on the music-hall circuit up north, keeping an eye on business, you know.' He gave Ralph a little wink.

Annie watched as he swallowed the amber liquid with gusto, making his Adam's apple bob up and down, before putting the empty glass on the bar for her to refill it.

She didn't have favourite customers, really, other than the musical-hall acts, who made her laugh and teased her. She'd got to know the drinkers who came in to pass the time, the punters who liked to settle down for hours playing cards and cribbage, as well as the silent regulars – the ones who never spoke and drank up quickly. But she started to look forward to seeing Stanley for a little chat at the bar every week, rather more than she would let on to anyone. He usually dropped by on Tuesday lunchtimes, or sometimes Wednesday evenings. So she was disappointed when he disappeared for a few weeks, without saying goodbye.

When he returned, softly calling her name while her back was turned to the bar, Annie was so delighted she almost dropped a bottle of brandy she was carrying.

'Did I scare you, Annie?' he purred. 'You look like you could use a drink yourself. Can I buy you one?'

'No, I don't think Mr Hartwood would like that,' she said, smiling because he had offered to treat her. Stanley glanced around the bar: 'Well, I don't see him anywhere. It could be our little secret.'

When he spoke, it was like being wrapped in a fur coat; his voice enveloped her in a kind of warmth.

Annie shook her head. 'I really couldn't, but thanks all the same.'

He took out a silver cigarette case and flipped it open. 'Perhaps I could find some other way of corrupting you.'

He selected one for himself before offering one to her. There was a gracefulness to the way he moved which was almost irresistible.

'Oh, I've never . . .' she began.

'Well, you should. All the sophisticated ladies smoke. Go on, give it a try.'

He placed the cigarette between his slender, manicured fingers and she hesitated for a moment before taking it from him and placing it between her lips. He took a match from the box on the bar and struck it, so that it flared, and then leaned towards her, lighting the cigarette, before returning it to his own.

She sucked on it a little bit, feeling the smoke snaking its way around her mouth, before self-consciously blowing it back out, giggling.

'Here, I'll show you how,' he said.

He pursed his lips and she couldn't help watching how his face changed, his features relaxing a little as he inhaled, almost as if he was swallowing something.

She tried again, drawing in, feeling the smoke burning its way down her airways so that she coughed and spluttered, and he had to pat her on the back.

'Oh, God, I'm useless at this!' she cried, holding the ciggie between shaking fingers.

'You'll learn,' he said. 'But that was terribly sweet to look at, all the same.'

Annie stubbed it out, grabbed the water jug on the bar and poured herself a glass, to try to take the awful taste away. As she sipped, he watched her closely.

Then, out of nowhere, he said, 'What do you want out of life, Annie?'

It was such a searching question, she felt like one of those butterflies in the museum, skewered with a pin. She had hopes, secret hopes, for the future but she'd always been so busy putting everyone else before herself, it didn't seem that there would ever be time – time for her to have fun, to meet someone, to fall in love, to have a family of her own, perhaps.

She smiled nervously. 'I don't expect much, I've never really . . .'

'What about marriage and children?'

That question just about knocked her for six. 'S'pose it might be nice, some day,' she said, as breezily as she could, a bit like one of the heroines in the talkies. It was an effort, an actual physical effort, to squash down all the pain she'd felt when Ed had dumped her for Vera, all her fears about getting pregnant if she went courting, all the loneliness, so much loneliness; night after night, day after day, just wishing she had someone to share her life with – to talk to, really, just about the little things. To get into bed and feel a man's arms around her and know that he cared, and that he'd always treat her right.

Stanley touched her arm and applied just enough pressure, so it was almost a caress, making her go quite weak at the knees. 'I'd like to see you again soon. We can talk some more about the future. I'm sure you've got plenty of dreams you can share with me.'

The trouble was, she knew she had. She was dying to share her dreams with him and everything else too. Her heart was pounding so loudly he could probably hear it.

'There's so much going on in that little head of yours, isn't there, Annie?'

Annie nodded mutely.

His mouth pressed itself into a little smile as he turned to leave, to get on with his very busy day.

When Wilf next popped into the pub, Annie asked him, rather self-consciously, if he'd been serious about helping her glam up a bit.

''Course I am, be delighted!' he said, clapping his hands together with glee. 'Is there some dish you've got your eye on, then? Go on, tell me!'

'No one really, I just think I could probably do with looking less like a laundrymaid and more like a barmaid, don't you?'

Wilf took a long look at her. 'You've got a nice bod and fantabulosa cheekbones, doll, but I reckon a bit more slap and you'll look like a film star. Come and see me in my parlour at the Royal and I can give you a quick tour backstage while we're about it, if you like?'

'I'd love to!' Annie had never been backstage in the theatre before and, although she wouldn't normally consider being alone in a room with a fella, she felt perfectly safe with Wilf. She'd been a bit shocked at first, when she'd seem him talking that Polari slang with other blokes, huddled in corners, laughing and giggling together. Ralph had whispered to her: 'It takes all sorts, Annie, remember that.' She'd guessed then, and if anybody was that way inclined, it was best not to discuss it, because the law could get involved and nobody wanted that. Wilf was a lovely bloke and she counted him as a friend.

On her next free afternoon, she hurried across the road to the theatre and he met her at the stage door. She followed him down a maze of dark corridors to his room, where all the costumes were kept, neatly hanging on rails.

A Singer sewing machine had pride of place next to a work table, where Wilf was repairing some breeches for one of the actors. His bed was a little sofa with a worn jacquard cushion and a patchwork quilt for a bedspread.

'It's hardly the Ritz, Annie, but it's home,' he said, gesturing her to sit down.

He'd pinched a bit of stage make-up – probably best not to ask where from – and started applying some rouge and lipstick and powder to her face. He outlined her eyebrows with a dark pencil, to define them. After a few minutes, he seemed happy with his work and said: 'Done!' He handed her a little mirror and she was so shocked she couldn't help but laugh when she saw herself. 'I look like Coco the Clown with all that slap on!'

'No, you don't,' he said, looking a bit hurt. 'Let's just sort your hair out, for Gawd's sake. You've got a lovely bit of curl going on. What about a hairband to lift it a bit? Or a ribbon?'

Annie ran her hands over her hair, self-consciously. She'd had the same style for the last ten years: a long bob which was wavy at the back and never really did what she wanted it to.

He rummaged in a box of scrap materials and pulled out a length of dark green ribbon, looping it under her hair at the nape of her neck and fastening it at the side, just above her ears.

'Hmm,' he said, appraising his handiwork, 'maybe not.'

He went over to the clothes rails and rifled through another box, emerging with some scary-looking tongs, with wooden handles and a metal prong at the end.

'How about curling your hair?'

Before she had time to change her mind, he had chucked an old copper kettle off its perch on the gas ring in the corner and was heating the curling tongs.

'Now, don't worry, I know what I'm doing,' he said, taking a section of her hair and wrapping it quickly around the barrel of the tongs, before releasing it.

'Can you smell burning?' said Annie, giving him a worried glance as the ends of her hair sizzled a bit.

'Only me fingers,' he said, shaking his hand where the tongs had singed him. After ten minutes of curling and primping, her new hair-do was unveiled. 'I love it!' she cried. 'I do look a bit like a film star, don't I?'

'Yes,' he said, warming to his theme, 'but now we need to get you some glad rags.'

He selected a bright red silk kimono from the rail and tossed it her way. 'Go on, try it on, I dare you!'

He pulled a huge feathered fan from a box of props and started fluttering it about in front of her face: 'Look! Fan-Ann! Try it on, be a devil!'

Annie glanced around for somewhere to change.

'Oh, I'll turn my back, don't worry,' he said, as she started to unbutton her blouse. But he turned around just as she was stepping out of her skirt and was standing there in her liberty bodice, drawers and stockings.

'Wilf!' she shrieked, suppressing a fit of the giggles. 'No peeking!'

'Oh, I am so naughty, Fan-Ann, but what the bleeding hell is that corset thing? You look like Queen Victoria in that get-up! What about some nice underwear? French knickers are all the rage, darling.'

Annie sat down on the clapped-out sofa, feeling its springs giving way underneath her. She was still wearing the liberty bodices she'd had as a teenager because she just hadn't been able to afford fancy underwear like the posh ladies. Now she had a little money saved from her wages, but it had never crossed her mind to buy fancy knickers and the like because there'd never really been any question of a man seeing her undergarments. 'I haven't got anything else,' she said, pulling the kimono to her, to cover her embarrassment.

'I didn't mean to hurt your feelings, doll, honestly,' said Wilf, sitting down beside her. 'But you have got to get yourself a nice brassiere, Annie. You have got a good figure, you just need to make the most of it.

'Come on, Fan-Ann,' he said, clasping her hands. 'We're going shopping!'

Gamages loomed over Holborn Circus, like a giant Aladdin's cave.

Annie had never been in a shop selling so many things; the window displays alone were enough to make her head spin. They had typewriters and bicycles, and that was just for starters. The ground floor was stuffed to the gunnels with hats, scarves and bags, and there were heaps of leather gloves of every size and colour, which they stopped to try on, just for a laugh.

Wilf was on a mission to get her underpinnings sorted, though, so they didn't linger long. Besides, the doorman was giving Wilf a few funny looks. 'They don't like the way I mince,' he whispered in Annie's ear, 'but they can get stuffed, because I don't care!' He was like a streak of lightning, brightening up the afternoon, making everything fun.

They made their way up a warren of little staircases, each one leading to another treasure trove; this one with fur coats and stoles and that one with gentlemen's suits. Finally, they found the ladies' lingerie department on the third floor. You could have heard a pin drop as the matronly assistant looked Wilf and Annie up and down. 'I presume the young lady requires assistance?' she said, sniffily, peering over the top of her horn-rimmed spectacles.

'Yes,' said Annie, as she was led away to the changing rooms and Wilf gave her a little wave goodbye.

She emerged, twenty minutes later, looking more womanly and quite pleased with herself. Wilf nodded his approval.

'Will madam be wearing it home?'

'Yes,' said Wilf, to the consternation of the shop assistant. 'Madam will!'

She tutted to herself and then said, 'I will just wrap this up for you,' folding Annie's old liberty bodice in some tissue paper. Annie pulled out her purse and unfolded a crisp ten-bob note, enjoying the feeling of being able to treat herself like this.

'Don't worry,' said Wilf, with a laugh. 'We'll give it a decent burial, won't we, Annie?'

They linked arms and left the shop, giggling like a pair of schoolgirls.

24

December 1934

'He's only gone and asked me to a dance at the Café de Paris!'

Annie was beside herself with excitement when she burst through the door into Wilf's room at the back of the Theatre Royal. Stanley had come back from his latest tour of the north with a promise to take her out dancing before Christmas, somewhere really special, and he had been as good as his word.

'Oh, Fan-Ann-fanacrapan!' cried Wilf, abandoning the costume he was working on and sweeping her into a hug. 'That's fantastic! What are you going to wear?'

'That's the problem,' she said, looking downcast. 'I haven't a clue and I can't really afford any of those fancy dresses up in Gamages.'

'Don't worry,' said Wilf. 'We'll get a pattern and some material and I'll help you run something up on my trusty sewing machine. Maybe I can make you look something like Ginger Rogers, in *42nd Street*? You could be Anytime Annie!' He guffawed at his little joke.

He was already pulling on his coat before Annie had time to tell him she hadn't even seen that film yet. 'Come on,' he said, tugging at her sleeve. 'Whatcha waiting for? Let's go and have a look down Berwick Street market before it gets dark.'

They scurried off towards Soho and the narrow market street, where stalls were crammed in so tightly together there was barely space to move. Wilf wanted all the juicy details about how Stanley had asked her out and they linked arms and chatted. The smell of roast chestnuts filled the air and Annie bought a bag for them to munch as they went along.

All the well-dressed ladies wandering down the market had mink stoles on, to take the chill off the winter afternoon air. Annie stopped in front of a stall which was thick with furs, hanging up there, swinging in the breeze, but Wilf knew that was just a pipe dream. 'Come on, Fan-Ann,' he chided. 'You can't afford those. Let's find you something jazzy for a nice gown.'

They stopped at a stall with rolls of material; it had silk by the yard, but that was out of her price range. Wilf ran some shiny rayon fabric through his fingers and dismissed it: 'Too thin.' Then he cast his expert eye over a bolt of cream-coloured rayon with black polka dots. The stall holder unfurled a length of it for him and he held it up to Annie's face. 'Perfect,' he said. 'We'll take four yards, no, five, if you will give us a bit extra for free?'

Annie's evening dress became her favourite project over the next fortnight. Wilf bought a dressmaking pattern from Gamages for a gown with flutter sleeves and a lovely V neckline and he showed her how to use the Singer machine, so she could get on with it when he was busy. Every spare moment she could, she'd steal away over the road to the theatre to sit there stitching and Wilf would pop in to keep an eye on her progress.

The night before she was due to go out with Stanley, she tried the finished dress on. It reached to the floor, so just the toecaps of her shoes were visible. 'Oh, no, Annie,' said Wilf, tutting at her old shoes as she swished about in it. 'You can't wear those old things.' He pulled out a box from under the rail of costumes and emerged trium-phantly, bearing a slightly scuffed pair of satin dance shoes. They were a bit big, so Annie had to stuff tissue paper down the end of each one, but they looked lovely, she had to admit, as she gave him a twirl in front of a full-length mirror.

'Cinderella, you shall go to the ball!' He laughed as she spun around. 'What time's he picking you up?'

'Nine o'clock,' said Annie, smoothing the dress down over her hips, not quite believing that she was going to wear such a beautiful garment. 'Ralph and Mavis have given me the night off.'

'I'll be over before then to give you the once-over and check you are looking the most fantabulosa you can pos-sibly be!' said Wilf. 'Now get that frock off before you spoil it!'

Annie was too excited to eat before her big night out, but Mavis forced some toast on her, all the same.

Her boss had a little heap of Christmas cards waiting to post on the kitchen table but had left one blank and sitting outside its envelope. 'Annie, love,' she began. 'I wondered if you'd like to send one to your folks, just to wish them all the best for the New Year?'

Annie glanced up at Mavis. She was never going to let the matter lie, always mentioning how a mother missed her children and how families should stick together, through thick and thin. Annie picked up a pencil and wrote the card, not to her mum and Bill, but to Aunt Clara and Dora. At least that way, she could pass on her best wishes and not reopen old wounds. Mavis gave a little satisfied smile as she stuck the card in the envelope and Annie wrote the address on the front. Annie started to look through her purse for a stamp.

'Oh, no need, love,' said Mavis, brightly. 'I'll post it for you in the morning. Hang on a tick, there's something I want to give you.'

She bustled off into her bedroom, re-emerging with a fox-fur jacket in one hand and a bottle of Coty perfume in the other. She gave Annie a little squirt of perfume on each wrist and then placed the jacket around her shoulders.

'I couldn't possibly . . .' said Annie.

'But I want you to wear it,' said Mavis, gently. 'I never get to go out anywhere these days and that jacket was made to go to the Café de Paris, even if I can't get there myself.' Annie fastened it up; it fitted like a glove.

'There's someone here to see you!' Ralph called up the stairs, setting Annie's pulse racing. But when she peered over the banisters, it was just Wilf grinning up at her.

'Come on, then, Fanny-Annie,' he said. 'Show us your glad rags!'

'Do you think I look all right?' she said, nervously stepping down the stairs; it wasn't that easy to walk in heels, let alone a pair that was a size too big.

'You look beautiful, Annie, really you do,' he said, giving her hand a little squeeze. 'I'd hug you, but we don't want to ruin the line of the dress now, do we?'

Stanley was twenty minutes late but when he caught sight of Annie, sitting shyly at the bar, his whole face lit up. He was dressed to the nines, in a white bow tie and tails and shoes so shiny you could see your face in them.

'Well, what a beautiful dress,' he breathed. 'You look like a film star.' He offered her his arm: 'Would you do me the honour of stepping out with me tonight?'

'Yes,' said Annie, smiling up at him. 'Don't mind if I do.'

Stanley escorted her across the pub, turning heads as they went, and once they got outside, he hailed a cab and held the door open for her as she climbed inside.

She'd never been driven anywhere in such style. London seemed to have sprung to life, with so many people out on the town; the taxi had to nudge its way through at a snail's pace. Annie didn't mind a bit, as Stanley paid her lots of compliments. Just being in a cab next to him was heaven.

'So, have you been practising your dance steps?' he teased.

'You might end up with bruised feet from me stepping on them,' Annie replied, with a laugh. 'I haven't really had the time.'

That was a fib, because Wilf had taught her some fancy

footwork, down the corridor which led to the stage at the theatre. They'd waltzed a bit and even tried a foxtrot, but she kept tripping over, so she was praying that Stanley wouldn't be too light on his feet or she'd never keep up.

'Don't worry,' he said, slipping his arm around her shoulders, 'I will be a strong lead and all you will have to do is follow.' She was tingling from the top of her head down to the tips of her toes at the very thought of that.

When they drew up at the Café de Paris, there were already queues forming on the pavement, but the door-man tipped his hat at Stanley and they were ushered through. 'Contacts,' Stanley whispered in her ear. 'It's not what you know, but who you know, in my business.'

The stunning polished circular dance floor and tables bedecked with pristine white cloths and silver cutlery almost took her breath away. A baby grand piano stood on a dais at the foot of two sweeping staircases, and there were musicians next to it, dressed in smart dinner jackets.

A waiter showed them to their table, on the balcony, which gave them a wonderful view of the scene below. Stanley started pointing out famous actresses and social-ites, but she really didn't have a clue who any of them were, only that they looked as if they belonged in another world. They were like exotic birds in the zoo, with their brightly coloured silks and taffetas and intricate bead-work on their dresses. Even their hair shone like gold under the light of the crystal chandeliers, and it looked so perfectly waved and set, it made the pin-curls she had so painstakingly perfected over the past few weeks look a bit amateurish really. Mind you, there was no way she was letting Wilf near her with those curling tongs. He'd nearly frazzled her hair off last time.

Stanley ordered them champagne, which she'd never tasted before, and as he raised a glass to her and she felt the bubbles fizzing on her tongue, she couldn't help noticing that some of the prettiest girls in the room were staring over at their table. Stanley was so good-looking, he just seemed to draw attention from women, and he nodded in their direction to acknowledge them before returning his gaze to Annie.

When the waiter returned with menus, Annie was completely flummoxed. She'd never eaten out before, other than fish and chips and the pie and mash shop; besides, it all looked so expensive. Stanley took charge and ordered them both a tenderloin of beef in a rich sauce. Annie watched the ladies downstairs picking daintily at their food and thought she'd better do likewise. She was almost too nervous to eat and it came as a relief when the band struck up and she could push her plate away.

First up was a barbershop quartet, the Yacht Club Boys, who had come all the way from America. They burst onto the stage singing 'We're Glad to Be in London!' which drew huge applause. Then Jack Harris and his band came on and the dance floor started to fill up. The best dancers went first, twirling around in a streak of silvery satin, with all eyes on them. When a dozen or so couples were up there, Stanley took her hand and kissed it, then he looked up at her and asked her: 'Would you like to dance with me?'

Annie was so nervous as she made her way down the staircase on his arm that she felt as if her feet weren't even touching the ground. He held her firmly around the waist with one hand and pulled her to him with the other, so she was looking up at him as they moved together to the music. 'How does it feel to be the prettiest girl in the room?' he said, smiling down at her. At that point, she honestly felt as if she was floating across the floor in his arms.

'Oh, don't be silly,' she managed to say. 'There's loads of girls who are miles prettier than me, and they only have eyes for you!'

He twirled her around gently and then pulled her even closer than before. 'I'm crazy about you, Annie, you must know that. Why don't you make me the happiest man in London and let me kiss you?'

She wasn't sure if it was the champagne or the thrill of just being with Stanley, but as their lips touched, the lights in the room seemed to burn that little bit more brightly.

As the clock struck one, Annie was struggling to stay awake and had no energy left in her legs for dancing, so Stanley hailed them a cab home. This time, they snuggled up close together in the back seat, his thighs pressing against hers, their hands intertwined.

When they got near Drury Lane he handed the cabbie a ten-bob note to pull over and disappear off for a quiet smoke. Then he turned to Annie and started to kiss her, passionately. She kissed him back and felt him sweeping over her, running his hands from her waist up over her bosom. It stirred something in her; she wanted to be lost in his embrace.

'That's right,' he said. 'You can give yourself to me, I won't hurt you.' He took her hand and pressed it down onto his crotch, so she could feel the hardness of him through his trousers. It panicked her. She pulled away.

She knew that was how men were when they wanted you, from the idle chatter at the washtubs. And she expected that the first time, it would hurt like hell, but then you'd get to enjoy it. Except, of course, there was the risk of getting a baby, so it was better to wait until you were married, after which you spent all your time fending them off so that you didn't have to hear the patter of any more tiny feet. And then there was what had happened to Vera . . .

'Don't worry, I can take my time,' he said. 'I can see you're a nice girl, aren't you?'

She nodded.

'Are you sure I can't persuade you back for a nightcap? I've got rooms just off High Holborn, we can be alone there, without anyone bothering us.'

'Perhaps I could come around tomorrow after work?' she said, biting her lip. She did want to be with him, she was sure of that, but she just needed time to think about it, that was all. It was happening in too much of a rush.

He laughed to himself and then said, 'Of course, I don't want to force you to do anything you're not comfortable with. I know nice girls like you want commitment.'

'Well, I have been saving myself for that, yes,' she said,

gazing out of the window, fearing she had spoiled the moment, or ruined everything between them.

'That's what makes me love you all the more,' he said, kissing her tenderly and very gently. 'I respect that, Annie. I respect you. A promise of engagement is something I wanted to talk about with you, very much . . .'

25

December 1934

Annie couldn't wait to tell Mavis all about her night on the tiles and her blossoming romance with Stanley.

She practically skipped into the kitchen the next morning.

'Don't tell a soul but I honestly think he might be about to ask me to marry him!' Annie gushed. 'He kissed me but when I told him he wasn't getting any further he said he wanted to talk to me about a promise of engagement!'

'Oh, Annie,' said Mavis, giving her a hug. 'That's wonderful. It's always good not to let them get what they're after, in my experience. Men don't respect women who give in too easy. Better to make them wait.'

Ralph sauntered in and picked up a piece of cold toast and chewed it thoughtfully for a moment: 'In my experience, fellas have to get used to waiting a lifetime once they're married . . .'

'Oh, the sauce of it!' said Mavis, flicking her apron at him.

They hushed up when little Daphne came in to eat her boiled egg; there were some subjects just not suitable for young ears. Annie took the little girl out for a long stroll by the river that morning and when Wilf didn't pop in at lunchtime, Mavis let her go and give him all the gossip, which she knew he'd be dying to hear.

She darted across to the Royal and let herself in at the stage door, calling for Wilf, but there was no reply. She knocked softly on the door of his room and pushed it open, to find him lying in bed, like a broken doll, with a busted lip and two black eyes.

'Annie,' he croaked. 'I didn't want you to see me like this.'

She rushed to his side and knelt beside him, taking hold of his hand: 'Whatever happened?'

'I thought my luck was in with a guardsman, a real dish,' he whispered. 'But when we went up an alley near the Seven Dials to get better acquainted, two of his mates were waiting for me.'

He closed his eyes. 'They called me a queer and then made me say it out loud as they took turns hitting me. I told them it was ungentlemanly, but they didn't stop, even when I was down on the floor. If you haven't woken up in the gutter with a dog pissing on you, you haven't lived, my dear.'

'I'm so sorry,' said Annie, who could feel a little knot of fury in her stomach at the injustice of it. 'Can you remember what they looked like?'

'Beautiful, all of them,' he said as tears slid down the sides of his face, which looked so small and frail, apart from the hideous bruising.

'Can you go to the police?'

His bright blue eyes were just visible through the

swelling, shining with indignation: 'Oh, for God's sake, of course not! I'd end up inside. I can't tell a soul, and you mustn't either. It's just the way things are for me in this life.'

He started to croon 'Two Lovely Black Eyes' but gave up after a minute because it made him cough: 'I think the swines have busted a rib or two.'

It seemed wrong to tell him about her big night out and how well things were going with Stanley, so she offered to go to the chemist's to get him some witch hazel to draw the bruising out and left with a promise to return later with something to eat.

'I hear congratulations may soon be in order, so this one's on the house,' said Ralph, pouring Stanley a large whisky and soda when he came in that afternoon.

He picked it up, with a look on his face which was nothing like delight, and then glanced over at Annie, who had bought herself a new lipstick at the chemist's shop and spent ages applying it, to get it just right, to look her best for her intended.

Stanley sank his drink quickly and looked at his watch before standing up and announcing: 'I'd best be off, one of my acts is having a spot of bother over at the Shepherd's Bush Empire, so I can't stay and chat, I'm afraid.'

Mavis put her hands on her hips and glared at him, as Annie stood there, open-mouthed, feeling very foolish.

When he'd gone she turned to Mavis. 'I think I've scared him off. I'm such an idiot! I shouldn't have told you. He's probably going to run a mile from me now. I've spoiled it all.'

'Nonsense,' said Mavis, folding her arms across her ample bosom. 'You are a wonderful woman and a real catch. He should be so lucky to be stepping out with you. Let's give him a chance and see what he's made of. He'll be back, you mark my words.'

But the week went by without any sign of Stanley. Annie spent her free time sitting with Wilf, bringing him whatever food Mavis and Ralph could spare, to save him having to go out and face the world. They got quite cosy at the theatre and the manager loaned him a radiogram set which crackled to life and filled the little room with the strains of the Palladium Orchestra or the Wireless Military Band, which set their toes tapping every afternoon. When he had costumes to sew, Annie stepped in to help, with Wilf telling her what to do and how to best stitch things; she'd learned so much from him, she was getting to be quite a dab hand with the Singer sewing machine now.

By New Year's Eve, Wilf was well enough to be up and about, and Annie was flat out busy working behind the bar for Ralph and Mavis's knees-up. They'd got an accordion player and hired someone to bash out tunes on the piano. Annie put on a brave face, but she wasn't really in a party mood. All she could think about was Stanley and how much she was missing him.

Her beautiful polka-dot dress hung forlornly at the back of the wardrobe. She picked it up and held it close for a moment, remembering the night she'd spent twirling in Stanley's arms. There was a gentle knock on the bed-room door and Mavis came in.

'Love, there's something I need to tell you and I think the sooner you hear it, the better.'

They sat down on the edge of the bed together and Mavis held her hand.

She loved a bit of gossip, did Mavis, but she wasn't taking any pleasure in delivering this piece of news, Annie could see that. You could have cut the atmosphere with a knife.

'It's about Stanley,' she said. 'I've been making some discreet enquiries with some of my market-trader friends about where he's got to, and it seems he's got a bit of a reputation with the ladies.'

'Well, that's no surprise,' said Annie, with a resigned sigh. 'He's the best-looking bloke this side of the water by a street mile. I'm not expecting any man to be an angel.'

'Just hear me out,' said Mavis. 'Seems he knocked up a Tiller girl a few years back.' She paused to let the news sink in. 'And that wasn't the worst of it. The poor mite fell head over heels in love with him, she did. She thought he'd do the decent thing, apparently, because he'd made a promise to get engaged.

'But it turned out he'd already slipped an engagement ring on someone else's finger too.'

'Who?' said Annie, whose leg was twitching, as if she wanted to get away, out of the room, so she wouldn't have to hear the rest of it.

'To a music-hall singer, good prospects,' Mavis continued. 'She was working long hours away on the circuit up in Leeds and Manchester and he was getting a pretty penny from her earnings, I can tell you. Well, Stanley knew which side his bread was buttered. He wasn't going to give her up for some hoofer earning ninepence for showing her all, was he?'

Mavis barely paused for breath before providing the answer, without waiting for Annie to reply. 'Not on your Nelly! He followed the money, right up the aisle, before his music-hall act had a chance to find out that the Tiller girl had a bun in the oven. Oh, he couldn't get wed quick enough.'

Annie's mouth had gone quite dry. 'What happened to her, the Tiller girl?'

'Oh, I think she had to go and live with one of her aunts in the country to have the baby, and that was that. He fairly ruined her, Stanley did. One of the other dancing girls went visiting and said it was like she'd aged twenty years overnight; hair like a haystack and not so much as a lick of lipstick on her face. Not that I'm one to judge, but I just thought you ought to know.'

'I'd never go anywhere near a married man, you know that!' Annie's cheeks were burning scarlet with humiliation. To think she'd almost . . .

'That's what I thought,' said Mavis, patting her on the arm. 'There's plenty more fish in the sea for a lovely looking thing like you.'

Annie looked away, so Mavis wouldn't see the tears which were stinging her eyes.

'Love, why don't you take a minute for yourself and

then you could pop down to the cellar and change that beer barrel for me? We've got a party to get ready for!'

It was as if a light had gone out in her world.

Everyone got as drunk as lords that night, linking arms, waving paper hats, cheering in 1935 as they sang 'Auld Lang Syne' at the top of their voices, spilling out into the street to wish each other 'Happy New Year!' Annie sang along with them, smiled her best smile and even had a little dance, but it was all an act. Inside, she couldn't wait for it all to be over, so she could just curl up in bed and cry. She wept hot, angry tears for her stupidity in trusting Stanley, and for fate, for making them meet after the Tiller girl and after he'd got married to the music-hall act.

The worst of it was, she couldn't get rid of the feeling that she was supposed to be with him. No marriage vows or even a baby born out of wedlock could change that. There was such a connection between them, he'd lit a spark of something in her and there was no going back.

26

February 1935

London laboured under leaden skies all month long.

Porters emerged from the freezing fog, scurrying like worker ants, rushing about with their baskets full of fruit and veg, but Annie could barely muster the energy to get out of bed.

She stopped bothering with her hair and her make-up and picked at her food. Mavis started to check how much she was eating, so Annie would take a big bite of a sandwich and when her back was turned, she'd chuck the rest in the bin. Her clothes seemed to hang off her skinny frame and the cold whipped through her coat, but still she felt nothing but heartache for Stanley.

Only Daphne kept her going, with her cheery little face and her inquisitive nature, seeing the world through excited eyes on their trips up to the art galleries and museums. The constant pull of that child on her arm when she'd seen something new forced her back to reality and, for a brief moment, she'd smile and laugh, but inside Annie was only half living.

Stanley occupied her mind, creeping into her thoughts at night and haunting her daydreams; every time she rounded the corner into Drury Lane, her heart would skip a beat, in the hope that she might catch a glimpse of him. The man with the straw-coloured hair and the smart jacket at the bus stop, the one hailing a cab, or inclining his head to light a smoke, all of them could be Stanley. But they never were.

She imagined angry exchanges with him, in which she slapped his face for the way he'd come on to her in the back of the cab. Or a shouting match, in which she revealed she knew about him cheating on his wife and knocking up the Tiller girl. But they all ended the same way – with him smiling at her, reaching out his arms and pulling her close. And each time she was powerless to resist.

One wintery afternoon, when the pub was closing, there was a loud knock at the door. Annie went off to answer, to tell the punter he'd have to come back later because there was no pulling him a pint now.

She held the door ajar and caught sight of her Aunt Clara, dressed in her best hat – the one she'd worn to Nanny Chick's funeral. Annie was so shocked, she didn't know what to say, but Mavis bustled up behind her and flung the door open wide: 'You must be Annie's auntie? Come on in, I'll put the kettle on.'

'Well, I don't know what they've been feeding you up here, Annie,' said Aunt Clara, huffing her way up the stairs, 'but it ain't enough because if you stand sideways, you'll disappear!'

Mavis gave her a knowing look: 'That's why I wrote to

you. I need you to talk some sense into her because, Lord knows, I've tried, and she isn't listening to me.'

'You wrote to my aunt?' said Annie. 'But how?'

'I may have made a note of the address you sent that Christmas card to,' said Mavis, pulling a little square of paper out of her tea caddy and waving it in the air. 'Just in case of emergencies. Well, this is an emergency, as far as I can see. We have got to get you over this moping about for Stanley or you will end up in hospital, the way you're going.'

'I'm perfectly fine,' said Annie, stiffening.

Mavis mouthed, 'She's not,' at Aunt Clara, as if Annie were a small child.

'Oh, Annie,' said Aunt Clara, giving her a hug. 'We've missed you so much and I've got so much to tell you! George is doing wonderfully at work and has moved out into lodgings down the Vale, and the girls are at secretarial college. You'd be so proud of them. Bill got a job too, down at C.A.V., the electrical factory, but the main thing is your mum is worried sick about you.'

'Does she know you've come to see me?'

'Well, no, not exactly,' said her aunt, fidgeting with the clasp on her handbag. 'I asked her how she'd feel if I were to bump into you up in town, if I were just shopping and we were to meet, just by accident. And she cried and said she'd be so overjoyed to know you were fine. But more than that, she would want to talk to you, properly, woman to woman, to explain things.'

Mavis had a look of rapt attention and drew up a chair. 'So, her mum'll have her back, then?'

'Of course she will, no question,' said Aunt Clara.

'Anyone would think you were trying to get rid of me, Mavis!' cried Annie, only half jokingly. 'That's nice, isn't it?'

'Oh, love,' said Mavis, patting her arm, 'I'm not, you know that. You've saved our bacon by being here with us, but a girl needs her family . . .'

'So, you *do* want rid of me!'

'No, I don't,' said Mavis. 'You have helped me through some very tough times, just by taking the weight off my shoulders, and now I'm trying to help you. Your family will always be your family, come what may, so it's best to heal rifts while you still can. And maybe that will take your mind off things round here. Why don't you just go and see your mum? You don't have to leave here, but it can't hurt just to go and talk, woman to woman, like your auntie says.'

The following Saturday afternoon, with her heart in her mouth, Annie boarded the bus to Shepherd's Bush.

From there, she climbed aboard the rickety old tram, which rattled its way back to Acton, past dreary soot-covered little houses. She was shocked at how drab everything looked after the bright lights of London, and how shabbily everyone was dressed compared to people up in Theatreland, stepping out in their finery.

She wasn't being snobby about it; she just saw the world through different eyes now. As she stepped off the tram on Acton High Street, she spotted a little huddle of kids, fighting over who was going to take an empty lemonade bottle back to the corner shop to get a ha'penny, while their mum pleaded with them to pack it in, or get a thick ear apiece.

Everything about the poor woman was sagging, from her stockings to her face. Only her hair seemed to have any energy left because that was sticking up in all directions, well – the bits that she hadn't managed to fasten back from her face with clips. She opened her mouth to say something as Annie stepped in between the little boys, who were wearing shorts three sizes too small and whose cheeks hadn't seen the damp end of a dishcloth in weeks, by the looks of it.

But before she could speak, Annie had produced an apple for each child from her bag; she'd stocked up on some fruit from Covent Garden to bring home for her family.

'I do feed 'em, you know!' said their mother, plonking her laundry bundle down on the pavement, her face red from a mixture of embarrassment and the sheer effort of hoicking the family linen down to the communal wash house.

'Got two little sisters myself,' said Annie, smiling at her. 'I know what it's like, with them fighting all the time, that's all.'

The woman blushed, and smoothed her hands over her creased housecoat, which was covered in stains. She looked Annie up and down. Annie realized then that she was like a stranger round here, in her smart coat and hat, and heels, with her neat handbag and its shiny metal clasp.

'Well, ain't you kind,' the woman muttered, to no one in particular.

'Kindness costs nothing,' Annie murmured, and she turned and headed across the High Street and down the lane, back to her home.

As she wandered down Fletcher Road to their front door, with its flaking green paint, she recalled the countless times she'd skipped up the front path as a little girl coming home from work, pushed it open and gone to chat to Nanny Chick in front of the fire.

Those days were long gone. Now she thought it only polite to knock.

The door swung open and before she knew it, she was being pulled into an embrace by her brother, George, who stood a full five inches taller than her. He seemed to have shot up. 'Gorblimey, Annie, don't you look the bee's knees!' he said. 'Where've you been hiding, then?'

'Oh, George.' She hugged him, feeling foolish for not having been in touch sooner. Ivy and Elsie were next down the hallway, surrounding her with questions about what it was like around Covent Garden, and could they go up West and go dancing with her? They had both blossomed into beautiful young women, with the same high cheekbones as their mum: Ivy brimming with confidence, with tumbling curls, and Elsie the quieter of the two but no less attractive for it. The look on Bill's face when he came into the hallway and overheard their plans to go out dancing quickly scotched their plans though.

He leaned over and gave Annie a little peck on the

cheek. 'It means a lot to all of us that you're here.' He cleared his throat, self-consciously, and turned to George: 'We'd best be off to the hardware store to pick up those nine-inch nails we need.'

'What nails are those?' said George, with a puzzled look on his face. Bill nudged him in the ribs and whispered, 'Women's talk.' And they disappeared out of the front door as Elsie and Ivy scurried off upstairs with a ball of wool and some knitting needles.

Mum stood on the threshold to the scullery, looking older and careworn.

She reached out her arms: 'Thank God, you're home.'

'Aunt Clara says the family you're working for are good people,' Mum said, settling herself down at the table, which had a freshly baked Victoria sponge waiting to be sliced. 'But she wasn't lying about you being thin as a pin, was she?'

'Oh, I've just been out of sorts, that's all,' said Annie, as Mum cut her a huge piece of cake and pushed it towards her.

'I've made your favourite. You'd better eat that, then, and you can tell me all about it,' said Mum.

Annie picked up the cake and ate some, savouring her mum's cooking and the sticky jam oozing out of the sides. It was the best thing she'd eaten in ages.

'Well,' said Mum, 'is he worth making yourself sick for?'

'I thought he was the one,' said Annie, 'and it hurt so

badly when it turned out he didn't want me because he was already married. It just didn't seem right, still doesn't.'

Mum clasped her hand. 'I know how badly love can hurt but you have got to keep going because another man will come along, the right one.'

It was so comforting to hear her mother's words of advice; Annie realized then how much she'd missed her. 'I want to be with him!' she said, as a great tidal wave of grief swept over her. 'He makes me feel differently to anybody else, I love him, Mum!'

'But he's married, isn't he?' she said, softly. 'You have to think carefully and don't let your heart rule your head. What's the point of wasting your life wishing on a bloke who's with someone else and, from what Aunt Clara heard, is a bit of a ladies' man, in any case?' Mum added, matter-of-factly. 'Now, eat another piece of cake. You still look peckish.'

Annie knew she'd couldn't just put her feelings to one side, but just speaking to Mum about it made it a bit better, at least.

Once the cake was eaten, Mum poured some tea from the huge brown teapot, which had a lovely new knitted cosy on it. 'I wanted to say sorry for how we left things before,' she said. 'It was wrong of me to slap you, but I was so shocked, I didn't know what else to do.'

'It's all right,' said Annie. 'I shouldn't have got angry with you like that and I just thought it would be better if I left.'

'I never wanted you to go,' said Mum. 'I'm still trying

to understand how you found out so much in the first place . . .'

'It was when I was sick with the scarlet fever,' said Annie. 'Aunt Clara told me some things.'

'Well, she kept that quiet!' said Mum, folding her arms. 'I thought you'd just found some address and an old photo in that sewing box, that's what she told me. I'll be having words with her.'

'Oh, Mum, please don't,' Annie implored. 'It's all water under the bridge now, surely? I was really ill and she was just telling me a story because she was worried about me. I can't even remember half of it, it was like a dream, or maybe I did dream it, but she told me about the old days in Notting Hill.'

'What did she tell you, exactly?' Mum's fingers were rapping lightly on the table in front of her.

'About the two Austin brothers, Arthur and Henry, and the sisters, Emma and Kiziah, and Clara, of course,' said Annie.

'I see,' said Mum, colouring up. Her fingers stopped moving. 'Well, it wasn't helpful of her to go raking over the past like that without telling me first or asking if I minded.'

'Maybe this was a mistake,' said Annie, rising to leave. 'I don't want you to get upset with Aunt Clara over this.'

'No, wait,' said Mum. 'Please, I'm sorry, don't go. It's just . . . you can't know what it's like, to love someone and lose them so young. I had to carry on somehow, build a new life. For all of us.'

'Oh, Mum,' said Annie, throwing her arms around her

mother. 'I can't imagine how hard it must have been to keep going, through all those years without him.'

'I worked my fingers to the bone to keep you, and so did your nan,' said Mum, staring into space. 'I'm not expecting a medal for that, Annie, it's just what families do – they keep going, they survive.'

'I've always been grateful for everything you've done,' said Annie.

Mum gave her a weak smile. 'There were certain things I kept to myself because I was afraid, Annie, afraid to lose you, I suppose. But it seems that life has a way of working things out, and I lost you anyway.'

'You haven't lost me, Mum, I'm right here,' said Annie, resolutely.

'I'll tell you everything, exactly as it happened,' said Mum. 'Just don't judge me, I've had enough judgement to last a lifetime . . .'

27

August 1914

'Britons! Your Country Needs You!'

Posters of Lord Kitchener appeared in shop windows all over Acton, his finger of military might calling on men to volunteer to fight Germany in the war.

Hope Cottage was alive with the gossip of who had enlisted during those early weeks of the conflict. It seemed that all the bright, enthusiastic faces on the High Street – the delivery boys, the apprentices – disappeared almost overnight to go and fight on the Western Front.

Bessie's boy, Thomas, caused a bit of a stir by turning up at the laundry gates in his khakis, with his cap perched on the back of his head. He was a tall, gangly lad and full of fun. 'Don't worry, Mum,' he told her, with a grin, as the laundrymaids flocked around him to admire his new outfit. 'It'll all be over by Christmas, you'll see.' But Bessie didn't think it was a laughing matter. She sobbed into her apron as he handed her a photograph he'd just had taken with his new army mates, up in Kensington, and made him promise to write to her often. The Missus was cross, too, because he was her best carman and now she'd have to rely on Bill, the laundry hand, to drive the cart for her and, God knows, he wasn't the most reliable.

The war seemed far enough away not to affect their lives too much, and Emma's daily battle was on the home front, just to make ends meet and keep the rent collector and the tallyman happy. She'd been on her own for nearly ten years now, since Henry died. It was a strange thing, grief, because although the years had rolled by, she still missed him as much as if it had only happened yesterday. She kept his picture on the mantelpiece in the scullery, so he was always watching over her, and kissed it goodnight before she went to sleep, longing to feel his arms around her. She'd hidden a little love letter he wrote her, long ago, in the back of the frame, to keep it safe forever.

A loud knock on the front door could still make her jump out of her skin, in case Felstone and his men had tracked them down and wanted to settle their debt, with no Henry to protect them any more. They'd kept themselves to themselves, as far as the neighbours were concerned. Her mum had told one particularly nosy woman down the road that Emma had been widowed young and was too upset to talk about it and, as she expected, word spread. Most folks had been bereaved in some way; life went on and the unspoken rule was that there were certain things that were not for children's ears. At least she could be sure of one thing: her little girl Annie was out of harm's way in Suffolk, with her Great-Aunt May, being well fed and looked after. Of course, there might come a time when Emma would tell Annie that her dad had died, but that day was a long way off. Besides, she only had a few precious days a year with her daughter and she wanted that time to be filled with happiness, not grieving. God knows, she'd cried enough for both of them when he'd gone. Life was hard enough without burdening her with the sadness of the past. That could wait until she was old enough to understand and there was no harm in that, was there?

Clara lived with her and their mum in Fletcher Road, and Kiziah and her husband Arthur were only a few streets away – not that anyone saw too much of him, mind you. He was often away working, decorating houses up in Hertfordshire and North London, and he'd stay away during the week if it was too far to travel home. Lately, he'd even been away for months, working up in Leeds. Kizzy said she didn't mind too much but Emma was worried about her sister, who'd just announced she was expecting again. Kizzy had lost three babies over the years and one quite late on in the pregnancy. It was a terrible heartache; she was desperate to have a little one of her own.

Nobody liked to talk about it, but they'd got to the stage when they all dreaded Kizzy getting pregnant again, in case she lost another baby. They lived in fear of seeing her doubled over with the cramps and the bleeding, when all they could do was tell her it would all be over soon. Mum would always say, 'There's time for you to try again, don't worry.' But everyone did, of course.

So, Emma was praying hard that this time everything would be just fine. Mum had told Kizzy to try to put her feet up a bit in those early weeks, but what woman could do that? Not a busy seamstress running the home and

working all the hours God sent, that was for sure. Emma
and Clara took it in turns to cook, to build her up a bit,
and tonight Clara had gone round there, taking liver and
onions for her tea.

'I don't know,' said their mum, her knitting needles
clicking away furiously. 'It just doesn't seem right when
there's so many children not wanted and they come into
this world just fine and Kizzy can't carry one to term and
she'd be the most wonderful mother.'

Emma nodded silently. Her mother never mentioned the
fact that life had been cruel to Emma too, by taking Henry
away when Annie was just a baby. Emma wasn't allowed
to dwell on her own sorrow, not even for a minute. Her
mother wouldn't hear of it. 'It's no good you wallowing,
my girl, you've got to make the best of it!' she'd say.

Clara came running in then, her face white as a sheet.

Mum and Emma leaped up: 'Is it the baby?'

'I don't know,' said Clara, hopping from one foot to the
other, as if she was jumping on hot coals. 'Something's
wrong with Kizzy. She's got a terrible fever and she's crying in pain, her head is killing her and I can't get any sense
out of her.'

There was a flurry of woollen shawls being pulled
around shoulders in haste, as the three women rushed out
of the house, but not before Mum had tucked her medicine bible, *Consult Me for All You Want to Know*, under
her arm.

Kizzy was lying in a darkened room in her nightdress and
groaning in pain.

Emma opened the curtains a bit, allowing a shaft of light to enter, so she could get a better look at her, but that only made her sister scream and clutch her head in agony.

'Have you had any bleeding?' asked Mum, sitting down at Kizzy's bedside. 'Is it the baby?'

'No,' she cried. 'The pain in my head, please make it go away!'

Emma went to fetch a cloth, running it under the cold water of the scullery sink, before returning to lay it carefully over her sister's forehead. Kizzy was scorching hot, as if she'd been lying among the embers, and a rash, like a bunch of little purplish pinpricks, had started to creep its way up her neck. Emma pulled the bedsheets back and saw another crop of the same little spots forming on her sister's arms.

'Clara,' she said, her heart pounding with fear, 'I think you'd better go and fetch the doctor.'

The doctor took one look at Kizzy; he announced she'd have to go to hospital straight away and Emma knew she'd been right to trust her instincts. He sent for the ambulance, a horse-drawn affair, and Kizzy was carted off out of the house on a stretcher with the whole street peering out of front doors and through curtains. Kizzy barely seemed aware of her surroundings any more and was mumbling and groaning the whole time.

Emma went with her to the Poor Law Hospital, the Union infirmary in Isleworth. Clara was sent off to see if she could find one of Arthur's building pals in the local pub who would get up to North London, sharpish, and tell him that he was needed at home.

'Sepsis'

The word was short, but Emma understood, from the glances the nurses gave each other as they tried to make Kizzy comfortable in white sheets stiff with starch, that it was very serious indeed.

Kizzy was suffering from meningitis and, from what the doctors said, the infection had got into her blood. Now her body was covered in purple welts, where the rash had joined together. She was feverish, her breath coming in short gasps, and she moaned in agony until the nurses injected her with morphia to ease the pain.

'She'll sleep now,' said the ward sister. 'Why don't you go home and get some rest. We'll take good care of her, I promise.'

'But will she get better?' said Emma, clutching at the nurse's arm before she had a chance to leave the bedside. 'And what about the baby?'

'I can't honestly say, dear.' She sighed. 'She's young and strong but the baby will be taking her energy at a time when she needs it the most. The best thing you can do is go and pray for her recovery.'

Emma did pray, at the laundry church on Acton Green, but God didn't hear her, because Kizzy took a turn for the worse a few days later and slipped into unconsciousness, with Arthur at her side. 'Come back to me, Kizzy, my love,' he whispered in her ear, with a look of such desperation that Emma almost fell to her knees. She'd been trying to be strong, for everyone's sake, but her resolve deserted her as her sister lay gravely ill.

Mum refused to leave Kizzy's side, despite the hospital's pleas for her to go home and rest. Instead, she clasped her home remedies book, poring over the pages in the hope of finding some tincture or herbal helper that the doctors hadn't thought of, to bring her daughter back round to the land of the living. Arthur sat mutely, stroking Kizzy's hair, which now coiled around her neck, dark and matted with sweat.

Kizzy clung to life for ten full days, and Emma and Clara held her hands and talked to her about the old days, back in Notting Hill, watching helplessly.

On the eleventh day, as birds heralded the arrival of the dawn, she died.

Several mourners almost fainted in the heat of a swelter-ing August afternoon at Kizzy's funeral. It all seemed so out of kilter, her dying in the prime of her life and the sun shining down relentlessly as her coffin was lowered into the grave; the flowers wilting, almost an insult to her memory.

Arthur sobbed uncontrollably as they turned to leave. Emma remembered him at his brother Henry's funeral, standing with a stiff upper lip, offering her his arm to lean on. Now, as he broke down, she went to his side, to be his support, and they walked together out of the cemetery. There was a wake to get through at the Railway Tavern and it would be a matter of pride for him to pull himself together for that.

After the last toast had been drunk in Kizzy's name, Mum and Clara dried their eyes and headed back to Fletcher Road to face up to life without her. Arthur finished up his drink and made his way over to Emma, who was sitting quietly in the corner, accepting the condolences of all the laundry girls, who were too shy to speak to the handsome widower.

'Might you come home with me?' he said. 'It's just I can't face being alone, not today. Not yet.'

'Of course,' she said. If the truth be told, she was glad of his company too, as Mum and Clara would intrude on her sadness, shake her out of it, perhaps, and she wanted to just be with the memories of Kizzy a while longer. As they strolled home through the streets of Soapsud Island, the years rolled away from them.

Sitting for hours together, in the dark depths of their grief, they found that the bond they had made in their younger years was like a thread, connecting them to their lost loves, Kizzy and Henry. Simply being together seemed to bring something to life, something that could pull them closer to the past. In the fading light, when there were no more words left to say, Arthur held Emma's face in his hands and kissed her.

'Forgive me,' he said, stammering and looking ashamed. 'I shouldn't have done that.'

She reached out, tracing her fingers over his features, so different to Henry's, but yet there were similarities: the curve of his cheek, the line of his brow. She placed her hands around his neck, losing herself in the strength of his embrace, as he pulled her to him.

28

January 1915

Emma had never been good at keeping secrets but the dread when she didn't bleed every month became a deep, dark worry she could share with no one.

At first, she tried to pretend to herself that it was just the upset of losing her sister, but by the third month, she'd guessed the truth of it. There was no sickness, not like when she was carrying Annie, but by the fifth month her stomach started to swell and no amount of lacing her corset could disguise it.

She was a regular visitor to Arthur's house, cleaning for him when he was away and doing his laundry, and he always popped around to them for his tea when he was home, but there was nothing for the neighbourhood gossips to talk about in that – she was just helping her late sister's husband out, in the way that good families did in times of need. Neither of them discussed what had happened between them the night of Kizzy's funeral. He hadn't made any attempt to do it again, and Emma was so guilt-ridden by it that she couldn't have, anyway. There had been such a comfort in it, being together, but she knew it was wrong and it would bring such a terrible shame on the family. With every passing day, she knew her pregnancy risked being unmasked – and then she'd have some explaining to do.

It was Bessie who noticed at first, sidling up to her at their break time in the laundry and whispering: 'Have you got a little secret to tell?'

Emma was horrified that she'd noticed and almost dropped her basket of ironing.

'Come on, then,' said Bessie, 'spill the beans – who's the lucky fella? Are we going to be hearing wedding bells soon?'

Emma shook her head and looked at the floor: 'It was a soldier I met down Chiswick High Road and we got a bit carried away, because he was going off to France the next day. It was just the once. He's over there now, in the trenches . . . fighting for King and Country.' The lies just spilled out, before she even had time to think about it.

'Oh, I see,' said Bessie. 'What regiment is it? The same as my Tom?'

'I'm not sure,' she replied. 'I'm terrible at remembering things like that. Could have been the London Regiment . . .' She was digging herself in deep, desperate to get out of this conversation.

'But you must write to him, tell him the good news,' said Bessie. 'He might get special leave to come home for a few days and you can get wed. Your mum will be delighted.'

'I don't think she'll see it that way,' said Emma. 'She's a real stickler for tradition. No putting the cart before the horse and all that. So, do me a favour and keep this between us?'

'Fine,' said Bessie, giving her a hug. 'I understand. Anything I can do, just say the word. But you are going to have to tell the old girl sometime, Em. That bump ain't getting any smaller!'

The following weekend, Arthur popped around as usual, for his tea, and they all struggled through one of Mum's meat pies; time had changed many things, but sadly Susan Chick's cooking wasn't one of them.

Emma got up to clear the plates and as her belly was just at eye-level with Mum's face, the penny finally dropped.

'Emma, my girl, what in the name of God . . .' said Mum, her mouth falling open. 'I thought you were looking a bit broad around the beam lately. But you're in the family way, aren't you? You've gone and got yourself pregnant, without a ring on your finger . . .'

Emma sat back down. Clara got up and scurried upstairs – she couldn't bear arguments – and Arthur looked as if he had just been shot, his arms and legs splaying as he reeled backwards in his chair.

'Well, there's no need to ask what you've been getting up to while my back was turned!' cried her mother. 'You'd better not have been doing it under my roof, you filthy slut! Where's the father?'

Emma took a deep breath and opened her mouth to speak. She'd been planning for this moment and had been getting her story straight, about the soldier, but now the time had come, her words had deserted her.

But before she could say anything, Arthur spoke: 'Don't be hard on her, Susan, please. It's my fault . . .'

'Oh, this is the living end!' she cried. 'My Kizzy barely cold in her grave and you two at it like rabbits!' She leaped to her feet and picked up her pie dish. She brandished it for a split second before hurling it towards Arthur, who dodged as it went flying past his ear and landed, with a crash, against the scullery wall. 'Oh, I can't bear it!' She sat back down and threw her head into her hands, wailing like an injured animal.

'Please,' said Arthur, 'give us a chance to explain. It only happened once . . .'

'It only happened once,' she mimicked him, with a horrible scowl on her face. 'You filthy whoremonger! To think I welcomed you into my home. You betrayed my Kizzy. And you!' She pointed a finger at Emma, who had frozen where she sat. 'I will not have his bastard child under my roof, do you hear me?' Mum snatched the picture of Henry, which was presiding over the whole terrible scene, from its special place on the mantelpiece. 'Well, you don't care about *him* any more, Emma! He'd be spinning in his grave to see this day.' And before Emma could stop her, her mother had cast it into the grate.

'Get out of my house, the both of you, and don't come back!'

Clara was sitting on the bed, rocking herself back and forth and sobbing, as Emma packed up her few belongings in a sheet and tied them into a bundle, before making her way downstairs.

Arthur was waiting for her in the street and he put his arms around her for a moment as they made their way through the freezing night air, before pulling away from each other. Even under the cloak of darkness, with the faint hiss of the gas lamps the only sound, they knew that neighbours could be watching, especially given the fracas they'd doubtless heard.

'Come to my house?' he said, taking the bundle from her.

'No,' she said. 'People will talk, Arthur, and it wouldn't be right. We can't see each other no more, you know that, don't you? I have to think about what is best for the baby now . . .'

He shifted from one foot to the other, but he didn't argue with her. He knew the women of Soapsud Island could be vicious if they felt someone had crossed the line. Cheaters were driven out, shunned, and whole streets could turn against each other. He didn't want that for Emma, or his child.

'We could leave, together?'

'And go where?' She almost laughed at the suggestion. 'This is my home. I've no money to start flitting off with you, Arthur. I have to think about Annie, keeping her safe, and this baby too. It's not about what I want, I've been selfish enough already – look where that's got me.'

'Don't say that . . .' He tried to put his arm around her again, to comfort her in some way, but she brushed it away. 'Where will you go, then?' he said, helplessly.

He walked her to the corner of Stirling Road and she turned, giving him a brief kiss on the cheek and a little wave goodbye before she knocked on Bessie's door.

She didn't hear him say, under his breath: 'I'll miss you, Emma.'

The weeks that followed, with both Mum and Emma working together at Hope Cottage, were awkward, to say the least. It wasn't long before the Missus clocked that something was up.

'Now, I'm not one to pry, Emma, but I can't help noticing you're not on speaking terms with your ma at the moment,' she said, whispering to her in the ironing room one morning, before the packers and sorters had come in. Emma was spending all the hours she could working, to save up for the baby. 'They ain't my business, family feuds, but I expect it's got something to do with her having the hump about you expecting the patter of tiny feet? When is it due?' She patted Emma's tummy.

Emma sighed. The whole laundry would probably be talking about her behind her back before long.

'A few months, around May, I think,' she said.

'And the father's not around?'

'No,' she said. 'He's in France, fighting the Hun. I barely knew him, just got a bit carried away one night.' She smiled to herself, ruefully, at the ease with which she now peddled her lie.

'Well, you're not the first woman who's got herself knocked up like this and you won't be the last. I just want you to keep working as long as you can and get back here sharpish after the birth. Where are you staying?'

'Bessie's putting me up,' said Emma. 'She's been a real pal.' They'd been great company for each other on the long winter nights, knitting socks for Thomas in France and little hats and shawls for the baby. Bessie loved reading Tom's letters out loud to Emma; he always sounded so chipper about life in the trenches, apart from the food, which was not a patch on his mum's cooking. That always made Bessie smile.

The Missus nodded. 'Seems like a good arrangement. I've got a woman I know can help you get the baby out when the time comes. If your mum wants to be a silly old fool about it, let her – you are always welcome here, Emma, and if any of my girls says a word out of line, they will be getting a boot up the backside from me.'

'Thanks, Missus Blythe,' said Emma. 'I won't forget it, I promise you.' She thanked her lucky stars for the rest of the day, because she knew there were women at other laundries who'd lost their jobs because they'd got themselves into trouble out of wedlock and that had been the road to ruin, with only the Poor Law to help them. She worked extra hard after that, even though her feet were killing her and her back ached from standing at the ironing board all day.

Every little kick of the baby inside her was a reminder of Arthur, but she saved those thoughts for the dead of night, when she was unable to sleep, because she knew she could tell no one, not even Bessie. Arthur had let her know that he'd had gone away on a job up in Leeds and would be there for the foreseeable. He'd dropped a note through Bessie's door, with a ten-bob note to help 'when the baby comes'. He'd apologized 'for everything', signing himself off with a kiss. Emma tried not to think about that, and how it had felt to be in his arms, being loved by him.

It was a secret she was determined to keep forever, not for her sake, but for this baby and, above all, for her daughter Annie, who must never find out the awful truth of what she had done.

29

May 1915

Bessie was busy putting together a food parcel for her boy, Thomas, whose last letter from France said he was going to the Front.

'Smokes, matches, corned beef, bar of chocolate, tea, evaporated milk,' she rattled off the list as she wrapped it all up in brown paper and tied it with string. She'd scrimped, saved and gone without to put it all together for him. 'And that lovely scarf you knitted him, Em, he'll be glad of that, won't he?'

But Emma didn't reply. She was clutching her stomach, like she was winded. 'Oh, good Lord,' she said, sitting down on the old armchair in the corner of the kitchen. 'I think the baby's coming.'

She'd got some things ready for the baby: a drawer lined with a straw-stuffed sack for a mattress, some linen, shawls, napkins, bootees and a hat. But because she was on her own, she just didn't feel ready for it, not like when she had her first, with her mum at her bedside, offering words of comfort and advice, with Henry excitedly pacing up and down in the scullery, waiting to catch a glimpse of his new baby. She'd heard nothing from Arthur since they parted, months back, and it was better that way, for all of them, but it left her desolate.

The Missus had given them the name of a local woman, a seamstress, up at The Steyne, who helped women in labour. She wasn't a popular figure, not someone people spoke to unless they had reason to, because she also helped women who were pregnant get rid of their unwanted babies, for the right price – but no one talked about that.

'Right-ho!' said Bessie, pulling on her coat. 'I'll go and get her. Just keep breathing deeply and walk about if you can. I found that helped me with my Tom and he was a big bugger when he popped out.'

Emma paced about the tiny kitchen, wishing that the woman would hurry up and get there because the contractions were getting stronger. This wasn't like her first, where she had spent the best part of the day sipping tea and even darning a pair of socks in between labour pains. Everything seemed to be happening much faster and, as she went to sit down, there was a gush of liquid down her thighs, as her waters broke. 'Ooh, sweet Jesus, help me,' she groaned, sinking onto all fours.

There was no time to mop anything up, the contractions were getting closer together, and all she wanted to do was bear down.

Suddenly, Bessie appeared, flushed from running, with a rotund little woman pushing her way through the door behind her. All her features were rosy and round apart from her eyes, which were flinty and hard, like two little pebbles.

'Now, Emma, isn't it? Let's have a look at you.'

'I can't move!' she cried. 'I feel like the baby's coming.'

'All right, dearie.' She felt the woman's hands lifting her skirts and pulling down her drawers. 'Oh, you're quite far along already. Yes, yes, the baby's head is here but it's important for you not to push until I say, or you'll rip yourself to bits, d'you see?' She plonked a basket down next to Emma on the kitchen floor and pulled out some linen cloths. 'Or I will have to be sewing you up, dearie, and I'm a dab hand with the needle but we don't want that if we can help it.' She mouthed to Bessie: 'Costs extra, you see?'

Emma nodded, but she could no longer speak. She just wanted this baby out. Now.

Bessie wrung out a dishcloth and dabbed some cool water onto Emma's forehead, whispering words of encouragement to her friend: 'Just breathe, breathe.'

'All right,' said the seamstress. 'He's face-up but it's too late to change that now. This baby is ready to be born. On my count, dearie, push.'

Emma pushed with all her might as her stomach went rigid with the contraction and the seamstress counted out loud to ten. 'And again!' she ordered. 'Keep going, push.'

The pain was searing through her, but she pushed with every ounce of her strength, screaming out all the anguish of losing Henry and the pain of betraying her sister Kizzy with Arthur. The next thing she heard were the cries of a newborn baby, as Bessie hugged her, saying: 'It's a boy! A beautiful boy!'

The first Zeppelin raids on London happened just days after the baby came, killing seven people in the East End, bringing the terror of war to their doorsteps.

'They bombed families and babies,' said Bessie, almost spitting with rage. 'It ain't right, Em. Makes me proud my Thomas is out there fighting them, filthy beasts.' She turned to the baby and picked him up, cooing: 'But you'll be safe here with us, won't you? Ain't it about time this child had a name Emma? I can't keep calling him "Baby" much longer.'

Emma hesitated. Yes, he was the image of Arthur because boys always looked like their fathers, she knew that, but part of Henry lived on in him too, she could feel it.

'I'll call him George, after the King, I think, because that's patriotic, isn't it?' said Emma, feeling the warmth of his tiny body next to hers as Bessie handed him to her.

'Yes,' said Bessie, glancing up at the mantelpiece to her son, who she prayed for every night. 'Any soldier worth his salt would be proud to have a son called George . . .'

'And his second name will be Henry,' said Emma as his tiny fingers gripped her hand, tightly.

When she took George down to Brentford to officially register his birth, the registrar asked: 'Name and occupation of father?' He glared at her for a moment, over his horn-rimmed spectacles.

Emma looked at the floor and said, 'Leave that blank.'

When the baby was a fortnight old, the Missus sent word from the laundry that she wanted to speak to Emma about coming back to work, so Bessie stayed at home and minded him while Emma heaved herself back into her corset and off to Hope Cottage.

The Missus was waiting for her, in the hallway, sitting in her rocking chair, with her ledger on her lap. And standing beside her, looking thunderstruck to see her daughter appearing through the front door, was Mum.

'I don't know what you think you're playing at, Eliza, but I ain't staying here to chat if she's here,' said Mum, making to leave.

'Oh, stay put and listen!' said the Missus, crossly. 'I pay both your wages, so I can call you here any time I like. I need Emma here to come back to work and she's got a baby at home needs looking after.'

'Well she should have thought about that before she went and got herself pregnant,' said Mum, turning her face away, so she didn't have to look at her daughter.

'The point is, I need her to come back to work and I need you to help her out by looking after the child.'

'That's meddling in our family business! You've no right!' Mum stamped her foot in fury at the sheer cheek of the Missus.

'I've every right to stop you doing something stupid out of stubbornness, Susan. Gawd knows, I have known you long enough. You've lost one daughter, it'd be careless to lose another wouldn't it?'

'You don't know the half of it, Eliza. It ain't what it seems. What will folks round here say?'

'Oh, pish,' said the Missus. 'Tittle-tattle. Who cares? Sticks and stones, Susan. They'll be gossiping all the more if you don't have your own flesh and blood growing up under your roof. Then folk'll start to talk – just see if they don't? More fool you for giving 'em something to talk about! And anyway,' continued the Missus, who was like a river in full flood by this point, 'no one at Hope Cottage dares say a bad word because they know they'll get their marching orders from me. A child is a good in itself, Susan, and it don't matter to me one jot how that baby came to be, and it shouldn't matter to you neither. Take her back. Make the rules, if you want, for her to live by, but take her back.'

'I don't know the first thing about the child,' said Mum, picking at her fingernails. 'Got no interest in it and, anyway, I've got to come to work here, or have you forgotten that?'

'That's the thing,' said the Missus, standing up and placing her hands, gently, on Mum's shoulders. 'You're not getting any younger, Susan, and I thought maybe I could give you a couple of quid to make life a bit easier just until you can get your granddaughter here to work for me at the laundry, to take your place, so to speak . . .'

'My Annie?' said Emma, alarmed by this suggestion. 'She's a bit young, not even twelve yet . . .'

'I'd turn a blind eye to that,' said the Missus. 'She can start after the summer. That way, we keep the laundry business in the family and everyone happy, don't we?'

Emma was horrified, but she knew she had little choice but to agree to it. The Missus had them all in the palm of her hand.

The Missus pulled out a couple of ten-bob notes from her pocket and handed them over to Mum, who then turned to Emma: 'This doesn't make it decent, you know.' She waved the money under her daughter's nose. 'You could give me all the tea in China and it wouldn't buy back my respect, my girl.'

As the leaves fell from the trees and the nights turned colder, the situation at the Front was so serious that the government started a new recruitment drive.

A crowd gathered outside the grocer's on Acton High Street as a new recruitment poster was hastily pasted up in the shop window.

MARRIED MEN! ENLIST NOW!
You have the Prime Minister's Pledge that you
will NOT be called upon until the young unmarried
men have been summoned to the colours!

SINGLE MEN!
Surely you will recognize the
force of the Prime Minister's statement
and ENLIST voluntarily.

All the talk was about Lord Derby's scheme, which wasn't too popular, as it involved canvassers banging on doors around Soapsud Island and cajoling or shaming men aged from eighteen to forty into either volunteering on the spot, or at the very least saying whether they would be prepared to fight.

Women like Bessie, with her son away at the Front, had little time for those who didn't promise to fight, even if they only chose to defer it. 'Skrimshankers and cowards, the lot of you,' she'd mutter at the washerwomen who complained about their boys being bullied into it.

Bill and the other laundry hands did their duty and signed up, returning to Hope Cottage, all proudly sporting a grey armband with a red crown on it, to show they were part of the Derby Scheme.

'I suppose this means I will be having boys who are wet behind the ears to deliver my laundry and be my dollymen if you lot have to go away and fight,' grumbled the Missus.

'Now, now,' said Bill, giving her a toothy grin. 'We're just doing what's right and we won't be in the trenches unless we're needed. In any case, I'm knocking on forty – who's going to want the likes of me?' He'd enlisted with the Duke of Cambridge's Middlesex Regiment, as a reservist, and been told he could return to work until called on.

Those armbands could be spotted all over Acton lately. Any single fella who didn't have one risked being given a white feather, publicly shamed as a coward. It took a lot of brass neck to live that down, and there were many boys would rather die on the Front than be shunned by their sweethearts for failing to get into khaki quick enough.

Anyway, Bill was nice enough, always making himself useful, even if he was a bit showy about his volunteering for the Army. When Emma had been big, carrying George, he'd offer to take baskets of ironing down to the sorting room for her. The story around the laundry was that her bloke was away at the Front fighting, and Bill seemed to feel it was his patriotic duty to keep an eye out for her.

She overheard him chatting with Bessie in the washroom

one day. 'Such a fine-looking woman, that Emma,' he said. 'I bet there's no bloke in France wishing for a speedier end to this whole war business than her fella, the lucky sod.'

That made Emma smile more than she had in a long while.

30

July 1916

Baby George took his first steps in the summer, toddling across the scullery, with Nanny Chick holding her arms open, ready to catch him if he should fall.

'Oh, who is such a clever little soldier?' she cooed, scooping him up and covering him with kisses.

Arthur had been as good as his word, keeping out of their lives, but at moments like this, Emma couldn't help wishing he'd been there to see his son. She'd not seen hide nor hair of him since they parted, but a week later Bessie sidled up to Emma in the ironing room one morning, clutching a letter.

'This came, addressed to you. I think it's from your fella,' said Bessie, conspiratorially. 'He must be home on leave, though, because the postmark is from Leeds. Ain't he coming to see his child?'

'Oh,' said Emma, who was completely flummoxed by this bolt from the blue. 'No, it's too difficult with things as they are indoors, with my mum, you know. But I'm so grateful to you for bringing it to me, Bessie. It means the world.'

Bessie gave her a wink. 'It's fine, you can rely on me. He

can write to you at my place, if it helps. I know you don't need no more trouble, Emma, but it's a shame a man can't know his own child, that's all.' Bessie knew better than most how that felt, because her fella was a bricklayer who turned out to have a wife in Shepherd's Bush, but not before he'd got Bessie up the duff. Nobody spoke about that.

Emma stuffed the letter down her corset for safekeeping and at tea break stole away into the lavvy in the back yard to read it.

Her hands began to shake as she read:

Dearest Emma,

I know I promised I would stay away, for all our sakes, but I've got my call-up papers for the Army and I fear I will soon be sent to France.

I had prayed that this day would never come, not because I am a coward, but because of the thought that I may not live to see you again.

Would you write to me and let me know that the child is well? It would help me face whatever war brings, just to have any news that you could give me.

With fondest affection,

Arthur x

She tried to keep her reply brief and to the point, but in her heart she yearned to feel his arms around her and for him to see the beautiful baby they had made.

Dearest Arthur,

The baby is a dear little thing and is running

rings round us all, as he is learning to walk. I think
he has a look of my Henry about him, but his eyes
are so like yours. He would make you very proud.
I have called him George.

   I am praying to God to keep you safe,
   Yours with fondest wishes,
   Emma

That was the start of regular correspondence between them, and a deepening of their friendship, which was something that Emma could never have foreseen. She kept the letters secret, tied with string in a tight bundle and hidden behind a chest of drawers in her bedroom. Arthur couldn't say too much about what he was doing in the war, but he'd been conscripted into the Lincolnshire Regiment and had found army life hard at first but was determined to 'keep his spirits up' and do his duty. There were route marches and drills and he learned to fire an ancient rifle that had last seen service in the Boer War. 'No one had any idea if we actually hit a target,' he wrote. 'It was freezing cold and we could barely feel our fingers.' She knitted him socks and a pair of fingerless gloves, telling her mum that they were for Bessie's boy.

After a month, he left for France and the tone of his letters changed; he became wistful, wondering how little George was getting on. Every time Bessie secretly passed her a letter, Emma's heart would skip a beat, just to know he was safe. 'We were terribly sick and cold on the crossing and it was a relief to be back on dry land. I never thought I'd say this, but the streets of Soapsud Island seem like a paradise in my mind and I dream of them a lot,' he wrote. 'I see George sitting with you and it is the most perfect, happy thought.'

The boredom of life in the Army training camps over there, with its endless drills and exercises and target practice, was soon replaced by the harsh reality of life on the front line at the Somme, with weeks on end spent in the trenches, but still he found time to joke. 'It was a sea of mud,' he wrote:

> *The first soldier I saw was covered in it, head to foot: How terrible, I thought. Now I am the same as him. We do what we can to keep the lice out of our clothes – a hot iron wouldn't go amiss. The land ahead of us, over towards the German lines, is full of the biggest shell holes, sloshing with filthy water. That reminded me of the Ocean, back in Notting Hill . . .*
>
> *The shells come over at all hours, making a screeching sound, and any man fool enough to pop his head up from his dugout is fair game for the enemy. Sentry duty is one hour on, one off, all night. I have lost friends, too many to mention, to the snipers' bullets.*

The gas attacks were what he feared most, or being 'buried by a shell', as some of his comrades had been.

Not long after the New Year of 1917, a letter arrived which shocked her. His handwriting, usually a neat copperplate, was a spidery scrawl.

My dear,
  It is as near to hell on earth as you could
imagine. Nowhere is safe. I only pray we may be
together again one day. Kiss the boy for me.
  Arthur xxx

She pulled out the bundle of letters from their hiding
place and was sitting on the bed, reading through them,
imagining what he had gone through, when she felt a
presence in the room. Glancing up, she saw her mother,
standing there, hands on her hips.

'What in the name of God Almighty have you got
there?' said Mum, rushing forwards to snatch the paper
from her. She read the letter. 'You lied to me!' she
screamed, slapping Emma's face. 'Well, this stops now, or
you are out on your ear, do you hear me?'

'He's away at the Front, there's no harm in it,' said
Emma, making to take the letter back. But her mother had
grabbed the whole bundle from her.

'Oh, you're leading him up the garden path. This one's
signed with kisses on it!' cried Mum. 'I ought to chuck
you out right now!' She took the bundle and marched
off downstairs, to the fireplace, with Emma hot on her
heels.

'Think about the children, Emma,' said Mum, who was
almost shaking with anger. 'You've already told Annie her
dad's away fighting. You are creating an unholy mess. It
ain't right. What will the neighbours think?'

Mum untied the string and cast it into the fire, where it
crackled and turned black. Then she started to throw each

letter in, one by one: 'This is for the best, it's the only way. We left all our troubles behind us in Notting Hill. It ain't right to be stirring up more problems now. You've got the family name to think about.'

'But what will I tell Annie, and what about George?' said Emma, watching helplessly, as the flames flickered over the papers and her secret correspondence went up in smoke.

'Well, the war has made widows of a lot of respectable women round here, from what I can see,' said Mum, wiping her hands on her apron.

Emma thought about it for a minute. There could be no future with Arthur, she could see that now. Mum wouldn't allow it and if word got out around the laundry about who had fathered George, it would bring shame on the whole family. Her children, sleeping soundly in the room above them, deserved better than that.

'I s'pose you're right,' said Emma quietly, sitting down by the fire, watching as Arthur's last letter turned to ash and drifted away up the chimney. 'There's plenty of good men went away to war and never came back. We can tell Annie tomorrow and get it over with.'

'Yes,' said Mum, giving her daughter a satisfied little nod. 'There's no shame in that.'

Perhaps it was the guilt of coming between Emma and Arthur, or just the fact that she was sick of the sight of her daughter moping around the house, but Susan Chick did everything she could to get Emma to go out with the other laundresses that summer. 'Go on and enjoy yourself!'

she'd say, popping another one of her pies in the range. 'I will take care of George, and Annie can help me around the house. You've only got one life, so go and live it.'

The girls at work liked a trip out to the varieties in Chiswick and Emma made a great pretence of enjoying herself, but inside she was broken, sick with worry about Arthur, who hadn't written since she'd told him about Mum burning the letters and threatening to chuck them all out in the street if their correspondence continued.

The war seemed to be rumbling on forever, and even the likes of Bill, the laundry hand, had been called on to serve. Although he was still only with the reservists, he was square-bashing down in Kent. He'd caused a bit of a fuss at the laundry the other week, because he'd rolled up fresh from a fortnight's training, looking quite dapper and trim in his uniform. He'd joined them on a night out at the Chiswick Empire, making a point of holding the theatre door open for Emma and squeezing in beside her in the stalls.

'It must be so hard to be left a widow with two little children,' he said. 'And George never even got to meet his father, did he?'

Emma stared straight ahead, wishing the ground would open up and swallow her whole. The news of her fella dying at the Front had travelled around the laundry wash-tubs like wildfire, it seemed. She wanted to die of shame for the lie of it.

'He's never got to slip a ring on that pretty finger of yours, either. Such a shame. Not that I'd ever mention anything to Annie or gossip with any of the laundry girls about it, that wouldn't be right,' Bill continued, leaning rather too close for comfort.

'Yes, well, I'm very grateful for that,' said Emma, stiffening.

'Oh, I've gone and put my foot right in it, haven't I?' he said, clapping a hand to his forehead, as her discomfort finally registered with him. 'I only meant to say, if you ever need anything, anything at all a man around the house can help you with, you can always rely on me. I know it can't be easy for you.'

Emma relaxed a little and turned to look at him. His inky blue eyes stared straight into hers, unblinking. He didn't mean her any harm, she could see that now, he was only trying to help in that clumsy way that fellas had sometimes, wasn't he?

'Thank you, Bill, that's very kind,' she said, giving him a little smile. He beamed back at her.

'Well, I'm ready to do my bit for King and Country,' he said, puffing out his chest. 'In fact, I'm as keen as mustard to get over there to France.' He sat there, like an eager little rabbit, watching her face for a reaction. Emma hadn't the heart to tell him of the horrors of war that Arthur had written to her about: the shattering noise of the shells, the gas, the fear of death and the trenches thick with mud. 'That's very brave of you,' she said.

'Do you really think so, Emma?' Bill replied, looking at her, earnestly. 'It would mean the world to me if you might let me write you a letter or two, when I go. All the Tommies have someone to write to, to keep their spirits up.'

Emma swallowed hard. 'Of course, that would be fine,' she said. 'Although I'm not much of a letter-writer.'

But Bill didn't go to France and he never saw a shot fired in anger. His military career came to an abrupt end when he tripped on a route march and injured his back, setting off a bad bout of lumbago. By autumn, he was dismissed on medical grounds and back in Soapsud Island, griping about his aches and pains, working as a dollyman at the washtubs. He still wore his grey armband, just in case anyone thought he was a shirker.

As Christmas approached, Emma put in lots of hours up in the ironing room, to try to get enough money together to pay for the extra coal they needed and buy a small gift for Annie and George. Late one evening, as she toiled away alone, there was a soft footfall on the stairs, and Bill poked his head around the door.

'I wanted to ask you something important,' he said, shuffling in, with his hands in his pockets. 'It's been on my mind a lot lately, but I just couldn't get up the courage to put it to you until now, because I wanted to do it properly . . .'

Emma put down her iron and looked at him.

He went on: 'I was hoping, I mean it would be my dearest wish, that you might have some kind feelings towards me, enough to make this man the happiest in the world, by agreeing to be my wife.' A smile flickered across his face then, as if his little speech had gone just as he had rehearsed it, pacing up and down on the creaking floorboards by his single bed at his mum's house. He struggled down onto one knee, clutching his back as he did so, and dipped into the pocket of his waistcoat, pulling out a thin gold band. He offered it to Emma. She hesitated.

What was love, to a widow with two children and an elderly mother at home? What was it, when the biggest worry each day was making ends meet? Love wasn't a teenage girl losing her heart to a boy who used to bring bread and cheese round to the laundry at lunchtime; it wasn't the bitterness of lost romance, of finding the one she was supposed to be with, only to have him cruelly snatched away by fate. It wasn't a night of blind passion, in some vain attempt to bury the grief of what life had stolen from her. It wasn't the tender companionship of letters penned in some Flanders field, building a relationship that could never be. No; love, real love, was doing the right thing for the living, for her two children, keeping the family going, against all odds.

She walked over to Bill. He'd never be the most handsome of fellas, but he was a good sort. He had a regular job, he didn't drink much, and he worked hard for his pay. He was on tenterhooks, waiting for her answer, wobbling a bit on one knee, looking quite desperate to stand up again.

'I will,' she said.

31

February 1935

It was nearly dark by the time Mum had finished her story, and she sat together with Annie in silence for what seemed like an eternity.

Annie hesitated for a moment before asking the question on the tip of her tongue: 'Did you love Arthur?'

Mum shifted in her chair and put her head in her hands for a minute. Then she looked up at her daughter. 'A long time ago, when I was little more than a girl, I fell head over heels in love with Arthur Austin, but the love of my life was Henry, your father – you mustn't doubt that,' she said. 'What happened with Arthur the night of the funeral was about grief and pain, two people taking comfort in each other. I'm not expecting you to understand it, Annie, or forgive it, but I don't think either of us really knew what we were getting into . . .'

'There's nothing for me to forgive,' said Annie. 'I've fallen in love with a man who got a girl pregnant while he was engaged to someone else, so I'm not judging you, I promise.'

Mum reached out and squeezed her hand. 'You've grown up such a lot. All I ever wanted was for you to be happy. There's still time for you, if you will just give your-self a chance to start again, back here, where you belong, in Soapsud Island.'

Annie wasn't ready to leave Drury Lane straight away but the bond with her family grew stronger over the coming months, and she spent her days off with them back in Acton whenever she could and wrote to Elsie, Ivy and her mum every week, sharing her news and becoming a part of their lives again.

She told no one what her mum and she had discussed that afternoon, but just knowing the truth lifted a huge weight from her shoulders. She understood at last the choices her mother had made and why she'd been so reluc-tant to share her secrets. It couldn't erase the past or right wrongs, but Annie saw, as a grown woman herself, that her mum and Nanny Chick had tried to make the best of things for the sake of respectability in a world which was quick to judge. Sometimes she'd lie awake at night and ponder whether she would have done anything differently, in her mother's shoes. Little by little, Annie began to realize that family was more than just who your father was, who'd made you: it was about who raised you. She counted herself lucky to have been born into a family of strong, determined women who were prepared to look life in the face and do their best for their kids.

Back at the pub, Mavis was delighted that Annie seemed more like her old self. 'I knew it was right for you to see your folks,' she clucked. 'There's no one more understanding when you're down in the dumps than your own mother!'

Wilf did his level best to keep her too busy to mope about Stanley too. He taught her everything he'd learned about costume-making, so that by the autumn, she was thinking about buying her own sewing machine and taking in piece-work for the West End shows, to make a little extra cash. 'I'll put your name forward, Annie,' he said. 'Then all you've got to do is let those little fingers work their magic. It's good extra money for you and it'll keep you out of trouble!'

Inside, in the quiet moments, Annie still yearned for Stanley, but the memory of the night she'd spent dancing in his arms grew more distant, almost like a film playing in her head when she was bored. She started to see him as Mavis and her mum saw him – a selfish man, someone who charmed the pants off women but with little thought for the consequences. In place of heartbreak, she took comfort in solitude; she'd be turning thirty this year, way past marrying age for most, and had resigned herself to the single life. Annie was someone who'd be there to support her mum as she got older and also to offer advice to Elsie and Ivy as they started their careers in secretarial work, which she was so proud of.

As the long hot days of a London summer gave way to the colder nights of autumn, Annie knew in her heart that the time was fast approaching when she would be ready to say goodbye to Drury Lane. Daphne would soon be starting school and that meant Mavis wouldn't need her as much. Although she always knew she'd be part of their life, the pull of her real family was growing stronger.

She spent Christmas back in Acton, enjoying every moment of decorating the house with paper chains, helping Mum get the dinner ready and having a glass of sherry and a natter with Aunt Clara and Dora. Bill was just slicing the turkey – serving himself and George first, of course – when Elsie said: 'When are you going to tell Annie the big secret?'

Annie almost jumped out of her skin and glanced over at Mum, who was smiling.

'Well,' said Mum, 'things have been looking up, with both girls working, as well as me and Bill, so we've rented a place up the other side of the High Street. We're moving in the New Year and you can have your own room!'

'And the best bit is, I've found a job for you at the factory,' said Bill, handing her a plate of turkey with all the trimmings. 'If you want it, that is . . .'

Grove Road was only up the street and around the corner, but it might as well have been another planet as far as Soapsud Island was concerned. It wasn't exactly posh, but it was a step up from the slums of laundry land.

They'd rented a smart three-bedroomed terrace, with a lavvy out the back. The yard was big enough to sit out when it was sunny. It had a gas stove – which might take a bit of getting used to after the range, but Mum was looking forward to that. On moving day, George borrowed a van from his mates down at White City and he and Bill heaved their furniture into the back of it, while

Mum, Annie and her sisters carefully wrapped up their china in old newspaper and put it all in a big tea chest. The whole street came out to see them off and a few of the neighbours made comments about them 'going up in the world', which Mum brushed aside, saying she'd see them down at the laundry tomorrow in any case.

Once the New Year was seen in, Annie told Mavis and Ralph about the job offer back in Acton and her plans to leave at the end of the month.

'You're always welcome here, love, and we will hate to lose you,' said Mavis, 'but it sounds like regular work with good prospects and you want to be at home with your mum, now, don't you?' Mum had spent ages getting her room ready, before she'd even said she was definitely coming home, so there was no going back, Annie knew that.

On her last night in Drury Lane, Mavis and Ralph held a surprise farewell party in her honour and Wilf did a turn which just about brought the house down, singing the old music-hall favourite: 'Goodbye-ee, Goodbye-ee, wipe a tear, baby dear, from your eye-ee . . . Bonsoir, old thing, cheerio, chin-chin!'

He clasped her hands and pulled her into a little dance routine as the punters clapped and cheered: 'Don't be a stranger, Fan-Ann,' he said, 'or I'll come and find you in Acton!'

32

August 1936

It took a while to get used to the rhythm of factory life, after the freedom of being a nanny and the fun of the London pub trade, but Annie didn't regret returning home.

Bill had treated her with renewed respect since she joined the factory workforce. He even made a point of making up her sandwiches every morning and they walked along Acton Vale together before clocking in at C.A.V., the electrical engineering works, housed in a sprawling four-storey red-brick building with arched windows.

It was different to the stifling and close-knit atmosphere of the laundry, being a massive factory, but there were little rituals – clocking in and out, the production line, tea breaks and chatter when the foreman wasn't watching – which broke up the monotony. Annie was never one for gossip, but she did look forward to the camaraderie of having other women to chat to, although many were a good deal younger than her and they were a bit of a flighty bunch. Still, no one dared to misbehave on the shop floor, with the foreman stalking about between the rows of work benches. Annie perched on a high-backed stool, like the other workers, and got on with the task in hand. If you needed to go to the lavvy and it wasn't your break time, you had to ask permission from the foreman or there'd be raised eyebrows.

She soon found herself being looked up to by a lot of the other factory girls, because she'd worked up in town. That sense of her being 'older and wiser' only increased when she was quickly singled out by the bosses for her nimble fingers and attention to detail. All that needlework that Wilf had taught her hadn't been in vain, it seemed, as she was chosen to test diesel engine fuel injection pumps, which required meticulous precision. All the workers had it impressed upon them that accuracy was key, because otherwise the engine would fail, so there was no chance of anyone sloppy being given such a crucial job.

Managing the section was a Geordie bloke, Harry, who was a few years older than Annie and didn't seem to say much – unless there was a union meeting. He was the branch secretary of the electrical engineers' union at C.A.V. and had no trouble calling the room to order and taking complaints to management about unfair treatment of the workers.

Bill was often to be found chatting outside with him at lunch, having a smoke together; it was probably more a case of Bill listening to what Harry had to say about the latest political situation while Bill nodded in agreement. Harry seemed to be more worldly and well read than any man Annie had ever met, and she was a bit overawed by him, to be honest.

'Aren't there any decent fellas for you to go out with up at that factory?' asked her mate Esther, as they strolled around Gunnersbury Park one Sunday afternoon. Esther was now pregnant with her third, and Leonard was growing into a charming little boy – until he yanked his sister Evelyn's pigtails.

'I think I'm over men,' said Annie, watching closely as the children threw some stale bread to the ducks, in case either of them fell in the water. 'They're just more trouble than they're worth. I'm happy enough.'

'Well, I envy you, in some ways,' said Esther, patting her growing tummy. 'All I've got to look forward to is more sleepless nights and washing nappies! At least you're using your brain. I know I shouldn't say it, but sometimes I'm just desperate to do something other than keeping house, but my Paul won't hear of it.'

Annie felt a pang of regret that she hadn't got married or had children like Esther, but she'd got her hands full helping around the house and going out to work. What was more, she'd been contacted by Wilf, who had been as good as his word and had got her some sewing work for a costumier who lived up at Shepherd's Bush. Even the fiddliest little jobs, like stitching on sequins for dancers' costumes, weren't too much for her.

'Do you ever see much of Vera?' asked Esther, as they wandered along.

'Not really,' said Annie. 'She was out the last time I called around and her landlady was a bit off with me.' That was an understatement: the landlady had used some quite choice language to describe Vera, who – from what

Annie could gather – owed a fortnight's rent and had even been in trouble with the law for rowdy, drunken behaviour.

Annie wanted to see her old friend, but she just wasn't sure how to help her; she seemed intent on boozing herself into oblivion. A guilty little knot sat right in her stomach at the thought that she was letting Vera down in some way, when they'd been friends for so many years. The conversation was brought to an abrupt end because Elsie and Ivy appeared, waving their arms like a pair of windmills, to get her attention.

'It's Mum!' said Elsie, gasping for breath. 'She fainted at home and Dad's gone to fetch the doctor.'

By the time Annie got home to Grove Road, the doctor was packing his stethoscope away and Mum was sitting on the sofa in the living room, looking very pale.

'It's exhaustion,' said the doctor, 'it seems to be making her heart irregular, which has led to the dizziness. I've advised that she should ease up on work, at once.'

'But I've got to go to work,' said Mum. 'We need my wages, for starters . . .' Resting up wasn't something that came naturally. She'd spent all her life working twelve-hour days in the laundries and then keeping house on top of that.

The doctor looked at her sympathetically but said firmly, 'I'm afraid I can't be responsible for the consequences which may arise if you don't stop putting too much pressure on your heart.'

Bill sat down next to her: 'Please, Emma, listen to the

doctor and listen to reason. We will find a way to manage.'
He cast his eyes around the room. 'We've got plenty of
space here. We could take in a lodger, just until you feel
well again?'

Mum nodded, and Annie went to sit by her, holding her
hand, while the girls fussed around with cups of tea.
Nobody said it out loud, but they all felt it. She was the
glue that bound their whole family together and the
thought that they might lose her was almost too much to
bear.

'Well, everybody, this is Harry.'

Bill introduced the Geordie union man as their new
lodger less than a week after Mum's funny turn and he
looked very pleased to have found a bloke he got on with.

'Hullo,' said Harry. He was softly spoken, with a kind
of magnetism which drew you in and made you want to
listen. He said he'd been looking for a place closer to the
factory as he had been travelling in from Hammersmith
every day, so this was 'just grand'.

Annie smiled politely. Whatever it took for her mum to
get the rest she needed was fine by her, even if it meant
having that union firebrand in the house. Mum, of course,
got up and started fussing around him, taking his coat,
offering him a bite to eat. After tea, he made himself
scarce, unpacking his few belongings in the front room.
Annie had spent ages getting the room ready, plumping up
the pillow and tucking in the sheets in the single bed
George had found at the second-hand shop down Acton
Lane. He'd be comfortable enough. As Annie watched him

close the door, she couldn't help hoping he wouldn't be staying too long.

Her fears of him intruding on their family life were short-lived. Harry kept himself to himself, to the extent that Mum got a bit worried about him: 'It isn't right, him shutting himself away like that,' she tutted. 'Anyone would think we weren't making him welcome.' She rapped gently on his door one evening to invite him to play cards with them. Elsie and Ivy had been learning canasta and it turned out he was a dab hand at that and, with the new radio set George had bought for them tuned into the BBC in the evenings, things got quite cosy in the kitchen. Annie wasn't one for games, so she sat in the rocking chair in the corner, working on her sewing, surreptitiously glancing over at Harry, as he concentrated on his hand of cards. He was quite striking in his way, with long, dark eyelashes and eyes which were greyish blue, and quite a fine nose for a man, really. Not that she was interested, of course, because she was too busy with her piece-work to pay too much attention.

After that, he regularly joined them in the kitchen after tea, sitting there, engrossed in his newspaper. Sometimes, he'd fetch a pen and a pot of ink from his room and start scribbling away, frenetically.

'What are you doing there, Harry?' said Mum. She was in awe of her house guest and his prolific writing. She was doing much better since she'd stopped working at the laundry, although she still took in some ironing for the Missus at home, and Annie had spotted her clutching her chest when she got out of breath at the top of the stairs a few times, which was a worry.

'I'm complaining to the *Evening News* about that tin-pot idiot Mosley and his Blackshirts,' said Harry. 'Their fascist views are dangerous and too much in line with Herr Hitler. People need to see it for what it is. They're already persecuting the trade union leaders over there, not to mention Jewish people as well – it's just intolerance of the highest order. If Mosley has his way—'

'Ta-da!' Elsie burst into the room, showing off the new dress that Annie had made for her on the sewing machine, cutting Harry off mid-rant.

'Oh, it's lovely, Elsie!' said Mum, as Elsie swished about in the dress, which had a pink rose-print pattern and a matching belt.

Harry glanced up at Annie, without smiling, and picked up his papers and stalked off to his room. Elsie raised her eyebrows: 'Oh, he's a funny one, ain't he?'

Annie shushed her: 'He'll hear you!'

The girls at work had been planning a big night out at the dance hall in Shepherd's Bush for ages, and Elsie and Ivy had begged to be allowed to tag along.

'Just think of all the good-looking blokes we might see!' said Elsie. They'd done each other's hair up in pins the night before and had been rewarded with a head full of curls each, to show off.

Annie had put on her polka-dot dress for the first time in years and found – to her relief – that it still fitted. Elsie was wearing her new rose-print outfit and Ivy had found some emerald-green rayon down the market, which Annie had run up into a frock for her, adding some lace at the collar, to finish it off nicely.

'Well,' said Mum, admiring her daughters as they got ready to leave. 'Don't you look the most beautiful bunch of sisters in Acton! But don't be back late or your dad'll have your guts for garters.'

They were just about to make their way into the hall when Harry came in, ashen-faced.

'We're off out dancing!' said Elsie, bubbling over with enthusiasm.

'I see,' he said, sitting down, his mouth pressing itself into a thin line. 'I've been up at Hyde Park, with the Jarrow marchers.'

'Who are they?' said Ivy, as Annie shifted uncomfortably, feeling him gazing at her.

'They're men from the North-East who are starving because they have no work and the government has all but murdered their town, that's what one of the speakers said today,' he said.

'Cup of tea?' chimed Mum, desperate to lighten the mood.

'I'm fine, thanks,' he said, flicking open his newspaper. 'I just want to see how biased the reporting of the march is.'

He looked up at Annie. 'Oh, don't let me keep you – off you go dancing.'

She felt so silly then, like some giddy girl going off enjoying herself while out in the real world, people were suffering terrible hardship. It shouldn't have mattered to her what Harry thought, but for some reason it did.

As she turned to go, he said, softly: 'You do look very pretty in that dress, mind.'

It was gone midnight by the time they got back from the dance.

As they pushed open the front door, with Elsie and Ivy giggling, their stomachs started to rumble as they smelt the most delicious whiff, of bacon frying.

Annie darted into the kitchen to find Harry, with his shirtsleeves rolled up, cooking up a round of bacon sandwiches.

'I thought you might all be hungry after your night on the tiles,' he said, handing a sandwich over to Elsie, who wolfed it down.

'I didn't know you could cook!' said Annie, completely flummoxed by the sight of a man at the stove.

'Well, you never asked me, so I never told you,' he said, giving her a little a wink.

33

May 1938

'I thang yew!'

The comedian Arthur Askey's catchphrase rang out across the kitchen as the whole family gathered around the radio to listen to his show, *Band Waggon*, on the BBC.

Harry had a funny way of laughing, clutching his sides a bit as he chortled, and he'd even taken to calling Ivy 'Mrs Bagwash', after the comedian's charlady, to tease her, which Annie and Elsie found hysterically funny. He'd relaxed into life at Grove Road and, as he did so, had allowed them to see he had a great sense of humour and it wasn't all serious politics with him, as Annie had at first thought.

'You used to know him, didn't you, Annie?' said Elsie, chewing on a piece of toast and jam.

'Yes, when I worked up in Drury Lane,' she said, catching Harry's eye. There was something about the way he looked at her which could just make her blush, even though she had nothing at all to be embarrassed about. Those days up in Drury Lane seemed like a distant memory now, although she wrote to Mavis and Wilf often and she loved flicking through her autograph book with her sisters, showing them all the famous people she'd met.

As it was the bank holiday weekend, work had organized a charabanc outing to Richmond-upon-Thames. Annie had never been down that way before and everyone was praying it wouldn't rain, as they were planning on a boat trip down the river. Bill didn't want to go – his legs were giving him gyp, and in any case, he was superstitious about going on water: 'Never set foot on a boat in my life and I'm not about to start at my age!'

So, it fell to her and Harry to set off bright and early the next morning to meet everyone at the factory in Acton Vale. He whistled as they went along and Annie found herself feeling a bit shy to be alone with him – there'd normally be three of them, and Bill and he did most of the chatting.

'What were you doing up in Drury Lane, then?' he asked.

'Working for a family, helping them run the pub and getting my heart broken, mostly,' she replied, with a laugh.

'I'm sorry to hear that, and more fool him, in that case,' he said, watching her intently.

'Oh, it's fine. I shouldn't have even mentioned it,' she said, slightly flustered that he'd paid her a compliment and that she'd told him something so personal. But part of her had wanted him to know, for reasons she couldn't quite fathom. 'I'm fine about it, really, I like my own company, although I'm not often on my own because I've got the family around me.' She sounded like she was gushing the last bit, falling over the words, in case she sounded desperate. 'So, what about you? You're a long way from the North, aren't you?' She was quite keen to shift the attention back onto him.

'I had to come down here to find a job, and I left my Mum and sister back up in Newcastle,' he said, lighting a cigarette. He blew the smoke out, thoughtfully. 'I've never been lucky enough to meet the right girl and settle down, but life's quite busy with work and all the union business.' He seemed a bit awkward and Annie regretted having said anything, as if she'd touched a bit of a sore point for him. It must have been tough, having to leave his folks. She took a long look at him – he must be more than five years older than her – but he was a handsome man.

When they reached the charabanc, Annie was quite pleased to strike up conversations with the factory girls, who'd dressed up in their best clothes for their outing. They admired the dress she'd painstakingly made – a cotton seersucker number with a nipped-in waist and some tiny pleats down the front that really showed off her trim figure. Someone was handing out white carnations as buttonholes for the women, and the men were loading crates of beer and bottles of pop onto the bus, which Harry got roped into helping with, rolling up his sleeves, joshing with the workers, but she felt his eyes on her as she clambered on board.

An accordion had found its way onto the charabanc and, as they set off, one of the machinists started to play 'The Sun Has Got His Hat On' and bottles of beer were popped open. Annie settled herself back in her seat as kids chased along the road after the bus, cheering.

It was going to be a great day out.

*

Down by the river at Richmond-upon-Thames was where all the posh people liked to promenade on high days and holidays and it wasn't quite prepared for a busload of rowdy factory girls and fellas, intent on having the time of their lives. They were in high spirits, singing at the top of their voices, which raised eyebrows among the well-to-do ladies in white tea dresses going for a scenic stroll by the white stucco houses which presided over the terraced lawns.

The river was alive with people on little skiffs and rowing boats, and there were beautifully polished pleasure cruisers cutting sleekly through the water, driven by smart-looking gents wearing peaked caps, slacks and open-necked shirts. It was such a different world down by the water's edge, with green fields and countryside all around them, and all just a few miles from the industry and slums of Acton.

Their boat was moored and waiting for them, and Annie felt her stomach do a little flip as Harry held her hand to guide her up the gangplank – but it was probably just because she was no longer on dry land. Everyone had brought sandwiches, ginger beer and lemonade; several of the factory girls declared themselves to be starving hungry and got stuck in early. This was a bit of a mistake because they'd barely been on the water half an hour when there were heads leaning over the side, chucking up.

The captain had a wind-up gramophone on the top deck and a space had been cleared for dancing, with seats around the edge. As the boat made its way downriver, one of the factory lads wound it up and put a record on and the music brought a stampede of people up top, to dance.

Annie was left sitting on the sidelines, tapping her feet, watching the girls pair off with the blokes until she got a bit bored and looked out over the fields and the meadows instead, to pass the time. Suddenly, she felt a hand on her shoulder, and spun around, coming face to face with Harry.

'Would you like to dance?'

'Dance? I didn't think you liked dancing,' she said, in astonishment.

'Whatever gave you that idea?' he replied, with a twinkle in his eye.

She took his hand and they started to move in time to the music. He smiled down at her and she found herself beaming back at him. It wasn't like the heady fizz of champagne, dancing with Stanley, but being in Harry's arms felt warm and familiar, as if she had come home at last.

That summer, Wilf kept his promise to come and visit Annie over in Acton. 'It's not the same down in Drury Lane without your cheery little face,' he wrote. 'Ralph's got no one to laugh at his jokes any more! It's as dull as dishwater in the pub.'

Mum got quite excited that Annie was having a gentleman visitor round for tea and had put on her best blouse and tidied her hair up into a neat little bun.

'The thing is,' Annie began, taking some scones she'd baked out of the oven, 'he is quite theatrical, so you mustn't mind the way he talks. He's not like all the blokes round here.'

'Oh, that's fine, love,' said Mum, glancing up from her knitting. 'All your friends are welcome here and I'm sure he's a very nice man. Didn't you used to go out with him, you say?'

'Well, yes,' said Annie. 'But not like that.'

'What other way is there to walk out with a fella?' said Bill, gruffly, swiping one of her scones and then putting it back down on the tray, quickly, as it burned his fingers.

There was a knock on the door and Annie heard Wilf calling 'Coo-ee! Fan-Ann!' through the letterbox. She rushed to answer, ignoring Bill's raised eyebrows.

'Ooh, look at you!' he said sweeping her into a hug. 'You've got a glow about you! Who's the lucky fella? Tell me everything!' They walked through into the kitchen, where Mum was pouring some tea into their best blue and white china cups and Bill sat, open-mouthed. Wilf was wearing his best suit, tailor-made to show off his slim figure, and a perfect red and white spotted bow tie at his neck added a splash of colour. With his blond hair slicked back, emphasizing his high cheekbones, he was very striking to look at.

'Such a pleasure to meet you!' Wilf cried, practically skipping across the floor to clasp Mum's hand. Bill stood up, stiffly, before Wilf could get anywhere near him. 'I'd better get on and mend those shelves, out in the yard,' he said, gesticulating over his shoulder. 'Can't sit around here all day chatting . . .'

'Do have a cup of tea and a scone,' Mum cut in, shooting Bill a filthy glance. 'You've come a long way to visit us, haven't you? Was the journey all right?'

'Yes, it was lovely, thanks,' said Wilf, sitting down at the table, just as Harry made his way into the room. He walked over and shook Wilf's hand. 'So, you're the handsome Wilf, who I've heard so much about,' he said. 'Sounds like you two had a champion time of it up in Soho. I'd love to know all about what Annie got up to. I bet she was quite naughty when she'd had a drink, wasn't she?'

Annie giggled and felt herself colouring up.

'Oh, yes,' said Wilf. 'Wicked as anything. Wait till I tell you what she got up to behind that bar, never mind leading me astray down the dark alleys of Drury Lane. It was a relief when she came back home to Acton, just so I could get a rest!'

By September, the mood in London had darkened, as the situation in Germany and the rise of Herr Hitler became the chief topic of conversation everywhere, from the pub to the factory floor. Annie and her friend Esther were quietly playing draughts at the kitchen table after work one day, while Elsie and Ivy took her kids out for a run around the park, to give her a rest. Meanwhile, Harry was absorbed in the headlines, which were enough to put the fear of God into Annie: HUMANITY FACES ITS BIGGEST CRISIS SINCE 1914!

'You would have thought they'd all have had enough fighting, with the last war,' said Mum, bustling about by the sink as Harry peered over the top of the newspaper.

'He seems to think Germany's got the right to have part of Czechoslovakia, but the question is, should we let him – and can we stop him in any case?' he said.

'Oh, I don't know, I just think nobody wants another war . . .' said Mum.

Bill sauntered in from the yard, his hands covered in oil because he'd been fixing Elsie's bicycle chain for her. He put his tuppenceworth into the conversation: 'If you'd told me after the war that we'd have all this bother from another German, I'd have laughed at you. We should have finished 'em when we had the chance, the rotten, stinking lot of them.' He glanced over to Esther, who looked rather taken aback. 'Sorry, no offence . . .' he muttered. He got up to leave.

'None taken,' said Esther, shrugging her shoulders. She turned to Harry, who was listening intently: 'You know, I'm not German, actually, although people always seem to think my family are. We're Jewish. My grandfather was from Belarus. He had a good trade as a shoemaker, but the Russians were persecuting Jews like us, and the family saved money to get him to England before the Great War. A lot of families tried to give one person the chance to start a new life somewhere safe. He had ten brothers and sisters who helped him escape here. He never got over the guilt of leaving them behind.'

'That must have been be terribly hard for you all,' said Harry. Annie remembered Esther's grandad then and how kind he'd been to both her and Vera.

'My mum is still in touch with her cousins – she writes to them. We're worried about Hitler and the Nazis coming, but they tell us they've lived through the pogroms under the tsars, so we mustn't fret.' She sighed. 'I try not to think about it too much. I've suggested we try to get them to come over here, but no one has the money and most of them don't want to leave their homes – and why should they?' Her question hung in the air and Annie had no answer. She imagined for a moment, her family having to pack up and flee, leaving everything behind, travelling to a foreign country and starting again, from scratch.

Within a few days, the Prime Minister Neville Chamberlain had flown to Munich to meet the dictator, returning with an agreement that he said secured 'Peace for our time'. Many people took that as a sign that war had been averted for good.

Harry wasn't so sure: 'We've gone and sold the poor Czechs out, giving Hitler what he wanted. It won't be the end of it, you mark my words.'

Regular trips to the riverside in Richmond on Sundays became a real lifeline to Annie in those heady weeks, when it seemed the world was teetering on the brink of war. Harry was only too happy to accompany her. She felt a bit guilty that she was trying to escape the drudgery of factory life and the claustrophobic atmosphere of home, but just to have a bit of freedom again seemed to breathe new life into her for the week ahead.

One day, as they were strolling along, Harry spotted a pair of swans gliding down the river and caught Annie by the hand, to point them out. It seemed only natural that they should hold hands for a while as they wandered along after that, not that she'd tell her sisters about it because they'd tease her mercilessly.

'Do you miss your family up north?' she asked him, as he gazed into the distance.

'Well, I write to them regularly, so I keep up with all their news, but I've been away from home a long time now, and I'm very happy down here in London, you see.'

She didn't want to pry but she couldn't help wanting to know a bit more. 'Didn't you ever have anyone special up there?'

He paused. 'No,' he said. 'I was away fighting in France in the war when I was a teenager and then it was just a case of finding a job when I came back, which brought me down here. I've always been into my union work, and I was just never lucky enough to find the right girl. Although, there is someone I've got my eye on lately.'

His piercing grey eyes searched her face. 'Might you think it was very foolish of me to say that I'm very fond of you, Annie? I don't want to spoil our friendship in any way, if it's not what you want, and I realize I'm a good eight years older than you . . .'

Annie's heart skipped a beat. She hadn't been looking for a relationship with anyone after Stanley and Drury Lane, far from it. But love seemed to have found her; in fact, it had come round to her house and moved into their front room. She always looked forward to spending time with Harry and she had got to know him, realizing that behind his serious side there was a warm, funny and kind man, who she had grown to care about a great deal.

'It is what I want, Harry. I'm certain of it, more than anything,' she said.

He brushed some hair away from her face and their lips met, in a tender kiss.

They were frequent visitors to Richmond after that, enjoying the bustle of the riverside and the quiet of the meadows, where they strolled hand in hand. One sunny Sunday afternoon the following summer, he got down on one knee in the fields near Petersham and pulled out a stunning engagement ring.

'Will you marry me, Annie?'

His eyes were full of hope, as she gasped at the sapphires and little seed pearls on the gold band. It was the most beautiful thing she had ever seen. He must have paid a small fortune for it.

'Oh, Harry, yes!' she cried. He slipped the ring onto the third finger of her left hand and, as he swept her into his arms, they kissed. Everything that had gone before – the heartache, let-downs and loneliness – all faded away. There was only now, here, with Harry.

It was all like a dream; the gentle dip-dipping of oars on the River Thames and the chug of pleasure boats, music drifting along, people lazing on the grassy banks. Kids were still turning cartwheels as the sun set on a hazy afternoon by the water and they walked on together. It was idyllic; it was England on a hot summer's day and they were just two people in love about to embark on the biggest adventure of their lives.

Epilogue

September 1939

The last of the wedding cake had barely been eaten when war broke out. Mum was wrapping a good chunk of it in brown paper and tucking it safely into a tin, to keep for those dark winter nights, when the news came.

Annie had just given up work, as married women were expected to do, when Britain declared war on Germany, turning their whole world upside down. Many of the men at the factory immediately joined up, but Harry, in his early forties, was too old for active service so he volunteered to be an air-raid warden. A gloom descended, with the BBC bulletins picked over and discussed at length with the family, who all feared what was to come and made regular trips up to Grove Road, to listen in.

Uncle Arthur had not long found himself a wife; a lovely widow from the Cambrian Laundry called Mary, who wouldn't say boo to a goose. She was kind and caring with him and seemed to relish having a man around the house because she'd been on her own for so long after losing her husband in the Great War. They stayed with Aunt Clara and Dora, taking the upstairs rooms. 'They're no bother,' Aunt Clara whispered to Annie. 'It helps with the rent and they barely speak.'

George called round to Grove Road that night. 'I've got some big news,' he said, his green eyes flashing with pride. 'I've joined up. I'm going off to fight the enemy, just like my dad did.'

Mum sat down at the kitchen table and put her head in her hands. 'But . . . you can't! What about your chest? Surely they won't take you?'

'Doctors say I've got some scarring on one lung but I'm fine to be a despatch rider in the Army, because I already know how to ride a motorbike. Don't worry, Mum,' he said. 'I can take care of myself. It will be fine. I'm doing the right thing, volunteering.'

Mum was crying, the tears of a mother fearing the worst for her only boy.

George looked a bit crestfallen and turned to Annie: 'There's worse things to be than a soldier, ain't there? I know our dad would be proud of me, wouldn't he? He gave his life fighting for freedom.'

Mum's sobs grew louder and she glanced up at Annie, with a look of desperation and sorrow, knowing she could say nothing to stop him going away to fight. Bill stood up and put his arms around her and Elsie and Ivy went to her side: 'Don't upset yourself, it's not good for your heart, Mum.'

Uncle Arthur turned away and stared at the wall, but his fingers started to rub at each other, relentlessly, and a muscle twitched in his cheek.

Annie looked around her. The blackout curtains were

already tightly drawn and their ration cards were neatly stacked on the sideboard, ready for the next trip to the shops. Harry's tin hat with 'A.R.P' painted on the front was perched next to a row of gas masks in cardboard boxes, which they had to take everywhere with them these days, just in case.

Annie knew then, that even the truth could not change what George needed to do, for his country.

'Yes,' said Annie, giving him a hug. 'We couldn't be prouder, George. Our dad was a war hero and he would tell you himself, if only he could.'

Author's Note

All families have secrets.

My mother was Annie and Harry's daughter and I grew up watching her carrying out painstaking genealogical research into her family to try to piece together the fragments she'd gleaned when she was a girl. Certain things were simply not talked about and as I grew into a very inquisitive teenager, I began to find out why; the choices made by one generation were sometimes deemed too shocking for the next to bear.

Looking back on the laundresses in my family, I feel a huge sense of pride. Learning more about the way they worked and where they lived brought home the sacrifices they were prepared to make, and I hope this book has gone some way towards bringing that to life. In a world of washing machines, tumble dryers and hot water from a tap, it is easy to forget just how long women had to spend keeping their families looking clean – not to mention all the other housework. But however tiring washday Monday might have been, it was nothing compared to the back-breaking, time-consuming and soul-destroying work in a laundry. I have one surviving photograph of my great-great-grandmother, the washerwoman Susan Chick, who was born in 1850. The photo used to scare me as a child because of her careworn, unsmiling face. Now I see it differently. This woman was extraordinary, pushing her handcart of laundry from Notting Hill to the mansions of Kensington and Belgravia to earn a few pennies more for her family, to help keep them all out of the work-house. I am fiercely proud of my great-grandmother Emma Chick, who was, by all accounts, a very caring and strong woman, who faced everything that life could throw at her with a quiet but resolute determination.

I was fortunate enough to spend my earliest years in the care of Annie Austin, later Annie Dickman, my nanny, who married Harry, the union man from Newcastle upon Tyne. Her kindness was infectious. Some of my happiest memories are still of her and her half-sister, my Great-Aunt Elsie, who told me stories about growing up in Acton and working in Soapsud Island. They were like a bridge to another time and another world – the years between the wars, which have always fascinated me.

I hope you enjoyed this book. And you can be sure of one thing: the story doesn't end here. I am busy writing the sequel, which will be published in summer 2019. Because in researching my family history, I discovered that Harry and his family had their secrets too . . .

The official Facebook account for all my book news is @beezymarshauthor and you can follow me on Twitter @beezymarsh. You can also sign up for book updates and all my news on my blog, Life Love and Laundry, at beezy-marsh.com.

Acknowledgements

Recreating a bygone era is never easy and I am very grateful to a number of people for their expertise and memories, which helped bring the years between the wars to life. I would particularly like to thank my Uncle John for sifting through his memories of Acton and our family at work in the laundries.

David and Amanda Knights and Maureen Colledge, of Acton History Society, were very kind to me and I would like to thank them for their help locating materials and memories to do with the laundries of Soapsud Island. The research of T & A Harper Smith, and their booklet *Soapsud Island*, detailing all the laundries from the area and lots of local history, proved invaluable. I am also grateful to Ealing Borough Council's local history section for images and research materials on Acton's laundries and local newspapers.

I was very lucky to be able to draw on the knowledge of Lou Taylor, Emerita Professor of Dress History at Brighton University, who taught me a lot about how working-class women dressed at the turn of the last century and the years leading up to World War Two.

I am grateful to Ingrid Connell at Pan Macmillan for being such a great editor at every stage of the process. It is a joy to work with such a professional team at Pan Macmillan. I would like to thank my agent, Tim Bates, at PFD for his unstinting support and enthusiasm for my writing and ideas.

Thank you to my husband, Reuben, and my boys, Idris and Bryn, for putting up with me while I spent months with my head in the last century. Likewise my friends Mark, Jo and Sally, who have had to endure me enthusing about various parts of the story, for what must have felt like an eternity.

Lastly, I would like to thank my readers, without whom I would have no audience. Thank you for picking up this book. I hope it transports you to a bygone age, and you are as gripped by life in a vanished London as much as I was while writing it.

Other research sources which proved invaluable were:

The Fabian Society, *Life in the Laundry*, London, 1902 (Fabian Tract No. 112)

Knights, David and Amanda, *Acton Through Time*, Amberley Publishing, Gloucestershire, 2012

Laybourn, Keith, *The General Strike of 1926*, Manchester University Press, Manchester, 1993

Skelley, Jeffrey (ed.), *The General Strike, 1926*, Lawrence and Wishart, London, 1976

Smith, Malcolm, *Democracy in a Depression*, University of Wales Press, Cardiff, 1998

Spring Rice, M., *Working-Class Wives*, Virago, London, 1981

Kemp Philp, R., *Consult Me For All You Want To Know*, W. Nicholson and Sons, London, 1900

Report of the War Office Committee of Enquiry into Shell Shock 1922, reprinted by The Naval and Military Press Ltd., East Sussex, and The Imperial War Museum, London

I also viewed archive material, films and pictures from the following sources:

The Wellcome Library

Pathé News and Getty Images

British Newspaper Archive

The National Archives at Kew

Forces War Records

Acton Gazette

Internet resources:

North Kensington histories, for memories of Notting Hill in the early 1900s: https://northkensingtonhistories.wordpress.com

Brentford and Chiswick Local History Society: www.brentfordandchiswicklhs.org.uk

The Long Long Trail website, for background on World War One regiments: www.longlongtrail.co.uk

The Great War Forum: www.greatwarforum.org/

THE *SUNDAY TIMES* AND INTERNATIONAL BESTSELLER

The moving true story of three sisters born into poverty and their fight for survival

Eva, Peggy and Kathleen were sisters born into a close-knit working-class family, living in a tiny terraced house in a street so rough the police would only walk down it in pairs. As they grew up between the wars, they dreamed of escaping their father's anger and the struggle of daily life in Waterloo.

Peggy was a studious and principled girl so appalled by conditions in the factories that she became a communist. Beautiful Kathleen, with a voice like silk, experienced tragedy too young and was destined to have her heart broken time and time again. Feisty Eva became a thief as a child so she could help their mother put food on the table – and never lost her rebellious streak.

As the years passed, the sisters stayed together, sharing each other's lives, supporting each other through hard times and protecting each other by whatever means necessary. *Keeping My Sisters' Secrets* is the rich, moving story of their fight to survive through decades of social upheaval – their love for each other the one constant in a changing world.

Out now in paperback and ebook